TANZANIA'S UJAMAA VILLAGES

RESEARCH SERIES, NO. 39

TANZANIA'S

UJAMAA VILLAGES

THE IMPLEMENTATION OF A RURAL DEVELOPMENT STRATEGY

DEAN E. McHENRY, JR.

INSTITUTE OF INTERNATIONAL STUDIES
University of California
Berkeley

International Standard Book Number 0-87725-139-8

Library of Congress Card Number 79-84636

❸   1979 by the Regents of the University of California

CONTENTS

CONTENTS

LIST OF TABLES

LIST OF TABLES

LIST OF TABLES

LIST OF TABLES

ILLUSTRATIONS

ACKNOWLEDGMENTS

This study would not have been possible without the assistance of many Tanzanians, to whom I would like to express my gratitude for their immense help and my respect for their impressive achievements. I would like also to acknowledge the support of the University of Dar es Salaam. The Department of Political Science, where I taught while conducting most of the research between 1974 and 1976, provided financial assistance for the survey work, and the Research Committee of the university provided funds to perform initial computer analysis of the data collected. Financial support for the field work also was provided by the Midwest Universities Consortium for International Activities (MUCIA). Special appreciation is owed to Professor Carl G. Rosberg and the Institute of International Studies at the University of California, Berkeley, for their interest and encouragement.

Chapter VI of this book draws heavily on an article entitled "Peasant Participation in Communal Farming: The Tanzanian Experience," which appeared in *African Studies Review*, Vol. 20, No. 3 (December 1977), pp. 43-63. I am grateful to the *Review* for permission to reuse parts of that article. Other material and data from portions of this study have been presented earlier in the following papers: "Policy Implementation in Rural Africa: The Case of Ujamaa Villages in Tanzania," a paper presented at the African Studies Conference, November 1973, Syracuse, New York; "Gaining Peasant Compliance: The Colonial Government's Implementation of Policies Affecting Rural Tanzania," a paper presented at the East African Universities Social Science Council Conference, 18-20 December 1974, Makerere University, Kampala, Uganda; and "Rural Policy Divergence: Communal Farming in Ujamaa Villages," a paper presented at the East African Universities Social Science Council Conference, 15-21 December 1975, University of Nairobi, Nairobi, Kenya.

D.E.M.

Urbana, Illinois
February 1979

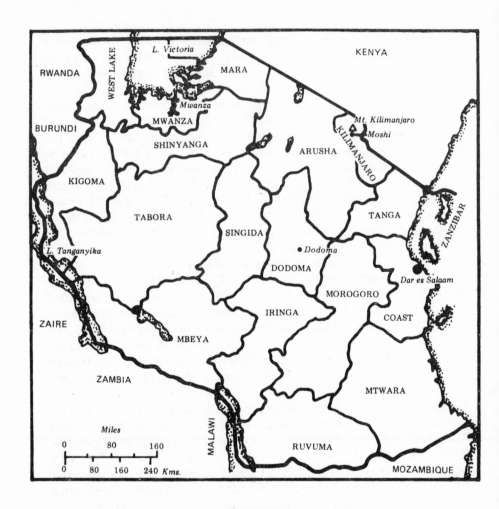

TANZANIA

Regions and Major Towns

THE FOCUS:
POLICY IMPLEMENTATION IN RURAL TANZANIA

A common objective of the leaders of many African countries is the creation of some form of socialist society. The achievement of such a goal requires the socialist transformation of the countryside. Attempts to effect such change, however, have met with innumerable obstacles. As a result, some participants and observers have begun to question the feasibility of the undertaking. One of the most important efforts to initiate a form of socialist change in rural areas is the subject of this study: the struggle to implement the ujamaa* village policy in Tanzania.

The policy was initiated by President Nyerere in 1967 with the aim of inducing the rural population to "live and work together for the good of all." A decade later, virtually all rural Tanzanians were living in villages and carrying on at least some activity collectively. The scale of the effort was impressive. Not since the massive collectivization campaigns in the Soviet Union during the 1930s and in China during the 1950s has such a high proportion of the peasantry of a country been so fundamentally affected by a public policy.[1]

The impact and relevance of the policy extends far beyond Tanzania's borders. It has attracted great attention from third world leaders seeking models for development. Delegations from Ghana, Burundi, Botswana, Zambia, Lesotho, Guinea, the Somali Republic, Sudan, Kenya, Liberia, Libya, Malta, Bangladesh, Jamaica, Surinam, and many other countries have visited Tanzania to examine the effort.[2] Most expressed great admiration for what they saw. The vice president of Botswana "said he had been tremendously impressed by . . . the country's Ujamaa villages."[3] Ghana's director of

---

*"Ujamaa" is the Swahili word for "socialism"—or in this context, "socialist." Literally, it means "familyhood."

community development and social welfare said he would apply what he had learned of the ujamaa village effort to his own program of rural transformation.[4] Delegates from Ghana, Peru, Cameroon, and India announced after a visit that "they would try to influence their Governments to introduce the Ujamaa village idea in their countries."[5] The prime minister of Surinam declared that the name of Tanzania was known throughout the world "because it is the cradle of the Ujamaa policy."[6] The vice-president of Bulgaria "greatly praised the development of Ujamaa villages in Tanzania and said such an encouraging trend should serve as an example to the development strategies in the whole of the African continent and the rest of the developing world."[7]

The policy is also relevant to those seeking explanations for the success or failure of public policy. The literature on policy implementation decries the limited attention given the subject and emphasizes its importance. Jeffrey Pressman and Aaron Wildavsky were virtually "unable to find any significant analytic work dealing with implementation."[8] Donald Van Meter and Carl Van Horn observed that "we know relatively little about the process of policy implementation."[9] Thomas Smith wrote of the "neglect of the policy implementation process."[10] Erwin Hargrove commented that "too little attention is given to implementation as a subject for inquiry."[11] Walter Williams declared that "the lack of concern for implementation is currently *the* crucial impediment to improving program operations, policy analysis, and experimentation in social policy areas."[12] The reason most frequently cited for the inadequate attention given to the implementation process is the implicit assumption that once a policy is formulated it will be implemented.[13] The error of such an assumption and the need to focus attention on policy implementation processes began to be realized in the 1960s with the failure of many development efforts in urban sections of the United States as well as in rural portions of third world countries.

THE SPECIFIC CASE

The situation in Tanzania to which the ujamaa village policy responded was virtually a model of underdevelopment. It included:

(1) *A large rural population.* In 1967 over 11 million people, 94 percent of the total population, lived in rural areas.[14]

(2) *A scattered pattern of rural settlement.* It was estimated in 1965 that 86.3 percent of the total or 91 percent of the rural

population lived in scattered homesteads—i. e., outside villages or urban areas.[15]

(3) *A relatively rapid drift of population to the towns.* Between 1957 and 1967, urban areas had experienced an average growth rate of about 6.4 percent per year, more than twice that of the country as a whole.[16]

(4) *The persistence of subsistence agriculture as the dominant form of rural production.* Between 1961, the year of independence, and 1967, the subsistence share of agricultural production declined only from 59.0 percent to 55.1 percent.[17]

(5) *A low level of technology employed in agriculture.* The hoe remained the primary tool of agricultural production.

(6) *A falling per capita income from agriculture.* The gross domestic product per capita (GDP/capita) from agriculture in 1961 was Shs. 242; in 1967 it was Shs. 239.[18]

(7) *Significant and growing inequalities in the distribution of income.* The decline in per capita income of those in the agricultural sector was accompanied by a rise in income of those outside that sector. As a result, the total GDP/capita rose from Shs. 411 (about $59) in 1961 to Shs. 568 (about $81) in 1967.[19] There was also wide variation in the distribution of income among districts. Those with cash crops had relatively high incomes—e. g., Kilimanjaro (Shs. 746), Shinyanga (Shs. 680), and Arusha (Shs. 934). Those with none had low incomes—e. g., Kasulu district (Shs. 177), Kibondo (Shs. 184), and Sumbawanga (Shs. 199).[20] In addition, especially in the cash-crop areas, observers found growing differentiation and the evolution of a class system.[21]

(8) *Limited services available to the people.* In 1967 there were only 373 doctors in the country, or one for every 31,842 people.[22] Only about 24 percent of children 5 to 14 years old were in primary schools.[23] In both cases there was a significant bias in the distribution of services to the urban areas.

(9) *A growing reliance on foreign assistance.* The proportion of the total development budget in the form of loans and grants from external sources rose from 35.3 percent in 1963-64 to 38.4 percent in 1964-65, declined to 36.3 percent in 1965-66, and rose again to 43.2 percent in 1966-67.[24] This meant a reduction in the freedom to decide the nature of development and an increase in indebtedness and dependence.

(10) *An increase in the centralization of authority.* Despite major efforts at increasing popular participation through village develop-

ment committees (VDCs) and district councils, there was what Cranford Pratt called "a persistent tendency toward oligarchy and authoritarian rule."[25]

(11) *A commitment by political leaders to building a socialist society.* Early in 1967 the President prepared, and the party approved, the Arusha Declaration, which explicitly directed the country's efforts toward building a socialist society.[26]

President Nyerere and other leaders maintained that the creation of ujamaa villages was a means to bring the scattered rural population together, slow the movement to towns, increase production, permit the introduction of new technology, increase peasant per capita income, reverse the trend toward greater inequality, provide better social services to the people, encourage self-reliance, and reverse the trend toward centralization. In other words, it was a means of overcoming the major problems hindering Tanzania's development.

Such problems were not peculiar to Tanzania. The similarity of the Tanzanian situation to that found in other African countries is shown in Table I.1. In almost all African countries the proportion of the population in rural areas is high; most people are engaged in agriculture; the per capita production from agriculture has generally declined in the last decade; services available to the population are few; and the average per capita income is low. As a result, many African leaders turned their attention to the implementation of the ujamaa village policy to see whether it might serve as a model for overcoming problems in their own countries.

THE GENERAL CASE

Although this study is concerned primarily with a particular policy which has practical importance to countries faced with similar underdevelopment, it is also relevant to the general process of policy implementation. An extensive literature associated with the process has been produced, centering around three principal concepts—"development," "policy," and "implementation."

DEVELOPMENT

The common solution to the problems of most developing countries usually is said to be "development," but so many meanings have been assigned the term that it has become virtually useless in analysis.[27] All definitions embody the notion of change, but

4

disagreement arises over the direction of change implied. On the one hand, the majority of social scientists define the term as changes toward ends which are independent of the choices of the people in the particular society in which they take place. For example, Lucian Pye has stated that

> development . . . can be usefully conceived of as being the replacement of the particularistic norms, functionally diffuse relationships, and ascriptive considerations of tradition-based societies with the more universalistic, functionally specific, and achievement oriented patterns of action of more modern societies.[28]

Other ends which are sometimes used to define this non-choice-oriented conceptualization of "development" include per capita income, level of literacy, number of hospital beds, etc. Definitions, of that kind, however, have been harshly criticized, especially by third world scholars. Characteristic of such criticism is that by Inayatullah, who has complained that such a conception

> rests on a unilinear view and interpretation of history. It presumes that all history is inexorably moving toward the same destiny, same goals, and the same value system as Western man has. . . . Marshaling evidence from the period of ascendancy of Western society and conveniently ignoring the vast span of technological development before this period which the "traditional" societies developed and transmitted to the Western society, it ignores the fact that technological and material development before this period was not always the product of a "combination of universalism, functional specificity, achievement orientation and affective neutrality.[29]

On the other hand, many social scientists define "development" as changes toward ends determined by people in a particular society. For example, J. P. Nettl observed that during the 1960s "an increasingly relativistic concept of development emerged. . . . people saw development as having to do with what was hopefully described as the attainment of specific and identifiable and societal goals."[30] Most political leaders and citizens of third world countries conceive of "development" in this way—i. e., as the process by which they obtain what they want.[31] Many ends which are a part of non-choice-oriented definitions may be a part of choice-oriented definitions. For example, overcoming poverty, ignorance, and disease would probably be considered "development" by those using both conceptions. There may be others, however, such as achieving

5

Table I.1

POPULATION CHARACTERISTICS OF SELECTED AFRICAN COUNTRIES: EARLY 1970s

Country	Population Est. 1974 (x1,000)	Percent of Population Rural	Percent of Labor Force in Agriculture, 1973	Per Capita Agri-cultural Production, 1972 (1961-65=100)	Population per Hospital Bed	Population per Physician	Average Per Capita National Income (in US dollars)
Tanzania	14,763	92.7% (1973)	86%	92	775 (1970)	27,572 (1973)	$110 (1972)
Cameroon	6,282	79.7 (1970)	82	110	305 (1970)	25,956 (1971)	179 (1970)
Ethiopia	27,239	88.7 (1974)	85	98	3,801 (1972)	73,314 (1972)	78 (1972)
Ghana	9,607	68.6 (1974)	55	85	695 (1973)	11,227 (1974)	220 (1972)
Ivory Coast	4,765	79.0 (1973)	81	120	496 (1970)	13,839 (1973)	391 (1972)
Kenya	12,912	90.1 (1969)	80	94	759 (1972)	16,292 (1973)	148 (1972)

Liberia	1,669	72.4 (1971)	74	105	509 (1967)	12,579 (1973)	211 (1972)
Nigeria	61,270	77.0 (1973)	67	96	1,378 (1972)	25,463 (1973)	187 (1972)
Senegal	4,315	74.0 (1973)	72	59	769 (1973)	14,668 (1973)	234 (1972)
Sudan	17,324	86.8 (1974)	80	99	1,098 (1973)	12,527 (1973)	109 (1970)
Uganda	11,172	92.9 (1972)	86	85	662 (1970)	35,443 (1973)	132 (1972)
Zaire	24,222	73.6 (1970)	78	104	327 (1973)	28,802 (1973)	118 (1970)
Zambia	4,751	65.7 (1973)	69	127	313 (1969)	13,518 (1969)	365 (1970)

Sources: Agency for International Development (AID), *Economic Data Book for Africa, 1973* (Washington, U. S. Department of Commerce, 1974); United Nations, *1974 Demographic Year Book* (New York: United Nations, 1975); and United Nations, *1975 Statistical Year Book* (New York: United Nations, 1976).

socialism or eliminating private entrepreneurs or expanding communal cultivation, which would not be considered development in some non-choice-oriented definitions but would be in some choice-oriented ones. Most commonly the unit of choice is said to be the state, and the individuals involved in making choices of ends are the leaders of the state. Thus when African leaders speak of the "development" of rural areas, they generally mean the transformation of them in a manner congruent with their objectives. Such objectives are most clearly stated in public policy.

POLICY

"Policy," like "development," has been defined in various ways. First, many equate the term with decisions for action by governmental agents. Yehezkel Dror defines policies as "major guidelines for action directed at the future, mainly by governmental organs."[32] In a review of Dror's book and Charles Lindblom's *The Policy-Making Process*, Theodore Lowi castigates the authors for equating policy with decision.[33] Nevertheless, in the same review he defines "policy" as "statements attempting to set forth the purpose, the means, the subjects, and the objects of coercion."[34] All these writers seem to suggest that a plan or decision toward which the government has committed its resources is a policy. Second, some writers equate the term with both decisions for action and action by governmental agents. Vernon Van Dyke summarizes what he sees as a widely used definition: "*policy* consists of several components: (1) goals; (2) a plan or strategy for achieving the goals, or rules or guides to action, or methods; and (3) action."[35] Third, the most common definition appears to equate policy with action by government agents alone. Ira Sharkansky states that "*policies* are actions taken by governments."[36] Lewis Froman maintains that the term is used to refer to either how government agents do things or what they do.[37] Inasmuch as we wish to distinguish between a plan and actions for carrying out the plan, the second and third categories of definitions given above are of limited utility. As a result, "policy" will be defined as a decision or guideline for action to which the government has committed resources. Even when defined in this way, however, so many different decisions may be encompassed in the concept of "policy" that few meaningful statements of general applicability can be made.

In order to overcome this problem, systems of policy categorization have been developed to distinguish among policies on the basis of specified characteristics—e. g., the institution making the policy (federal, state, or local), the group at which the policy is aimed (farmers, businessmen, or elderly people), the ideological content of the policy (socialist, liberal, or capitalist), the areas of applicability of the policy (urban or rural), the purpose of the policy (reduce unemployment, plug tax loopholes, or stimulate agricultural production), and so on.* Since these policy categories were not devised for studies of implementation, it is not surprising that they do not involve distinctions crucial to the process of policy implementation.

A policy-categorization system relevant to implementation requires a criterion permitting distinctions as to *how* the policy ends are to be achieved. The major determinant of the manner in which goals are attained is the nature of resources made available to attain them. For example, in a country such as the United States, when a school is to be built or people are to be moved for an expressway, a contractor is hired or people are paid. That is, the direct use of money is the key to implementation. But in a poor country such as Tanzania, when a school is to be built or people are to be moved into villages, the money available is often insufficient. Alternative tools of implementation must be used.† Even *within* wealthy and poor countries, the resources available for particular policies vary

---

*See Lewis Froman, Jr., "The Categorization of Policy Contents," in *Political Science and Public Policy*, ed. Austin Ranney (Chicago, 1968), pp. 41-52. Van Meter and Van Horn have suggested that a system of policy categories useful in the study of implementation might be based on two variables—the amount of change required and the extent of goal consensus among participants. They argue that the extent of change required is less important than the extent of consensus among participants for effective implementation, and that the continuum from more effectively implemented to less effectively implemented policies might be divided into four categories on the basis of the two variables—i. e., low change/high consensus, high change/high consensus, low change/low consensus, and high change/low consensus. The basic problem with such a system is that goal consensus continually changes for each policy during the process of implementation. In fact, the degree of consensus is in many ways merely a measure of the degree of implementation; hence little is contributed by such a categorization. (See Donald Van Meter and Carl Van Horn, "The Policy Implementation Process," *Administration and Society* 6, 4 [February 1975]: 458-62.)

†In the Arusha Declaration, President Nyerere stated that "we are trying to overcome our economic weakness by using the weapons of the economically strong—weapons we do not possess. . . . A poor man does not use money as a weapon" (Julius Nyerere, "The Arusha Declaration," in Julius Nyerere, *Freedom and Socialism* [Dar es Salaam: Oxford University Press, 1968], p. 235).

greatly, thereby necessitating the use of alternatives to money as mechanisms of implementation. Policies therefore might be distinguished on the basis of the relative use of paid versus unpaid compliance required for implementation.

Finally, the role of policies in the political process is complex. Normally the values of those who hold governmental power are incorporated in the vision of means and ends contained in policy. These values are not, however, necessarily different from those of a majority of citizens. Most policies continuously undergo reform in response to shifting social, political, and economic forces. Some are mere facades or gestures which are not intended to be seriously implemented. Others may be intended for serious implementation but turn out to be ineffective. In African countries, the 1960s and 1970s have been filled with great plans that have not been realized.

IMPLEMENTATION

"Implementation" is the process of transforming the visions contained in policy into realities. The concept is essentially the same as the choice-oriented definition of "development." Both exist when progress is made toward achieving the ends specified in public policy, and the key to both is the altering of popular behavior so that it will be directed toward achievement of the new goals. The most general approach to the study of behavioral compliance is through a form of cost/benefit analysis. An individual may be expected to act when benefits are greater than costs. The basic problem with such analysis is the difficulty in determining individual and group valuation. Yet some approximation may be made, and cost/benefit assessments are useful in understanding many propositions regarding implementation.[38] For example, it is sometimes asserted that the more an individual participates in making a decision, the more likely he is to comply with demands resulting from that decision.[39] On the one hand, democratic decision-making may lead to policies that are congruent with widely held values. As a result, demands for compliance do not require much adjustment in an individual's cost/benefit assessment to achieve success. On the other hand, democratic decision-making can serve as a socialization forum to alter the valuation of those who would be asked to comply. An individual's cost/benefit assessment of compliance may be sufficiently altered so that little adjustment is required by implementers.

There are, of course, problems. Sometimes what appears to be real participation in decision-making is only pro-forma participation.

Leaders may feel that the resulting policy has maximized value congruence when it has not. Even when real participation does take place, participants may later change their assessments of the costs and benefits of compliance. In both cases, successful implementation becomes more difficult than expected.

Three concepts are particularly relevant to the study of behavioral alterations required for the implementation of public policy:

(1) *Persuasion*: The obtaining of desired behavior by making known the possibility of benefits should the appropriate behavior follow, or of costs if it does not follow.

(2) *Inducement*: The obtaining of desired behavior by making known the imminent likelihood of the offering of an incentive, defined as something which produces pleasure or gain, should the required behavior follow.

(3) *Compulsion*: The obtaining of desired behavior by making known the imminent likelihood of the imposition of a sanction, defined as something which produces pain or loss, should the required behavior *not* follow.

These concepts are useful for several reasons. First, they are related to a broad theoretical literature on behavioral change. Second, they are frequently used in literature on third world development. And third, they deal with the crucial link between the agents of implementation and the persons whose compliance is necessary for successful implementation.

"Persuasion" is the most widely used of the three mechanisms of implementation. Unlike "inducement" and "compulsion" it does not involve the likelihood of immediate costs or benefits. It operates in two principal ways. First, by bringing a person (or persons) to recognize the value of an action he/they had not recognized previously or by changing the intrinsic value of an action, compliance with a policy demand may be obtained. Second, compliance may follow as a result of indefinite suggestions of the possibility of future incentives or sanctions. The success of "persuasion" depends to a large extent on the legitimacy and credibility of the implementation agent.

When compliance does not follow from the use of persuasion, it can be "sweetened" by incentives. That is, something of value to those whose compliance is sought is offered along with the request for compliance, thus tilting the cost/benefit calculation so that compliance follows. Although incentives in poor countries, such as

11

Tanzania, are very limited, their impact can be augmented through skilled use. For example, "action chains" can be initiated by minimal incentives to induce forms of behavior which will alter the valuation of other forms to eventually lead to the type of compliance sought. Some critics of the use of incentives argue that no value alteration may take place, so that continued provision of incentives becomes a requisite for compliance.

The opposite technique to "sweetening" by incentives is to "sour" noncompliance by sanctions. This raises the cost of not complying and therefore the relative benefit of complying. There are obviously many degrees of sanctions that might be imposed. Generally, they are less expensive in monetary terms than incentives, but most writers suggest that they have other costs to the regime that imposes them, such as reducing legitimacy.

Progression in the use of compliance techniques for policy implementation appears to move by stages from persuasion to inducement to compulsion. However, the costs to regime maintenance go up with each step. Before the third stage is reached, the government may decide that these have become so great as to bar carrying on the policy, but regimes have methods to reduce the cost. One is the pursuit of other policies which win back support; another is the decentralizing of responsibility for the use of compliance mechanisms and/or the pursuit of goals that are unpopular with the people. As we shall see, Tanzania has had long experience with such activity.

The type of compliance required partly determines the utility of the various mechanisms. Some policies require continuous compliance over a long period of time; others require only a short period of compliance. The kind of mechanism used may vary because of this difference. Compulsion is more feasible and less costly when used for short- than for long-term compliance, for in that case costs will not last long and resistance will have less time to develop. In rural areas of third world countries, the carrying out of sustained compulsion is likely to be difficult, and the costs to the maintenance of rule engendered over a period of time would probably be prohibitive.

THE FOCI OF ANALYSIS

The purpose of this study is to examine *specifically* the implementation of the ujamaa village policy in rural Tanzania and *generally* the policy implementation process. It seeks to describe what happened; to analyze why it happened; and to evaluate the applicability of the Tanzanian experience to other areas. Because the success or failure of policy implementation hinges primarily on peasant compliance or noncompliance, special attention will be given to the methods used to gain popular adherence to policy directives. These concerns are reflected in the organization of the study. Chapter II will describe historical precedents for the ujamaa village policy— i. e., the British efforts to introduce concentrations during the colonial period, the Tanzanian attempt to establish village settlements in the early postcolonial years, the ambiguous encouragement given to marketing cooperatives and the several policies requiring joint or "communal" labor during both time periods. Chapter III will examine the situation in Tanzania from which the policy evolved and in which implementation was sought. The socioeconomic and politico-administrative systems set parameters which had significant effects. Chapter IV will examine the character of the ujamaa village policy and its modifications in the years following its initial exposition by President Nyerere in 1967. The policy was a blueprint for action, defining goals and means to those goals. Chapter V will be concerned with the implementation of one of the two primary objectives of the policy: the movement of the rural population into villages. The resettlement of the peasantry was the most dramatic aspect of the implementation process. Chapter VI will deal with the implementation of the second objective: the expansion of socialist activities in the villages. Getting people to work together on projects in the village and on production in the fields was the most *crucial* aspect of implementation. Chapter VII will summarize previous chapters, assess a variety of arguments that participants and observers have presented to account for the degree of success achieved, and consider the implications of the Tanzanian experience for its own future development and for the general process of policy implementation elsewhere.

It is to the past that we first turn to begin this study of Tanzania's most significant and ambitious policy for rural transformation.

Chapter II

THE EXPERIENCES:
PREVIOUS ATTEMPTS AT RURAL POLICY IMPLEMENTATION

The rural problems described in Chapter I were not new in 1967, nor was the ujamaa village policy the first attempt to deal with them. Moving people into villages was sought during the period of colonial rule through the concentration policy and during the early years of independence through the village settlement scheme.* During those years, efforts to induce people to work together included encouraging cooperative societies and initiating widely diverse projects requiring joint labor. This chapter contains an examination of these historical precursors of the ujamaa village policy.

MOVING PEASANTS INTO VILLAGES:
THE CONCENTRATION AND VILLAGE SETTLEMENT POLICIES

Many explanations have been offered to account for the scattered nature of the rural population noted in Chapter I. The one most frequently encountered is that prior to colonization people lived in defensive communities.[1] The people in them dispersed for various reasons, including the suppression of tribal wars, the devastation caused by the demands upon villages for porters during World War I, and the desire of individuals to free themselves from governmental control and exactions.[2] Although the dispersion may have been a consequence of colonial rule, it appears to have been an unintended one. In order to overcome a number of rural problems, governments—both colonial and independent—sought to bring people back into villages. The most important efforts—the concentration and village settlement policies—may be compared on many

*According to H. Fairbairn: "The areas in which the people are resettled were originally called 'sleeping sickness concentrations.' It has been found that some Europeans are inclined to think of these settlements in terms of Axis 'concentration camps,' and it is now considered advisable to call them 'sleeping sickness settlements'" ("The Agricultural Problems Posed by Sleeping Sickness Settlements," *East African Agricultural Journal* 9 [1943-44]: 17). The term initially used is retained in this study.

bases, including motives for, modifications in, targets of, techniques for, politicization in, organization of, governance of, and cost and size of the undertakings.

MOTIVATIONS FOR THE POLICIES

The range of problems that settlement was supposed to help solve was narrower for the concentration than for the village settlement policy. During the early years of British colonial rule, tsetse flies had spread over much of the territory and had become a major threat to man and his animals. The flies carried sleeping sickness, which broke out in a series of epidemics. The major outbreaks between 1922 and 1954 were as follows:

1922: A serious outbreak in Maswa district.
1924: An outbreak near Lake Rukwa, which by 1930 had spread to most of Western and Lake Provinces.
1932: Central Province affected.
1939: Ukerewe district infested.
1943: Northern Province, especially along the Great North Road, infested.
1954: Ngara and Karagwe districts affected.[3]

An obvious solution to the problem was to separate man from the flies. A major outbreak in Uganda at the turn of the century was controlled by the massive movement of population. The Maswa outbreak in 1922 also was dealt with by moving people into fly-free areas,[4] but such areas were not large enough to accommodate the affected population in Western Province. As a result, the policy of establishing concentrations was initiated. The first sleeping-sickness officer, C.F.M. Swynnerton, defined a concentration as a group of people "sufficiently closely scattered to bring about and maintain automatically, with the aid of their animals, country practically devoid of visible brush."[5] Such a concentration would eliminate the cover required by the flies to survive, with the result that the community would be free of flies and fly-caused sickness. Obviously, the policy was aimed at dealing with a specific problem.

The village settlement policy did not grow out of the problem of a particular disease but out of dissatisfaction with the slow rate of general development in rural areas. In an attempt to increase rural production, the British undertook a massive mechanical-farming effort in the late 1940s which became known as the groundnut scheme.[6] So many problems arose that the project turned out to be one of the greatest failures in colonial development history. By the early 1950s, small-scale tenant farming was initiated in each of the three major areas cleared for the groundnut scheme—i.e., Naching-wea, Urambo, and Kongwa. By the late 1950s, the effort to assist the development of "yeoman" or "progressive" farmers through the tenant schemes received considerable government encourage-ment.[7] Nevertheless, the Tanganyika Agricultural Corporation (TAC), which had taken control of the groundnut-scheme lands from the Overseas Food Corporation, was never able to attract more than a few hundred tenants. The idea was picked up in the 1959 World Bank team study entitled *The Economic Development of Tanganyika*, which argued that rapid transformation of rural areas was more likely with "systematic programs of planned settlement of empty or thinly populated areas suitable for agricultural develop-ment."[8] This was followed in early 1961 by a study of the poten-tialities by an Israeli expert, Benjamin Kaplan. Kaplan suggested the concentration of population into villages in both inhabited and uninhabited areas; like the World Bank team, however, he stressed the importance of the latter.[9] Nyerere, in his inaugural address as President of Tanzania in 1962, argued that unless people moved into villages,

> we shall not be able to provide ourselves with the things we need to develop our land and to raise our standard of living. We shall not be able to use tractors; we shall not be able to provide schools for our children; we shall not be able to build hospitals, or have clean drinking water; it will be quite impossible to start small village industries; and instead we shall have to go on depending on the towns for all our requirements; and even if we had a plentiful supply of electric power we should never be able to connect it up to each isolated homestead. . . . If we do not start living in proper village communities then all our attempts to develop the country will be just so much wasted effort.[10]

Nyerere stressed the gradual concentration of the population in villages in *inhabited* areas. The speech was heralded, however, as sup-port for the ideas contained in the World Bank study and emphasized by Kaplan—i.e., resettlement in *empty or thinly populated* areas.

Shortly thereafter, another Israeli expert, E. Yalan, devised an organizational framework for the development of agricultural settle-ment in Tanzania. He suggested that a settlement authority be attached to the President's office with an advisory body to the director composed of representatives from pertinent ministries.[11]

After the bureaucratic structures were established, a set of highly capitalized pilot settlement schemes were decided upon. Although the location of settlements and the capital-intensive approach differed, the broad objectives were similar to those sought by President Nyerere: to move people into villages so that services such as health, education, communications, and water could be provided at moderate cost, inasmuch as "they are essential prerequisites to higher production, better living and increased capital accumulation for the general economic development of the country"[12]—i.e., a purpose much broader than that of the concentration policy.

MODIFICATIONS OF THE POLICIES

Demands for an extension of the scope of the concentration policy were less successful than those for an extension of the scope of the village settlement policy. Those seeking a broadening of the concentration policy were, for the most part, members of the colonial administration. Twenty years before President Nyerere called for people to settle in villages, the sleeping-sickness officer—H. Fairbairn—urged the general resettlement of all scattered people "even though they may not have been exposed to Sleeping Sickness." He argued that the policy of resttlement was the only one that could lead to the improvement of "agricultural methods . . . and raise thereby the general economic standard of the people, and hence of the Territory as a whole."[13] A year later he argued that "the prevention of Sleeping Sickness is only the first, and ultimately the least, of the benefits which the people derive in these compact settlements." Others include medical facilities, larger-scale farms, protection from game, better administration, education and religious services, shops, and the incentives to production that all these involved.[14] Later that year he forwarded to the secretariat his suggestions that the "grounds for resettling the population should not only be medical ones (or even medical ones at all) but resettlement should be undertaken as part of the Government's deliberate policy to improve the social and economic welfare of the people for whom they are responsible."[15] The matter was considered with some skepticism by the secretariat, where a complaint was raised about the possibility that privileged settlements would result, thereby furthering rural inequality.[16] The governor reacted more favorably, though he felt that a detailed analysis of the scheme would have to await the conclusion of the war.[17] In 1945 a senior provincial commissioner, J. Rooke Johnson, revived the issue:

All things considered, I am convinced that the policy of closer settlement can be beneficially applied to large areas of Tanganyika and that it is indeed a condition precedent to real progress on the part of much of the African population. I even go so far as to suggest that it should become part of the declared policy of Government, and an integral part of post-war development.[18]

The issue moved forward to a discussion of a law that would permit the compulsory resettlement of Africans. It was argued in the secretariat that the government was already continuously moving people not only for sleeping sickness reasons, but also to establish forest reserves, relieve soil-erosion problems, etc. In each case, orders issued through the native authorities were relied upon because there were no other mechanisms.

Furthermore, it was contended that it was unfair "to continue to use the Native Authority Ordinance for purposes beyond its intended scope and to make Native Authorities bear the local odium."[19] When the executive council was asked to approve the "Resettlement of Natives Ordinance" in August and September 1947, all members supported it.[20] The governor, however, hesitated to accept the recommendation. He consulted officials in other British African dependencies and found that none had such a law.[21] Eventually, the attorney general advised against it,[22] and by 1948 the issue of expanding the scope of the concentration effort was dropped.

All those involved in the early suggestions for the village settlement policy urged that its application be confined to pilot schemes for several years,[23] but as time went on, pressures for its expansion increased. By 1965, in addition to the pilot settlement schemes, there were four other types under the Rural Settlement Commission: assisted settlement schemes, established and sponsored by regional administrations but provided with some central-government assistance; voluntary or unplanned settlements, created by peasants partly as a consequence of the President's call in 1962 for movement to villages; ex-Tanganyika Agricultural Corporation schemes, started on lands cleared by the ill-fated groundnut scheme; and Agridev schemes, initiated by the Agricultural Development Company (International) of Israel in cooperation with the Tanzanian government.[24] Regional pressure to create more schemes was intense. In addition, the second five-year plan called for a substantial increase in the number of settlements over what was initially planned. By 1969/70 there were supposed to be sixty-nine such villages, each costing about £150,000.[25] Thus pressures for expansion of the policy beyond the limited pilot schemes were successful.

THE EXPERIENCES: PREVIOUS ATTEMPTS AT IMPLEMENTATION

PLANNING FOR IMPLEMENTATION

Planning for implementation of the two policies differed considerably. In the case of the concentrations it centered primarily on the movement of people; in the case of the village settlements it concerned mainly the development of the village after movement.

Fairbairn has described planning for concentrations, once sleeping sickness was found, in terms of the following steps:

(1) The number of people who would have to move would be determined.
(2) The people affected would be asked to suggest possible sites for the village.
(3) A sleeping-sickness surveyor with the help of elders would locate the most suitable area.
(4) The choice would be put before the chief and the people affected to agree to the site or an alternative one.
(5) Boundaries would be marked, enclosing eight acres per family.
(6) Arrangements would be made for transportation of peasants and their possessions.[26]

Although the appearance was one of democratic planning, the reality was one of domination by government officers.

Local involvement in the planning for the village settlement policy appears to have been even less. The Rural Settlement Commission, for its part, recognized that its planning was frequently incomplete.[27] Nikolaus Newiger, in a study of the settlement scheme, found numerous examples of poor planning.[28] In the last half of 1965 a scheme-by-scheme evaluation was made and "in most cases it was discovered that Schemes were not economically viable."[29] The inadequacies of the plans involved what to do with the settlements once they were established more than how to get people to move into them. Among the causes of the planning problems that have been identified were bureaucratic difficulties in the recruitment of planners and overcentralization of decision-making in Dar es Salaam. The consequence was to reduce the chances that the settlements would become viable.

POPULATION INVOLVED IN IMPLEMENTATION

The target population whose compliance was necessary for implementation also differed. The concentration policy called for all those who lived in designated sleeping-sickness areas to resettle.

The village settlement policy had selective criteria. Recruitment was to be based on the following characteristics: (1) farming experience, (2) receptivity to new ideas, (3) capacity to work hard, (4) previous contact with the monetary economy, (5) willingness to live together with others, (6) a wife and children, and (7) age between 25 and 40.[30] However, the criteria did not bind the regional and area leaders, who were primarily responsible for actual recruitment. In the process of implementation, the target group for the village settlement scheme was expanded to include other groups not conforming to the original criteria.[31] Many of these were not found suitable for the success of the village settlements.

MECHANISMS FOR GAINING POPULAR COMPLIANCE

To cause the target populations to move into concentrations and village settlements, different types of recruitment campaigns were conducted. In the case of concentrations, not only were persuasion and inducement involved, but compulsion as well. There was no real disagreement among administrators over the first two. When Swynnerton first argued the case for concentration as a way of dealing with the sleeping sickness problem, he proposed four incentives to induce people to move: (1) exemption from government-demanded work, (2) exemption from poll tax, (3) cleared land, and (4) plowed plots.[32] When he later suggested, however, that it was regrettable that more force could not be used, controversy arose. The government asked for the opinions of provincial commissioners (PCs) on Swynnerton's suggestion. Those from both Central and Tabora Provinces expressed opposition to the use of compulsion. In Central Province the PC said that one must proceed with "the utmost circumspection" because the "whole economic and social equilibrium of the tribe might be upset by compulsory moves." Instead he suggested that "by building huts and presents of small stock we should do everything to attract voluntary settlement . . . but compulsory migration is a double-edged sword and may fearfully maim or even destroy the native authority employing such a weapon."[33] In Tabora Province, the PC argued that force should not be used because the natural attraction of the settlements with schools, dispensaries, and freedom from tsetse flies was sufficient to attract people.[34] As a result, a policy was established in 1928 that limited the forced movement of people to significant cases involving sleeping sickness or "prejudicial congestion" of men or cattle.[35] The controversy did not end there, however. Eventually it led to the celebrated Circular No. 40 of 1934, in which Chief Secretary Mitchell sought to define more explicitly the government position on the issue:

> I have heard a certain amount lately about our "concentration policy," which aims at inducing natives to settle in productive areas and develop them, rather than to eke out a precarious livelihood in unproductive areas. Stated in those terms the policy is unexceptionable and deserving of full support; but there seems, and not unnaturally perhaps, to be a certain measure of variety in the interpretation accorded to such words as "induce" and "persuade." Can inducement and persuasion legitimately pass into compulsion in certain circumstance, or can it not?[36]

The answer was that it could, but *only* in such exceptional circumstances as the presence of famine, serious crimes such as cattle raiding, persistent danger to life, or endemic diseases and tsetse flies.[37]

In practice, all three techniques were employed. An example is a case from Western Province during 1936/37. At a public meeting, attended by the acting chief secretary, the provincial commissioner, and the district commissioner, the people were told that they would have to move to a concentration being established nearby. The people who had gathered responded with several of their own demands: that they be permitted to remain together under their chief; that the government promise not to forcibly move them again; that food assistance be given; and that a hospital be built. The government leaders accepted all the requests except that for a hospital. In addition, they agreed to exempt the people from the hut and poll tax for a year, to transport their possessions at government expense, and to build a house for their chief. Although most of the people moved, some fled toward the west and had to be brought back forcibly.[38] Persuasion, inducement, and compulsion were combined in this effort.

In the case of village settlements, recruitment campaigns were launched in various parts of the country to persuade people to join. When the response appeared to be insufficient, two additional steps were taken. First, promises of free food and "other delights" were made as incentives to induce applications to the settlements.[39] Second, the criteria for selection were not rigidly applied. Instead, members often were recruited by regional officials to solve their own problems of unemployment in towns and overpopulation in other areas.[40] As a result, many of those who joined were not really interested in making the settlements a success. In Ellman's words, the settlers considered themselves "rather as temporary and under-paid employees on Government estates, whose aim was to do the least possible work and to exploit the Settlement Agency for what they could get out of it."[41]

It appears that for selective recruitment (e.g., in the case of the village settlement scheme), persuasion and inducement are sufficient and that for general recruitment (e.g., in the case of the concentration policy), compulsion is necessary.

POLITICIZATION OF SETTLERS

Once the villages had been established, little effort was made in the concentrations to directly politicize the settlers to accept values necessary for the development of the village. In the village settlements the responsible ministry and the political leaders were aware of a need to politicize, but found many of the settlers unreceptive. Nellis criticizes leaders for not recognizing that politicization is a long-term proposition. He notes that "after half a year of repeated doses of verbal exhortation failed to elicit revolutionary productive advances, what was altered and discarded was not the method, but the programme."[42] That is, the difficulties experienced were seen as a consequence of the policy rather than of the techniques used to implement the policy. In neither case was politicization used effectively for increasing the responsiveness of the peasantry to the suggestions of government leaders concerning activities likely to promote development.

ORGANIZATION OF PRODUCTION

The policies also differed in the organization of production once settlement had taken place. Although in some concentrations an attempt was made to regulate production through requirements for the rotation of crops, such efforts were said to have "not only failed but produced discontent and unrest, with a tendency for settlers to run away into the bush, where it was difficult to find them."[43] As a result, most attempts were abandoned, and scattered private plots came to form the basic productive units.

In the village settlements, there was more control over the unit of production. Although the system varied from settlement to settlement, there was a tendency toward individual plots in block farms which would involve more and more cooperatively undertaken tasks.[44] There were problems, however. In the only settlement that engaged in communal production of its major crops, Upper Kitete, the amount of work an individual did was not related to the amount of income he got from his effort for at least the first two years. The recruitment propaganda in 1963 suggested a target income per family of £150 ($429). In 1963/64 the Village Settlement Agency paid £100 ($286) and in 1964/65 it paid £68 ($194), but in neither year was the actual income from the sale of the crops near these levels. Rather, the Village Settlement Agency estimated what it thought was necessary to keep the settlers on the scheme. Inasmuch as payment was not directly tied to the amount or quality of work on the communal farm, it did not serve as an incentive to make communal production successful.[45] Thus, in neither the concentrations nor the village settlements was a system of organization for production created that promoted a significant increase in production.

GOVERNANCE OF SETTLEMENTS

The limited control by settlers over planning and organization reflected the limited form of democracy practiced. The governance of the concentrations remained under the native authorities, whereas that of the village settlements was under a manager appointed by the Rural Settlement Commission. Yet some of those in government felt that the degree of participation in decisionmaking was directly related to the degree of compliance with decisions made—i.e., that the virtual absence of democracy interfered with the achievement of village goals. In the village settlement policy there was a plan to democratize governance by transforming settlements into village settlement cooperatives that would be self-governing, but the government appeared very reluctant to promote such a transformation. A Treasury expert, Landell-Mills, stated explicitly that "it is not intended for a very long time if at all, to relinquish the power to appoint the Manager or his right to veto any decision considered harmful to the scheme taken by the elected cooperative committee."[46] The Village Settlement Commission, for its part, was unhappy with the "interference" of the precooperative committees (i.e., those set up prior to formal recognition of the settlements as cooperatives) in the affairs of the manager.[47] There was thus an absence of broad popular participation in the governance of both the village settlements and the concentrations.

COSTS OF IMPLEMENTATION

Part of the reason for the government's hesitancy to pass control to the village settlement scheme settlers was its fear that they would not handle responsibly the vast sums of money involved. The estimated cost per village settlement was £150,000 ($428,571).[48] Only a few of the best settlements had any prospect of retiring such a debt, even over twenty-five years. A very large part of the money obtained came from foreign sources, including the Commonwealth Assistance Loan funds, the Oxford Committee for Famine Relief (OXFAM), and the Irish Freedom from Hunger Committee. According to the commission, "there is no doubt that without aid from overseas it would have been impossible to launch Government's village settlement programme."[49] This high cost and dependence on foreign sources was not a feature of the concentration scheme. In fact, it conformed closely to the relatively low money/labor type of policy common in third world countries, whereas the village settlement scheme conformed more to the high money/labor type of policy common in developed countries. The consequences were important. In April 1966 Prime Minister Kawawa announced that no more village settlements would be established, chiefly because of their inordinate cost. The shift of orientation from money-intensive to labor-intensive efforts was an important principle in the Arusha Declaration, which followed in early 1967.

SETTLEMENTS ESTABLISHED

Although the cost of the concentration policy was much less than that of the village settlement scheme, the number of people involved was much greater. Estimates of the total population affected by the two policies vary substantially, but most indicate that at least ten times as many people were involved in the concentrations as in the village settlements.[50] One representative estimate of the population of the former in 1945 is given in Table II.1. The Village Settlement Commission's estimate of the population of settlements in 1965 is given in Table II.2. In addition to the totals given in Table II.1 and Table II.2, several unplanned and peripheral village settlements and concentrations were established that were never included in the official figures.

The concentration policy was, therefore, initiated to solve a specific problem, whereas the village settlement scheme was started to solve a more general problem; the scope of the former was not

THE EXPERIENCES: PREVIOUS ATTEMPTS AT IMPLEMENTATION

Table II.1

POPULATION OF CONCENTRATIONS IN TANGANYIKA: 1945

District	Number of Settlements Established	Period When Established	Approximate Population[a]
Tabora	8	1920s	19,064
Ufipa	2	1920s	6,009
Kahama	20	1920s	37,759
Kibondo	4	1930s	36,488
Kasulu	4	1930s	16,332
Biharamulo	8	1930s	22,724
Mwanza	7	1930s	11,487
Mahenge	9	1940s	37,188
Mbulu	1	1940s	1,386
Liwale	1	1940s	6,600
TOTAL	64		195,037

Source: Calculated from a chart included in a letter to the Director of Medical Services from the Sleeping Sickness Officer (Fairbairn), 14 November 1945 (TNA: 11771, vol. 2).

[a]These figures are approximate because they are based on Fairbairn's estimate of 3.3 persons per taxpayer and because there was movement into and out of the concentrations after they were established.

expanded, but that of the latter was; in neither was there much popular consultation in planning; the target population of the concentration effort consisted of all people living in a given area, whereas that of the village settlement scheme consisted of a group that was supposed to have met specified qualifications; selective recruitment in the latter case meant reliance on persuasion and inducement, whereas force was added to gain the compliance of those in areas subjected to the former; little politicization was sought in the concentration policy, whereas in the village settlements politicization was attempted but proved ineffective; governance of the concentrations remained under the native-authority system, whereas managers controlled the activities of the village settlers; costs of the latter scheme were much greater than those of the former, yet relatively fewer people were affected by the village settlements than by the concentrations. Just as some pre-1967 policies were directed toward

25

Table II.2

VILLAGE SETTLEMENT SCHEMES: SEPTEMBER 1965

Village	District	Year Founded	Approximate Population
Pilot Village Settlement Schemes:			
1. Upper Kitete	Mbulu	1963	400
2. Rwamkoma	Musoma	1963	456
3. Mlale	Songea	1963	880
4. Kingongurundwa	Lindi	1963	600
5. Kabuku	Handeni	1964	724
6. Kerege	Bagamoyo	1964	764
7. Bawakria Chini	Morogoro	1964	120
8. Kiwere	Iringa	1963 under TAC	936
Assisted Schemes:			
1. Buyombe	Geita	1963	304
2. Matwiga	Chunya	1964	400
3. Mkata	Morogoro	1963	364
4. Galu	Ukerewe	1964	316
5. Amani	Muheza	1965	(a)
Ex-TAC (Tobacco):			
1. Urambo	Tabora	1956	5180
2. Lupatingatinga	Chunya	1962	720
Ex-TAC (Ranching):			
1. Kongwa	Mpwapwa	1962	600
2. Matongoro	Mpwapwa	1962	360
Ex-TAC (Mixed Farming):			
1. Ichonde	Ulanga	1960	1000
2. Sonjo	Ulanga	1960	1000
3. Kichangani	Ulanga	1960	1000
4. Nachingwea[b]	Nachingwea	1952	528
AGRIDEV:[c]			
1. Nyatwali	Musoma	1963	200
2. Kalamera	Mwanza	1963	400
3. Mbarika	Mwanza	1963	200
TOTALS: 24 schemes			15,412

Sources: Nikolaus Newiger, "Village Settlement Schemes, The Problem of Cooperative Farming," in *Smallholder Farming and Smallholder Development in Tanzania*, ed. Hans Ruthenberg (Munich: Weltforum Verlag, 1968), pp. 256 and 268; and P.M. Landell-Mills, "Village Settlement in Tanzania, An Economic Commentary," University of Dar es Salaam, Economics Seminar 1965/66, Paper No. 2 (9 November 1965) [mimeo], p. 21. The "approximate population" figures are estimates determined by multiplying by four (an estimate of family size) the number of settlers given in the above-mentioned sources.

[a] 108 families were proposed but not selected by September 1965.

[b] About to be closed at the time.

[c] AGRIDEV schemes were started by the Agricultural Development Company (International) of Israel.

getting people to live together, others were aimed at getting people to work together.

GETTING PEOPLE TO WORK TOGETHER: PRE-UJAMAA VILLAGE POLICIES

As we have noted, a major problem with the implementation of the village settlement policy was the post-settlement task of getting people to work together. There is considerable disagreement as to the extent of joint work prior to the intrusion of colonialism. In the President's paper outlining the ujamaa village policy in 1967 he explicitly stated that working together was a basic aspect of traditional African family life. Others have argued, though, that the scope and form of such labor was not the same as that demanded by the ujamaa village policy. As one Tanzanian scholar observed:

> Ujamaa—in the strict sense of (1) communal production, (2) equitable sharing of communally produced goods, and (3) communal ownership of the means of production . . . was possible only at the primary family and, in some cases, extended family levels. What existed beyond these levels was ujima rather than ujamaa. *Ujima* is a Swahili word which refers to the habitual practice of the cooperation of villagers in certain "peak" seasons . . . or in cases of emergency.[51]

Government policies during the colonial period that necessitated collective work outside the family for their implementation may be divided into two general types. On the one hand, efforts were made to get Tanzanian peasants to work together to market their crops. On the other hand, there were efforts to induce them to apply their labor to productive tasks such as clearing brush outside concentrations, keeping up roads, preventing soil erosion, stopping grass fires, and building government buildings. The government's role was much more tentative and the peasant response much more hesitant in the former than in the latter.

WORKING TOGETHER: COOPERATIVES

When modern cooperative ideas spread to Africa in the 1920s and 1930s, Tanzania was one of the first countries on the continent to encourage the movement. In the 1920s, the Kilimanjaro Native Coffee Planters' Association was established among coffee growers in the Moshi area.[52] This cooperative (later to be known as the Kilimanjaro Native Cooperative Union) became one of the most powerful cooperative organizations in Africa. The government sought to regulate the growth of cooperatives through the Cooperative Societies Ordinance, passed in 1932. Its attitude toward cooperative expansion, however, was ambiguous.

In 1934 an officer was sent abroad to be trained in cooperative work. By the time he returned, government enthusiasm for encouraging the movement had diminished.[53] The marketing system of the 1930s, with a few important exceptions, was controlled by Indian traders. The decline in government support for cooperatives involved a shift of support from the leading African farmers to the Asian traders. So great was the shift that in 1944 the registrar of cooperatives complained bitterly that "the attitude of the Tanganyika Government towards the fostering and the advancement of the cooperative societies has been entirely negative."[54] In the postwar period, however, the colonial government began cautiously to foster the movement. On the one hand, it appeared to want to encourage the progressive farmers through cooperatives, but on the other hand, it feared that the movement might become a political tool aimed at its demise.[55] After independence, the government urged the formation of cooperatives with renewed vigor. No longer was there hesitancy to eliminate the Asian traders. The expansion of cooperatives was seen as "proof of TANU's penetration of the rural areas and of its success to capture the marketing system of agricultural produce. For the new party lieutenants in the regions and in the districts each new cooperative society meant an increasing opportunity for a rise to further prominence."[56] The growth of cooperatives and cooperative membership is shown in Table II.3.

Government assistance to the cooperative movement took the form of advice, training, and encouragement. Persuasion was an effective mechanism to get many peasants to work together in cooperatives, but it was not sufficient to induce them to apply their labor to tasks set by the government.

WORKING TOGETHER: LABOR

The application of joint labor to achieve policy objectives during the colonial period was the subject of considerable controversy. Although the formal debate concerned "legitimacy," the real issue seemed to be "utility." That is, the question appeared to be what was the least costly and most beneficial way to get people to

THE EXPERIENCES: PREVIOUS ATTEMPTS AT IMPLEMENTATION

Table II.3

GROWTH OF THE COOPERATIVE MOVEMENT IN TANZANIA:
SELECTED YEARS, 1934-1973

Year	Number of Societies	Number of Members
1934	23	16,800
1938	37	33,474
1943	45	44,717
1948	77	58,012
1953	198	156,276
1958	546	318,900
1963	1201	458,953
1968	1694	643,720[a]
1973	2299	873,620[a]

Sources: Data for 1934, 1938, 1943, and 1948 are from Tanganyika, *Annual Report on Cooperative Development*, 1949 (Dar es Salaam: Government Printer, 1950), p. 3; for 1953, from Tanganyika, *Annual Report, 1953* (Moshi: KNCU Press, 1954), p. 4; for 1963, from *Annual Report, 1963* (Dar es Salaam: Mwananchi Publishing Co., 1966), p. 3; for 1968, number of societies from Herbert C. Kriesel et al., *Agricultural Marketing in Tanzania: Background Research and Policy Proposals* (Michigan State University, June 1970), p. 63; for 1973, number of societies from Cooperative Union of Tanzania, "Structure of Agricultural Marketing in Tanzania," January 1975 (mimeo), p. 2.

[a]The number of members is based on an average membership per society of 380 (the average for 1963, 1964, and 1965 was 382, 384, and 400 respectively).

work together for particular ends. Cost and benefit were calculated in a broad sense to include regime stability. The technique used for gaining compliance was partly reflected in the descriptive terms used, which include communal labor, tribal turnout, requisitioned labor, conscripted labor, and forced labor.

Forced labor supposedly had been ended after World War I by Article 5 of the League of Nations mandate, which stated that the mandatory (Great Britain) would "prohibit all forms of forced or compulsory labour, except for essential public works and services, and then only in return for adequate remuneration."[57] The prohibition was reaffirmed in the International Convention on Forced or Compulsory Labor, sponsored by the International Labour Organization (ILO), which was made applicable to the territory in the early 1930s. The convention was interpreted to mean that the government could not use force to gain the labor it required to implement policies, except for what might be considered "minor communal services." The colonial administration, however, devised various methods of circumventing such restrictions and applying the full range of compliance techniques.

One method was to interpret very broadly what was voluntary and very narrowly what was forced. For example, in Central Province in 1936 the PC asserted that a large labor turnout was voluntary and not forced because "the native authorities only saw fit to punish 90 men out of a total of 32,190 men employed. In as much as 90 men refused to work, the labour is requisitioned, but in as much as 32,100 men worked willingly, the labour is voluntary and communal."[58] A similar view was expressed by the PC, Southern Highlands Province, who argued that compulsory laborers were only those who refused to be persuaded and had to be punished.[59] This meant that activities which many would consider forced were interpreted as voluntary. Such a practice avoided overt contravention of the convention.

A second method was to interpret broadly the meaning of "minor communal service" and thereby expand the types of activities in which force could be used. One way the expression was defined was as those activities "which are rendered in the interests of the persons giving them."[60] Clearly there was almost no limit to what might be included under such a concept. Another way was to list the kind of activities considered "minor communal services." For example, before he became governor, Mitchell wrote: "By communal labour we do not mean any form of labour for Government. . . . We mean labour employed in the cleaning and repair of village roads, the clearing of tsetse bush, repair of main irrigation furrows and the like."[61] In 1931 the advisory legislative council, consisting principally of government officials, added the sanitary care of villages and drives to destroy vermin that were damaging crops.[62] In fact the list continued to expand during the colonial period. Governor Cameron defined the expression in another way, saying that it was labor ordered by the chiefs for the general betterment of the community, from which the workers could return home at night.[63] Although such a limitation narrowed the physical range within which work could be required, it left open the type of work. That the interpretation in Tanzania was broader than that in Kenya is illustrated by an incident in 1945. At that time Kenya was considering legislation to facilitate the clearing of brush for tsetse eradication. Kenyan officials did not see how they could get around the labor convention in order to require the necessary labor to participate in the work. They contacted their colonial counterparts in Tanzania to discover how they had done it.[64] A member of the Secretariat replied that "we have only 'managed to get round the International Labour Convention' as you put it" by interpreting such labor as "minor communal labor."[65]

A third method used during World War II was to conscript labor and then send the conscripts where needed. The first such labor appears to have been assembled in August 1942.[66] Despite the fact that the rationale behind the practice was primarily the desire to increase wartime production, it continued for some years after 1945. In fact, it was simply another mechanism to broaden the range of tools available to the government to direct labor toward policy ends.

A fourth method of avoiding the restrictions on the use of compulsion to get people to work together in implementing policies was the use of tax labor. The problem of extracting tax from the peasantry in Tanzania was compounded by the fact that the monetary economy had not embraced the whole country. Some people simply had no money with which to pay taxes. When the first British tax legislation was proposed in 1921, it called for labor if taxes could not be paid in money. This provision prompted the secretary of state for the colonies, Winston Churchill, to respond:

> I am unable, on the grounds of policy, to accept the proposal that compulsory labour should be introduced even in the form suggested, in the case of natives who fail to pay their hut and poll tax. The retention of this provision would, I fear, lead to difficulties and I must request that it may be removed from the Ordinance.[67]

However, Governor Byatt presented a strong personal plea for the inclusion of the clause and Churchill consented, demanding only a change in the wording concerning the purpose of the labor from "to perform services of public utility" to "on any public works and services authorized by the Government."[68] When the practice was questioned during discussions concerning the Forced Labour Convention in 1929, Governor Cameron stated that "the Tanganyika Government would not wish to depart from its practice of extracting work in lieu of nonpayment of tax."[69] The secretary of state for the colonies, however, urged that the tax law be changed because it violated the spirit of the convention to which they were agreeing. The administration in Tanzania argued that "labour *in default of payment* cannot be authorized on account of the convention, but labour *in lieu of tax* . . . is desirable."[70] The Native Tax Ordinance, 1934, restated the policy of requiring tax to be paid in labor if money could not be produced. In fact, as late as 1951 the administration observed that "Tanganyika is now the only colonial territory left in Africa in which there is legal provision for discharge of tax obligation in this manner."[71] The Native Tax (Amendment) Order, 1951, finally ended the payment of tax in labor. Table II.4 indicates the sizable amount of labor obtained in lieu of tax.

Table II.4

LABOR OBTAINED IN LIEU OF TAX PAYMENTS:
TANGANYIKA, SELECTED YEARS

Year	Number of Men	Number of Man-Days
1936	28,307	924,980
1938	13,441	370,151
1941	15,299	505,372
1950	1,127	44,498

Sources: Figures for tax defaulters for 1936, 1938, and 1941 are from "Returns of Tax Defaulters Employed by the Government," TNA: 24744, Vol. 2; for 1950, from Tanganyika Territory, "Annual Report for the Period Ending 30th June 1951 on the International Labour Convention" (mimeo).

PEASANT COST/BENEFIT ASSESSMENT OF COMPLIANCE

The willingness of the peasant to comply with work demands apparently varied with his cost/benefit assessment of the action. It should be noted, however, that the mixture of factors affecting this assessment was and is very complex.

Differing customs, for instance, imply differing values. Swynnerton found that the Sukuma responded well,[72] but the labor commissioner noted that the Masai "will undergo any sort of punishment rather than perform manual labour."[73]

Differing wealth also implies differing values. For example, a coffee officer in the Kilimanjaro area required porters to carry his equipment to another part of the mountain. Instead of complying by contributing their labor, the peasants collected money and hired a truck.[74]

Furthermore, differing needs imply differing values. It was always much more difficult to gain the necessary work compliance during the planting season, when a peasant's food supply was at stake, than during the dry season, when there was little competition for his time.[75]

Values are also affected by leadership. Swynnerton noted during a "turnout" in Singida that those who worked under one chief labored much harder than those who worked under others. He attributed the difference simply to "a matter of leadership."[76]

Finally, differing benefits affect the willingness to comply. Many policies tended to require more labor from those who benefitted least than from those who benefitted most. Three examples illustrate this point. First, costs and benefits were unequally distributed under the policy that required peasants to contribute their labor to maintain roads. A colonial official observed in 1928 that in Tanga the roads were used mainly by European planters and administrative officers. The official noted that this meant "that the work done by the natives is not merely for their own comfort and economic development." For the sake of equity, he saw "no reason why they should be the only ones to work or pay to provide roads."[77] Nevertheless, the practice continued, at least on local roads, for decades. Second, the policies that required peasants to turn out for general reclamation work did not normally spread the costs and benefits equally. This fact was observed by the PC, Lake Province, in the Shinyanga area in 1935:

There is little doubt that reclamation work, whether it be for the purpose of creating extra grazing, settlement, water supply or to combat soil erosion is being undertaken for the benefit of the whole tribe but the actual and visible results at present appear to the onlooker only to favour wealthy stockowners. The immediate results of such work no doubt favour the stockowners who would lose large number of stock through starvation unless they can obtain extra grazing for their stock.[78]

To offset some of the inequalities, stockowners offered to contribute cattle for consumption by communal labor engaged in the reclamation work. The offer reduced the inordinate benefit to the stockowners and cost to the government and workers.[79] Third, certain groups were exempted from the requirement that they contribute their labor toward joint projects. In the case of Shinyanga cited above, many of the cattleowners did not join in the work because of their age. At the time of the 1956 turnout in Kondoa, exemptions involved (1) those with year-round paid employment, (2) "a reasonable number" of bush schoolteachers in each village, (3) members of the local government advisory committee, (4) skilled workmen who worked for the native authority or missions during the dry season, (5) one "helper" for each native authority, and (6) half the unskilled labour of the missions.[80] If one did not qualify for exemption on any of these grounds, he could do so by either paying Shs. 60 or contributing a number of cattle.[81] The point to be made here is that the costs and benefits of working together required for the implementation of government policy did not fall equally on Tanzania's rural population. Although in most cases peasant assessment of costs and benefits of compliance is difficult to reconstruct, available evidence suggests that it is the primary factor accounting for differing responses to compliance demands.

LEADER COST/BENEFIT ASSESSMENT OF ACTION TO GAIN COMPLIANCE

Implementation of policies that required significant labor inputs was affected not only by the complex of peasant values, but also by the values of the colonial officers. Technical and administrative officers apparently differed with regard to the importance they attached to "means," probably because of differences in responsibilities. The technical officers were employed to clear land to prevent tsetse infestation or to reduce stock to prevent soil erosion— i.e., to accomplish specific policy ends. The administrative officers were employed to maintain law and order and colonial rule—i.e., to accomplish tasks that might be made more difficult by disregarding the effect of particular means on the achievement of such policy ends.

A case in point is the large-scale tsetse-clearing campaigns in the late 1920s and early 1930s. The tsetse-control people, including Swynnerton and Bax, wanted quick and massive clearing operations. When the fly was found in Central Province, Bax insisted that "tsetse martial law should be declared and every resource of the area be at our disposal to fight the advance. Anything less, I'm afraid, will lead to certain failure."[82] His attitude clashed with that of the administrative officers, who feared the political consequences of the demand for such compliance. By Circular 55 of 1926, primary but not complete control of reclamation and labor turnouts was put in the hands of the provincial commissioners.[83] Nevertheless, the tsetse-control people pushed their urgent cases to the secretariat. In 1927 Sayers, a member of the secretariat, wrote:

> I sincerely hope that we are not going to be dragged in as a buffer state between the [tsetse-control people] . . . and the PCs in the proposals submitted by the former. . . . Mr. Swynnerton talks gaily in some of his letters to PCs of demands for ten thousand men![84]

The governor reacted by further centralizing tsetse control. Beginning in April 1929, he declared, all tsetse reclamation "will be conducted by Government as an administrative measure. Decisions relating to the execution of these measures will be exclusively a matter for the Administration."[85] The difference in valuations of joint labor led to a further clarification in 1938 by the acting chief secretary, who stated explicitly that "the functions of Agricultural Officers in a matter of this kind are advisory. . . . It is from officers of the Administration that the 'drive' and initiative must come, and it is mainly upon them that the responsibility for giving effect to Government's policy will rest."[86] It is quite clear that the colonial government was very concerned about the political consequences of the techniques used for getting people to work together for policy ends.

Differences existed among administrative officers in regard to the importance they attached to the same policies. This was a major problem at provincial and district levels when officers were moved. As early as 1925, the government attempted to bring about some uniformity by informing all administrative officers that

> it is not fair to the natives and the rest of the community that the policy of a District should be constantly changing according as this officer or that is in charge of it. . . . An officer succeeding to a district must not alter the policy which he finds obtaining in the district when he takes over, without obtaining sanction from headquarters.[87]

The same problem nevertheless continued until independence. Liebenow has vividly illustrated this situation, which he refers to as "White Man's Madness" (*Wazimu wa Mzungu*), in Mikindani district.[88]

Technical officers sometimes changed their minds as new information became available. We have noted the plea of Fairbairn,

the sleeping-sickness officer, for an extension of the policy of concentrations in the early 1940s so that they might lead to general
social and economic development.[89] He based his assessment on his
belief that local soils could be maintained fertile, but discovered a
few years later that, in fact, it was not known how to accomplish
this.[90] As a result, he did not advocate extension of the scope of
the policy as vehemently as he had previously.

There were also differences between higher- and lower-level
officers. A suggestion from above was often taken below as an
order. Higher costs involved in gaining compliance to achieve a policy
end were sometimes deemed warranted by the lower-level officer
than would have been deemed warranted by the central administration. It was for this reason that the administration demanded that
local officers obtain approval before orders for tribal turnouts were
issued with legal backing.

The complexity and uncertainty of peasant and administrator
calculation of costs and benefits of actions led the government to
be wary of implementing policies that required the labor of large
numbers of peasants. Errors in assessing operative values had led to
problems. In 1907 the governor of German East Africa, Freiherr
von Rechenberg, reported in a dispatch to the Colonial Office in
Berlin that it was his belief that the Maji Maji rebellion of 1905-7
was a result of the attempt to get people to work on communal
cotton plots that were unlikely to benefit them.[91] In 1927 the
British governor, wary about the political consequences of demands
for labor in tsetse-fly work, sent a memorandum to all PCs arguing
that where evasion was likely, a statutory order under the Native
Authority Ordinance should be issued so that authority would not
be undermined by noncompliance. In fact, the potential danger of
the implied use of force was so important that he required personal
approval in every case: "Such order must not be made . . . until the
sanction of the Governor has been obtained . . . and even if fly
reclamation work is regarded as voluntary the Governor's sanction
must be obtained before embarking on any scheme."[92] In 1928
the secretary of native affairs supported the Central Province PC's
view that "the turning out of communal labour on such a large scale
is subversive to the authority of the chiefs."[93] When the demands
for very large turnouts in Shinyanga and Kwimba reached the secretariat, it was observed by an officer that "even the most tractable
tribes in Africa will not put up with this sort of thing for very
long."[94] By 1955 the wariness had increased, and when planning
the tribal turnout that year, the DC observed that

The imposition of unpaid communal labour is a platform which political societies are now beginning to use to create trouble with traditional forms of local Government, and the greatest care must be taken that projects have full consent and cooperation of local authorities at the lowest possible level.[95]

This insecurity led the colonial government to devise mechanisms for implementation which would decrease the likelihood that problems would arise because of governmental demands for compliance. The most important was decentralization.

DECENTRALIZATION FOR COMPLIANCE

Decentralization for policy implementation involved the transfer of authority to the provincial and district commissioners and to the native authorities. There was very little territory-wide legislation requiring communal labor during the colonial period. Most was rejected as impossible to implement, and such as was passed was discretionary—i.e., it applied to only parts of the country. Two examples are the Native Liquor Ordinance and the Grass Fires Ordinance. The decision to extend such legislation to a given province or district required a request from the provincial commissioner and the consent of the governor. Much more important than legislation were circulars to and discussions with provincial and district officials urging them to take action to promote various objectives. The decision to take action, however, was normally at the discretion of provincial and district officials, as was the manner in which that action was undertaken. Even at these levels, though, dangers were seen in demanding popular compliance. As a result, responsibility was further decentralized to the native authorities.

Although the practice of decentralizing responsibility for policy implementation to African administrators goes back to the German period, it was the British administration that made it a basic principle. Governor Byatt, the first British administrator, is reported to have written that

It is beyond the bounds of possibility that a single European officer can properly administer his district or subdistrict except with the assistance of the tribal chiefs as intermediaries, and it is therefore the policy of the Government to support and strengthen the authority of the chiefs among their people. . . .[96]

Governor Cameron, who is usually given credit for this policy of indirect rule, wrote similarly: "It is quite impossible for us to administer the country directly through British officers. . . . Why then destroy an instrument that we *must* use?"[97] Nearly all policies affecting the peasantry, from tax collection to soil-erosion measures to tsetse clearings, were carried out through the native authorities. The manner of delegation of responsibility varied. An extreme example is illustrated by a case in Central Province:

> Native Authorities are informed of the communal tasks which are required to be performed during the year and are instructed to call out all able-bodied taxpayers available in their areas. A schedule is prepared for their guidance as to the number of taxpayers who may be expected to be turned out. Depending on the area concerned, this varies between 50% and 80% of the number of taxpayers on the books.[98]

The vast array of possible responsibilities that might be devolved to these administrators was given in the Native Authority Ordinance. These initially included matters dealing with intoxicating liquors, gambling, breaches of the peace, spread of diseases, migration of people, livestock movement, grass burning, tsetse flies, cultivation of crops, minimum acreages, and many others. In the administration's notes on the ordinance it is indicated that these matters were specified not only to clarify native law, but also "to draw attention to particular matters upon which the Government expects Native Authorities to exercise the duty of control."[99] The governor kept adding to this list. By 1952, twenty more matters for general application and forty-eight for restricted application were added.[100] Failure to comply was initially punishable by a maximum penalty of 200 shillings or two months' imprisonment, or both. By 1952 the two months' imprisonment had risen to three. Throughout the period of colonial rule the administration frequently circulated "model" orders which the native authorities were expected to promulgate.

The system did not work perfectly for the colonial administration. In some cases, the native authorities were unable to act; in others, they refused to act as instructed. Nevertheless, the policy of decentralizing to the provincial and district levels and to the native administration overcame some of the difficulties caused by limited resources and the wide range of values that existed in rural Tanzania.

The nature of collective work made possible by decentralization can be illustrated by two examples, one from Lake and the other from Central Province. A massive anti-tsetse operation was undertaken in Kwimba during 1928. First, chiefs and headmen were ordered to bring able-bodied men to specified camps. A total of 14,800 men were recruited in this way. Government supervisors were assigned to each camp. Then, with the help of the native-authority officials, the men were put to work. At the end of ten days, twenty square miles of land had been cleared. Overall responsibility for the operation was in the hands of the Mwanza provincial commissioner, who asserted that "Politically the effect of the turn-out has been excellent. The various factions have been brought together and worked side by side for the common weal of the tribe, tribal pride has been fostered by friendly rivalry . . . [and] close touch was maintained between the Chief, Sub-Chiefs and people."[101]

In the later years of colonial rule, the turnouts were more modest. The tribal turnout in Kondoa in 1955 was initiated with a demand by district officials that each village produce 30 percent of its taxpayers to work thirty days, and 20 percent to work ten days. The headmen compiled the lists, but then a problem arose. When the people on the lists were called up, it was found that many had moved from the area. As a result, according to the district commissioner, "people were seized at the last moment and bundled off to the clearings without having time to prepare their flour, and in some camps one was faced with every variety of hardluck story which one could only ignore. . . ." Nevertheless, "the atmosphere in the camps was generally healthy; it was accepted that the tsetse clearing had to be done and most men were prepared to work hard, pocket their 16/- and go home to their wives." According to the DC's reports:

> The only serious complaints were that, due to nepotism on the part of the headmen and to the activities of the "wide-boys" who ran off to Arusha, the same people were sent to the clearings every year, and that as a result of being seized without notice, their food was insufficient and a nice degree of chaos prevailed at home.[102]

Obviously, the colonial administrator was the initiator of the policy and the native authorities were the ones who were primarily responsible for the major task of getting the people to come to work together.

AVOIDANCE TECHNIQUES

Numerous avoidance techniques were devised to deal with colonial demands. The two most common were to flee the area or simply to refuse to comply. It was to deal with these situations that the use of force became important. Often there was no way to deal with those who ran off, but sometimes they were pursued. As previously noted, those who fled the concentration efforts in Western Province were tracked down. Those who fled the Kondoa turnout described above were dealt with similarly. The district commissioner reported that he sent a messenger to Moshi with warrants

> of arrest for a number of Warangi who are believed to have run away . . . after being detailed to attend barazas for tribal turnout selection. . . . This is an essential part of our policy to make the impact of tribal turnout as equitable as possible and it will provide a salutory lesson if we could catch even half a dozen of the spivs who evade their responsibilities to the community.[103]

Several were caught. Flat refusals were encountered in cases where legal sanctions were not available. Many examples could be cited, but in the early 1950s the Lake Province PC put the argument for statutory sanction in the following way:

> All responsible and public spirited persons are in favour of tribal turnouts. . . . I submit that it is the very essence of democracy that the minority should be bound by the wishes of the majority. . . . It may well happen, however, that a nucleus of idle, ill-informed, or selfish men may refuse to cooperate. Public Opinion is not as yet a sufficiently effective instrument to coerce this minority, and government may no longer rely, as it once did, on the influence or personality of the chief. If such persons do not contribute their share towards the output of their fellows they should, in my opinion, be punished. Otherwise, the "workers" will soon tire of doing more than their fair share, will become disgruntled at seeing others who refuse to assist go unpunished, and the rot will set in.[104]

It is clear that once the decision to implement was made, the government proceeded by stages in the application of techniques of implementation, although the shift from persuasion to compulsion often was a rapid one.

By the late 1950s, the importance of compulsion, which had been so great during most of the colonial period, began to decline markedly with the growth of the nationalist challenge to British rule. As we have noted, the use of compulsion was seen by the government as a potential threat to law and order and the maintenance of governmental authority. With British control of Tanganyika already threatened, there was hesitancy to do anything that might increase that threat. "Persistent persuasion" was an expression used to describe the predominant means for gaining peasant compliance in the late 1950s.[105] Compulsion continued to be deemphasized throughout most of the period prior to the initiation of the ujamaa village policy.

CONCLUSIONS

The experiences with policy implementation in rural Tanzania prior to 1967 involved both settlement and getting people to work together. The concentrations were shown to be a low-cost effort to deal with a problem that was solved by mere settlement. The village settlements were seen as a high-cost effort to solve problems for which settlement was only a necessary step. The concentration effort showed that it was possible to use compulsion to move masses of peasants from certain areas into villages. The settlement scheme indicated that incentive recruitment of villagers was possible but that it posed many problems for post-settlement activities. Policies encouraging peasants to participate in cooperatives were much more enthusiastically received than those requiring collective labor. Implementation of the latter was characterized from the early years of colonial rule until the late 1950s by emphasis on the use of compulsion, whereas from the late 1950s until after the initiation of the ujamaa village policy, inducement was stressed.

There appears to be a relationship between the mechanisms used to gain compliance and both the target population and the resources of the government. When compliance of the general population in an area is sought, compulsion appears relatively more useful than inducement; the reverse may be true when compliance of selected individuals in an area is sought. For example, compulsion was probably a necessary condition for the successful implementattion of the concentration policy, but not for the selective resettlement required in the village settlement scheme. Government use of particular mechanisms is also related to the type and amount of resources it is willing to use. The primary costs of inducement are financial resources, whereas in compulsion they are government stability. The colonial government was particularly concerned with the maintenance of rule. As a result, policies were applied to limited areas, compulsion was used hesitantly, responsibility for its use was decentralized, and its employment was halted when political pressures became great in the late 1950s. The Tanzanian government's limited financial resources were insufficient for more than a few peasants in the village settlement scheme. Moreover, incentives for those few were often ineffective because they frequently were not directly tied to the desired behavior. These historical experiences with policies requiring living or working together, or both, constitute one set of factors that affected the formulation and evolution of the ujamaa village policy. There were, in addition, many social, economic, and political factors, to which we turn in the following chapter.

Chapter III

THE CONTEXT: SOCIAL, ECONOMIC, POLITICAL, AND ADMINISTRATIVE FACTORS AFFECTING IMPLEMENTATION

The concentration, village settlement, cooperative, and "collective" labor policies of the colonial and early independence periods, which were the subject of Chapter II, were affected by diverse environmental factors that contributed to both the manner of implementation and the degree of success achieved. Some of these factors, such as the dispersion of the population, had existed for many years; others, such as government's willingness to provide substantial resources for the building of village settlements, were relatively new. Environmental factors most relevant to the ujamaa village policy and its implementation may be grouped under the headings "socioeconomic situation" and "agents of implementation." Both the former, which was dealt with briefly in Chapter I, and the latter, consisting primarily of the party and government, will be examined in this chapter. Attempts to generalize from the experiences of implementing the ujamaa village policy in Tanzania to the process of implementation must take these specific contextual features into account.

THE SOCIOECONOMIC SITUATION

Among the most important socioeconomic features in Tanzania are the prevalence of peasant cultivators, the existence of some economic differentiation in rural areas, substantial ethnic diversity, historical experiences with shifting residences, a rapidly increasing African population, the availability of unused land, a stagnant agricultural sector, growing government domination of the economy, and continued dependence of the economy on trade with capitalist countries.

(1) *The population of Tanzania consists predominantly of peasant cultivators.* That the population affected by the ujamaa village policy is the largest group in Tanzania can be easily estab-

43

lished by looking at the proportion of families engaged in farming, the proportion of economically active people engaged in agriculture, and the proportion of the gross domestic product (GDP) derived from agriculture. The 1967 census found 86 percent of the country's households engaged in farming.[1] Ninety-eight percent of these were engaged in smallholder cultivation and 2 percent in large-scale farming.[2] The proportion is even higher if one considers only the economically active population, as indicated in Table III.1. Of those active in agriculture, 97.5 percent were engaged in cultivation, 1.8 percent in animal husbandry, 0.6 percent in fishing, and 0.1 percent in forestry.[3]* Likewise, the percentage contributions by sectors to the GDP indicate that agriculture continues to predominate, as shown in Table III.2.

Table III.1

ECONOMICALLY ACTIVE POPULATION IN
MAJOR OCCUPATIONAL GROUPS, MAINLAND TANZANIA: 1967

Occupation	Number	Percent
Agriculture	5,063,303	91.3%
Labor	154,121	2.8
Service	97,583	1.8
Professional, technical	62,842	1.1
Sales	54,323	1.0
Communication	47,207	0.9
Clerical	36,574	0.7
Administrative, executive	23,426	0.4
Mining	3,700	0.1
TOTALS	5,543,079[a]	100.1[b]

Source: Tanzania, *Statistical Abstract, 1970* (Dar es Salaam: Government Printer, 1972), p. 57.

[a]In addition, the census recorded 34,337 for whom no occupation was specified.

[b]Percentages have been rounded off to the nearest 0.1 percent.

*Despite the fact that only a small percentage of the agricultural population considers its occupation to be animal husbandry, approximately ten million head of cattle, four million goats, and three million sheep were recorded in 1965 (Tanzania, *Statistical Abstract, 1966* [Dar es Salaam: Government Printer, 1968], p. 86).

THE CONTEXT: FACTORS AFFECTING IMPLEMENTATION

Table III.2

PERCENTAGE OF CONTRIBUTION OF SECTORS TO THE GDP IN
MAINLAND TANZANIA: 1964, 1967, 1970, 1973[a]

Sector	Years			
	1964	1967	1970	1973
Agriculture, hunting, forestry and fishing	46.7%	43.6%	41.7%	39.2%
Mining and quarrying	2.5	2.8	1.3	1.0
Manufacturing and handicrafts	7.1	8.4	9.3	10.0
Electricity and water supply	0.9	1.0	1.2	1.4
Construction	3.4	4.3	4.3	4.9
Wholesale and retail trade and restaurants and hotels	11.9	12.0	12.8	12.2
Transport, storage, and communications	6.9	7.9	9.5	10.0
Finance, insurance, real estate, and business services	10.2	10.4	9.9	9.7
Public administration and other services	11.0	10.9	11.3	13.0
Less imputed bank service charges	0.6	1.3	1.3	1.5
TOTALS	100.0	100.0	100.0	99.9[b]

Source: Tanzania, National Accounts of Tanzania, 1964-1972 (Dar es Salaam: Bureau of Statistics, February 1974), table 8, p. 21.

[a]At 1966 prices.

[b]Percentages have been rounded off to the nearest 0.1 percent.

Because the target group of the policy comprised the overwhelming majority of the population, the significance of possible success and the risks of possible failure were substantial. The peasant population, however, is by no means homogeneous.

(2) Economic differentiation in rural areas has developed to only a moderate extent. The question of the existence of rural differentiation may be divided into two subsidiary questions: "Are there differences in rural wealth?" and "Are these differences significant?" As to the first, there is general agreement. Differences do exist, as shown in Table III.3, which summarizes data collected in the government's household-budget survey (1969). Few observers deny that during the 1950s the British sought to create a group of

Table III.3

INCOME DISTRIBUTION IN RURAL AREAS OF
MAINLAND TANZANIA: 1967

Annual Cash Income	Percent of Population
Shs. 0 -Shs. 249 ($0-$36)	46.0%
Shs. 250-Shs. 499 ($36-$71)	19.6
Shs. 500-Shs. 749 ($71-$107)	10.6
Shs. 750-Shs. 999 ($107-$145)	5.9
Shs. 1,000-Shs. 1,499 ($145-$214)	7.3
Shs. 1,500-Shs. 1,999 ($214-$286)	4.1
Shs. 2,000-Shs. 3,999 ($286-$571)	4.6
Shs. 4,000-Shs. 5,999 ($571-$857)	1.2
Shs. 6,000-Shs. 7,999 ($857-$1,143)	0.5
Shs. 8,000-Shs. 9,999 ($1,143-$1,428)	0.1
Shs. 10,000-Shs. 19,999 ($1,429-$2,857)	0.2

Source: Tanzania, *National Accounts of Tanzania, 1964-1972* (Dar es Salaam: Bureau of Statistics, February 1974), table 29, p. 38.

"progressive farmers" who acquired greater wealth than other peasants. Several researchers in the late 1960s and early 1970s found substantial differences in the distribution of wealth, especially in the form of land, in various parts of the country. For example, John Sender, after a study in Lushoto district, concluded that "It would be flying in the face of the vast majority of the evidence from socio-economic surveys to suggest that the degree of unevenness in the distribution of land found . . . was untypical or in any way unusual in rural areas of Tanzania."[4] However, the fact that differences exist does not necessarily imply that they were significant.

In a study of the household-budget survey data, Manuel Gottlieb concluded that the magnitude of differentiation indicated was not really very substantial.[5] Issa Shivji has argued that though the more wealthy peasants may have been politically important in a few local areas, they have never played a significant role nationally.[6] Henry Mapolu goes so far as to say that the problem with implementation of the ujamaa village policy was that differentiation was not leading to class struggle, something which was necessary for real socialist construction.[7] The absence of a recognized "enemy" distinguishes Tanzania from most countries in which collectivization efforts were undertaken. Differences in wealth did, however, produce different cost/benefit assessments of compliance and led to differences in readiness to move into ujamaa villages. Besides economic differentiation, tribal differences provided another potential cleavage within the peasantry.

(3) *Substantial ethnic diversity characterizes the Tanzanian population.* Both the party and the government have worked hard to reduce the impact of "tribalism." Partly as a result of their efforts and partly as a result of the degree of diversity, it has not been as significant a factor in Tanzania as in other African countries. Because of the difficulty in distinguishing among many ethnic groups, the number identified has varied with every census: 68 were recognized in 1921, 137 in 1931, 117 in 1948, 123 in 1957, and 130 in 1967.[8] The ten ethnic groups with the highest population in 1967 are listed in Table III.4. Although the rank order has changed slightly since the 1948 and 1957 censuses, the percentage of total population has remained almost constant.

In general, the fewer the ethnic groups in an area, the more telling the impact of any one of them; hence the importance of a single ethnic group tends to be greater at lower levels of the administrative structure than at higher ones. As shown in Table III.5, in only 29.4 percent of the regions, as contrasted with 56.7 percent of the districts, does a single ethnic group constitute more than half the population.

Table III.4

ETHNIC GROUPS IN MAINLAND TANZANIA: 1967

Rank Order	Ethnic Group	Population	Percent of Total Population
1	Sukuma	1,529,917	12.8%
2	Makonde	476,136	4.0
3	Chaga	440,239	3.7
4	Haya	412,356	3.5
5	Nyamwezi	405,976	3.4
6	Ha	383,021	3.2
7	Hehe	360,686	3.0
8	Gogo	360,131	3.0
9	Nyakusa	306,786	2.6
10	Shambaa	271,536	2.3

Source: Tanzania, *Statistical Abstract, 1970* (Dar es Salaam: Government Printer, 1972), p. 42.

TANZANIA'S UJAMAA VILLAGES

Table III.5
ETHNIC HOMOGENEITY OF REGIONS AND DISTRICTS,
MAINLAND TANZANIA: 1967

	Percentage of Total Population of Unit Represented by Largest Tribe									
Political Unit	0-9	10-19	20-29	30-39	40-49	50-59	60-69	70-79	80-89	90-99	Total
District:											
Number	0	2	5	11	8	8	9	4	7	6	60
Percent	0.0%	3.3	8.3	18.3	13.3	13.3	15.0	6.7	11.7	10.0	99.9
Region:											
Number	0	0	2	6	4	0	3	2	0	0	17
Percent	0.0%	0.0	11.8	35.3	23.5	0.0	17.6	11.8	0.0	0.0	100.0

Source: Calculated from Stephen Lucus and Gerard Philippson, "Ethnic Characteristics," in *The Population of Tanzania*, Census Vol. 6, eds. Bertil Egero and Roushdi Henin (Dar es Salaam: Bureau of Resource and Land Use Planning [BRALUP] and Bureau of Statistics, 1973), pp. 166-67.

Table III.6
CHANGES OF RESIDENCE IN MAINLAND TANZANIA: 1967

Region	Percent Moved from Birthplace	Percent Moved Outside Region	Percent Moved Within Region
Tabora	61.9%	16.9%	45.0%
Shinyanga	60.2	12.3	47.9
Singida	55.2	14.8	40.4
Ruvuma	50.8	12.7	38.1
Mara	43.8	6.5	37.3
Kigoma	42.5	11.0	31.5
West Lake	42.2	6.1	36.1
Mtwara	41.8	5.8	36.0
Arusha	41.1	4.7	36.4
Morogoro	40.4	9.8	30.6
Coast (including Dar)	37.3	7.1	30.2
Tanga	37.3	7.7	29.6
Mbeya	36.9	6.7	30.2
Dodoma	33.9	7.1	26.8
Iringa	26.2	8.3	17.9
Mwanza	26.2	14.1	12.1
Kilimanjaro	22.3	8.1	14.2
ALL REGIONS	38.8	8.8	30.0

Source: Claes-Fredrik Claeson and Bertil Egero, "Migration," in *The Population of Tanzania*, Census Vol. 6, eds. Bertil Egero and Roushdi Henin (Dar es Salaam: BRALUP and Bureau of Statistics, 1973), table 4.8, p. 68.

Cooperation among leaders of different ethnic backgrounds was obviously a necessity at all administrative levels above the very lowest. Yet ethnic diversity implies cleavages, and these have the potential of distorting or hindering rural development efforts. Important, too, is the fact that Tanzania has had long experience with population movement.

(4) The migration of peasant cultivators has characterized Tanzania for many years. Two types of movement of the rural population have occurred in Tanzania—that within rural areas and that from rural to urban zones. The tradition of shifting cultivation, the need to earn money through wage labor, and the lure of the towns all have contributed to this migration. Nearly 40 percent of the people have changed their residence; almost 9 percent of those have moved out of the region in which they were born. The extent of migration varies considerably among regions, however, as shown in Table III.6. In general, the greater the movement within a region, the more people move out of the region, and the more wealthy the region, the less the movement of any kind.

The migration to urban centers from rural areas led to a rate of growth of the former (6.4 percent) approximately double that of the latter (3.1 percent) in the period 1957-67.[9] Contending with this influx presented the government with a major problem. As a short-term solution, there have been repeated campaigns to round up and transfer the unemployed to rural areas. For example, in Dar es Salaam in 1973 the government initiated "Operation Kupe," and in Mbeya in 1976 "Operation Kila Mtu Kazi" was undertaken to relocate unemployed people.[10]* Procedures vary from operation to operation, but a Dar es Salaam effort in 1970 involved photographing those rounded up so that they could be identified and sent to court should they return, providing them with warrants to their home districts, and requiring them to report to the area commissioners on their arrival.[11] A high percentage of the migrants to urban areas consists of youths. The President has repeatedly called upon educated youths to abandon the practice of using education as a "passport" to leave the villages and move to the towns.[12] The same point was made in an editorial in the government newspaper: "There is still the task of making our youths, the school leavers, believe in the ultimate benefit of life in villages."[13] One of the functions of

---

*The Swahili word *kupe* means tick or bloodsucker; "Kila Mtu Kazi" means everyone works.

the ujamaa village policy is to reduce the need and opportunity of movement to urban areas.

Thus the movement involved in establishing ujamaa villages was not as much a change of tradition as was the limitation on movement implied by life in those villages.

(5) *The African population of Tanzania has been growing rapidly*. The large increase in the country's population, especially in the ten years after 1957, is shown by the following figures (rounded to the nearest thousand) for the censuses conducted between 1913 and 1967:[14]

1913:	4,145,000
1921:	4,107,000
1928:	4,741,000
1931:	5,023,000
1948:	7,401,000
1957:	8,672,000
1967:	11,837,000

The rate of increase between 1948 and 1957 was 1.8 percent per year, whereas between 1957 and 1967 it was 3.1 percent.[15] Although, as we shall see, arable land is still available, this increase has put a considerable burden on the government to provide more services and opportunities.

The non-African element of this population has been small but important. Until independence, Europeans dominated the administration and Asians controlled trade. As a result of moves to Tanzanianize the administration and to reduce the role of private traders in the economy, Europeans and Asians began to emigrate, as indicated in Table III.7. In 1948 only 0.9 percent of the Tanzanian population was non-African; this rose to 1.3 percent in 1957 and declined to 1.0 percent in 1967.[16] The size of the non-African population was therefore never very great.

The internal distribution of Tanzania's population is uneven. In one writer's words, it is "highly concentrated into a few, small core zones separated by extensive tracts of sparsely populated country."[17] The density varies from a high of 94.7 persons per km.^{2} for Kilimanjaro district to 1.3 for Mpanda. The national average is about 14 per km.^{2}.[18] During the twenty years prior to the initiation of the ujamaa village policy, the distribution of the population had not greatly changed.[19] This absence of national land shortages but presence of local ones has necessitated different

Table III.7

NON-AFRICAN POPULATION OF MAINLAND TANZANIA:
CENSUS YEARS, 1913-1967

Year	Arab		Asian		European		Total Number
	Number	Percent	Number	Percent	Number	Percent	Number
1913	4,101	21.7%	9,440	50.0%	5,336	28.3%	18,877
1921	4,041	24.2	10,209	61.1	2,447	14.7	16,697
1931	7,059	17.5	25,144	62.2	8,228	20.4	40,431
1948	11,074	16.3	46,254	68.0	10,648	15.7	67,976
1952	13,025	14.4	59,739	65.9	17,885	19.7	90,649
1957	19,088	16.4	76,417	65.9	20,534	17.7	116,039
1967	29,775	24.5	75,015	61.5	16,884	13.9	121,674

Sources: Tanzania, *Statistical Abstract, 1970* (Dar es Salaam: Government Printer, 1972), p. 171; Tanzania, *Statistical Abstract, 1966* (Dar es Salaam: Government Printer, 1968), p. 23; and Tanganyika, *Report on the Census of the Non-Native Population Taken on the Night of 25th February, 1948* (Dar es Salaam: Government Printer, 1953), table X, p. 11.

policy-implementation strategies for different areas. In that connection, the availability of land was an important consideration to those seeking to build ujamaa villages.

(6) *A substantial amount of unused land remains available for development in Tanzania.* Tanzania is a country of great physical variety, ranging from a long coastline to an extensive plateau to high mountain ranges to vast lakes. Its climate varies from the warm and humid Indian Ocean coastline to the perennial snows on Mt. Kilimanjaro. Its rainfall has produced arid Dodoma (23 inches per year), moderately well-watered Dar es Salaam (45 inches), and wet Bukoba (82 inches), yet each area is subject to substantial variation from season to season and year to year. Estimates of land use indicate considerable untapped potential, as shown in Table III.8.

Estimates of the extent of cultivated land range between 5 and 10 percent of the total land area, and the percentage of potentially cultivable land is much more. Within the country, however, there is considerable variation from region to region. For example, the 1970 data indicate that small-holder cultivation ranges from 20.9 percent of the land in Mwanza Region to 1.7 percent in Arusha, and that large-scale cultivation ranges from 4.9 percent in Kilimanjaro and Tanga Regions to none in Kigoma, Mara, Mwanza, Ruvuma,

Table III.8

LAND USE IN MAINLAND TANZANIA: 1963 AND 1970

1963		1970	
Type	Percent of Total Land Area	Type	Percent of Total Land Area
Closed forest	1.3%	High-altitude forest	0.4%
Forest-woodland intermediate	0.5	Other woods, forests	42.6
Woodland (miombo)	34.7		
Woodland-bushland intermediate	4.3		
Bushland and thicket	11.7		
Wooded grassland	26.9	Rough grazing	50.1
Grassland	9.9		
Desert and semi-desert	0.6		
Vegetation actively induced by man	8.8	Small-holder cultivation	4.4
		Large-scale cultivation	0.7
Swamp	1.3	Urban, rocky, swampy	1.8
TOTAL	100.0	*TOTAL*	100.0

Sources: Calculated from Tanganyika, *Statistical Abstract, 1963* (Dar es Salaam: Government Printer, 1964), table A3, p. 3, and Tanzania, *Statistical Abstract, 1970* (Dar es Salaam: Government Printer, 1972), table A3, p. 3.

Shinyanga, and Singida Regions. Rough grazing land occupies 92.9 percent of Arusha, but only 0.5 percent of Ruvuma Region. Savanna forests/woods occupy 96.6 percent of Ruvuma and 67.5 percent of Tabora, but none of Kilimanjaro or Mara.[20] Although tsetse flies infested much of Tanzania, their presence did not prevent cultivation. In almost all regions, large acreages of potentially cultivable land are unused.

The rights to use the land were determined by the operative land-tenure system. This varied both in time and from one part of the country to another. Until the post-independence era, changes tended to adhere to what is known as the "evolutionary thesis of land ownership," which holds that rights to use tend to shift to rights to own and that group rights tend to shift to individual rights.[21] Although most areas had not progressed very far in these directions, the ujamaa village policy sought to reverse what movement had occurred.

The colonial period affected the tenure arrangements through "alienation" of land. The Germans gave about 1.3 million acres and the British about 1.4 million to Europeans as alienated land.[22] Compared with the alienation of land in other colonial possessions, this was relatively little, but in several areas it was substantial. With the aim of regaining control of this land after independence, the government converted all freehold titles to leaseholds in 1963 and then to rights of occupancy in 1969. Since then, much of the land has been nationalized by the government.

Until the late 1950s, colonial policy regarding most of the land of the territory sought to protect customary tenure and prevent its erosion or abuse. This policy was stated in 1945 by the director of lands and mines, R.C. Northcote.[23] He said that every effort should be made to prevent:

(a) Absentee landlordism;
(b) An absolute freehold right, where a man can do what he likes with the land which he occupies even to the detriment of the community;
(c) The uncontrolled use of the land;
(d) The unearned increment accruing to the individual instead of the community;
(e) The uncontrolled sale of the land with which is connected compensation for unexhausted improvements;
(f) The sale of trees and perhaps buildings apart from the land;
(g) Bad farming and soil erosion;
(h) The agricultural community being loaded with unproductive debt.

The customary system of land allocation involved the possession of power by an authority (e.g., a chief or village headman) to allocate land to individuals or families for their use. Since independence, the powers of the traditional allocating authorities have disintegrated. The power was assumed in different places by a wide variety of agencies—e.g., RCs, ACs, committees of the district council, and district executive officers. The process, according to one observer, became "veiled in obscurity."[24] One effect of the ujamaa village policy was to standardize the system and assign the power to the village leaders. There were some exceptions of local import to the customary system of land allocation, perhaps the best known of which was the Nyarubanja system in Bukoba district. This was a landlord/tenant arrangement. The landlords consisted of traditional chiefs, middle-class owners, and missionaries with land acquired by force, money, or grant.

All governments have viewed the system as exploitative. Rules or laws in 1930, 1941, and 1956 attempted to protect tenants, and those of 1954 and 1968 sought to give the land to the tenants. The need for this series of measures spread over forty years indicates the difficulty of eliminating the system.[25] In other densely populated areas, such as Kilimanjaro district, there was de facto, though not de jure, ownership. One legal loophole was the right to sell improvements to the land. Such local deviations from communal tenure systems which were customary in much of the country created resistance to the establishment of communal ownership through ujamaa villages. The greater the changes according to the "evolutionary thesis," the more difficult the task of implementation.

(7) *The agricultural sector of the economy has been virtually stagnant for the past decade.* Despite the fact that the development of rural areas has been the major domestic concern of the government at least since the initiation of the ujamaa village policy, the rural economy has remained stagnant. Although the GDP/capita has tended to increase, that derived from agriculture has not, as shown in Table III.9. Part of this stagnation is a consequence of the low crop prices accompanied by marked inflation. The prices paid to farmers for major crops are shown in Table III.10. In general, these price increases have fallen behind the cost of living.

Table III.11 shows that inflation has been worst for wage earners in Dar es Salaam. Between 1970 and 1976, the cost-of-living index for middle-grade civil servants in the capital rose from 100 to 221, whereas the national cost-of-living index for the same period rose from 100 to only 200.6. Both of these rises, though substantial, were considerably below the figures for the Dar es Salaam wage earners. The immense increase in the index between 1974 and 1975 was due chiefly to the substantial increases that occurred in October 1974 in prices of basic commodities, which are shown in Table III.12. The factor contributing more than almost any other item to the rise in the cost of living was the price of food.

The combination of relatively high inflation rates and relatively low producer-price increases obviously did not encourage production. This problem was reflected in the stagnation of per capita income from farming over the past decade.

(8) *Government control over the economy has increased significantly since independence.* The resources at the disposal of the

Table III.9

GROSS DOMESTIC PRODUCT PER CAPITA, MAINLAND TANZANIA: 1964-1975

(based on 1966 prices)

Sector		1964	1965	1966	1967	1968	1969
Agriculture, hunting,	Shs.	263	253	267	248	252	246
forestry, and fishing	$US	38	36	38	35	36	35
Total GDP/capita	Shs.	562	567	590	569	583	578
	$US	80	81	84	81	83	83

Sector		1970	1971	1972	1973	1974	1975
Agriculture, hunting,	Shs.	248	239	252	248	236	235
forestry, and fishing	$US	35	34	36	35	34	34
Total GDP/capita	Shs.	595	605	621	634	628	622
	$US	85	86	89	91	90	89

Sources: Tanzania, *Statistical Abstract, 1966* (Dar es Salaam: Government Printer, 1968), p. 24 (for population in 1964 and 1965); Tanzania, *Quarterly Statistical Bulletin* 26, 1 (June 1975): table 1 (for population in 1967-74—population in 1966 is a mid-point between the 1965 and 1967 data). GDP figures from Tanzania, *National Accounts of Tanzania, 1964-1972* (Dar es Salaam: Bureau of Statistics, February 1974), p. 20; Tanzania, *Quarterly Statistical Bulletin* 26, 1 (June 1975): table 5; and Economist Intelligence Unit, *Quarterly Economic Review*, Annual Supplement 1977, pp. 4 and 6.

Table III.10

AVERAGE PRICE PAID PER TON TO PRODUCERS OF PRINCIPAL CROPS, MAINLAND TANZANIA: SELECTED YEARS, 1965-1973

Year		Maize	Finger Millet	Sorghum	Rice	Mixed Beans	Cassava	Groundnuts
1965	Shs.	260	500	320	480	440	260	980
	$US	37	71	46	69	63	37	140
1967	Shs.	263	492	278	439	370	214	872
	$US	38	70	40	63	53	31	125
1969	Shs.	254	389	305	540	517	228	950
	$US	36	56	44	77	74	33	136
1971	Shs.	253	519	334	549	622	293	1028
	$US	36	74	48	78	89	42	147
1973	Shs.	300	517	371	575	692	238	1172
	$US	43	74	53	82	99	34	167

Sources: Tanzania, *Statistical Abstract, 1966* (Dar es Salaam: Government Printer, 1968), table G6, p. 85; Tanzania, *Statistical Abstract, 1970* (Dar es Salaam: Government Printer, 1972), table G6, pp. 112-13; Tanzania, *Quarterly Statistical Bulletin* 26, 1 (June 1975): table 43.

Table III.11

RETAIL PRICE INDEX OF GOODS CONSUMED BY WAGE EARNERS IN DAR ES SALAAM: 1961-1976

1951 = 100			1970 = 100		
1961	=	126	1970	=	100
1962	-	127	1971	=	103
1963	=	119	1972	=	114
1964	=	120	1973	=	124
1965	=	134	1974	=	163
1966	=	137	1975	=	243
1967	=	140	1976	=	294
1968	=	144			
1969	=	147			

Sources: Bank of Tanzania, *Economic Bulletin* 9, 3 (December 1976): 56; Tanzania, *Statistical Abstract, 1970* (Dar es Salaam: Government Printer, 1972), p. 170.

Table III.12

PRICE INCREASES OF STAPLES, MAINLAND TANZANIA: OCTOBER 1974

Staple	Before	After
Packaged maize flour (kg.)	Shs. 1/40 ($0.20)	Shs. 2/- ($0.28)
Unpackaged maize flour (kg.)	Shs. 1/25 ($0.18)	Shs. 1/75 ($0.25)
Rice (kg.)	Shs. 2/- ($0.28)	Shs. 5/-[a] ($0.70)
Wheat flour (kg.)	Shs. 2/40 ($0.34)	Shs. 4/55 ($0.64)
Bread (loaf)	Shs. 1/10 ($0.15)	Shs. 1/90[a] ($0.27)
Sugar (kg.)	Shs. 3/- ($0.42)	Shs. 6/- ($0.84)

Source: *Daily News* (Dar es Salaam), 31 October 1974, p. 1.

[a] A few months later, the price of bread was reduced to Shs. 1/80 and that of rice to Shs. 4/-.

government have not stagnated. They have notably increased at the expense of those in the private sector. This trend is illustrated by changes in the composition of the GDP and in the source of gross capital formation over the several years. As Table III.13 indicates, the share of the public sector in the generation of GDP nearly doubled between 1966 and 1972. The greater portion of the increase came from public enterprises. Between 1965 and 1972, the share of public as compared with total capital formation more than doubled. In 1965, the former accounted for 30.5 percent; in 1966, 35.6 percent; in 1968, 46.2 percent; in 1970, 59.8 percent; and in 1972, 71.4 percent.[26] Increasing state dominance of the economy, reflected also in Table III.13, suggests the parallel growth of central government power. The economic base of potential opposition has been undermined. As a result, one might expect a decline in the vigor of opposition to the ujamaa village policy. Despite the growth of state control of the economy, however, that economy remains closely tied to Western nations.

(9) *The economy of Tanzania is dependent to a great extent on trade with capitalist countries.* Critics of the ujamaa village policy point to the contradiction implicit in the attempt to build a socialist economy in a situation of continued dependence on the capitalist world. The importance of imports and exports as a percentage of Tanzania's GDP is shown in Table III.14. Most of this trade has continued to be with countries of the capitalist world, with the exception of imports from China in the early 1970s connected with the building of the railway to Zambia. The percentages of imports from and exports to Tanzania's major trading partners outside East Africa are shown in Table III.15. Within East Africa, the dominance

Table III.13

PUBLIC AND PRIVATE SECTOR PERCENTAGE SHARES OF THE GROSS DOMESTIC PRODUCT, MAINLAND TANZANIA: 1966-1972

Source	1966	1967	1968	1969	1970	1971	1972
Government administration	8.1%	8.3%	8.3%	8.5%	9.1%	9.7%	9.3%
Public enterprises	6.6	10.4	10.8	11.7	12.3	14.4	13.9
Subtotal	14.7	18.7	19.1	20.2	21.4	24.1	23.2
Private enterprises and households (including cooperatives)	85.3	81.3	80.9	79.8	78.6	75.9	76.8
TOTAL	100.0	100.0	100.0	100.0	100.0	100.0	100.0

Source: Tanzania, *National Accounts of Tanzania, 1964-1972* (Dar es Salaam: Bureau of Statistics, February 1974); calculated from table 9, p. 22.

Table III.14

MAINLAND TANZANIAN EXPORTS AND IMPORTS
IN TERMS OF VALUE AND PERCENTAGE OF THE GDP:
1964-1975

Year	GDP at Factor Cost[a]	Value of Exports[a]	Exports as Percent of GDP	Value of Imports[a]	Imports as Percent of GDP
1964	5,594	1,428.3	25.5%	879.5	15.7%
1965	5,671	1,281.5	22.6	1,000.9	17.6
1966	6,514	1,692.2	26.0	1,285.0	19.7
1967	6,735	1,586.9	23.6	1,300.5	19.3
1968	7,182	1,626.8	22.7	1,531.7	21.3
1969	7,460	1,688.5	22.6	1,418.8	19.0
1970	8,215	1,689.0	20.6	1,939.0	23.6
1971	8,845	1,792.2	20.3	2,414.4	27.3
1972	10,090	2,027.2	20.1	2,597.6	25.7
1973	11,558	2,238.3	19.4	3,139.5	27.2
1974	13,749	2,489.4	18.1	5,407.1	38.5
1975	16,534	2,589.3	15.7	5,288.1	32.0

Sources: Tanzania, *National Accounts of Tanzania, 1964-1972* (Dar es Salaam: Bureau of Statistics, February 1974), p. 11, for GDP between 1964 and 1970; Tanzania, *Statistical Quarterly Bulletin* 26, 1 (June 1975): table 4, for GDP between 1971 and 1974; United Nations, *Yearbook of National Accounts, 1976*, Vol. 1 (New York: United Nations, 1977), p. 1147, for 1975 GDP; Tanzania, *Statistical Abstract, 1970* (Dar es Salaam: Government Printer, 1972), p. 70, for imports and exports, 1964-69; Tanzania, *Statistical Quarterly Bulletin* 26, 1 (June 1975): table 26, for imports and exports, 1972-75; Economist Intelligence Unit, *Quarterly Economic Review, Tanzania and Zambia* 3 (1971): appendix 2, for imports and exports, 1970; Bank of Tanzania, *Economic and Operations Report*, June 1976, pp. 91 and 93, for imports and exports, 1975.

[a] Millions of shillings.

Table III.15

PERCENTAGES OF MAINLAND TANZANIAN IMPORTS FROM AND EXPORTS TO MAJOR TRADING PARTNERS: SELECTED YEARS, 1961-1976

Country	1961 Imports	1961 Exports	1964 Imports	1964 Exports	1967 Imports	1967 Exports	1970 Imports	1970 Exports	1973 Imports	1973 Exports	1976 Imports	1976 Exports
United Kingdom	37.6%	35.8%	33.1%	30.6%	28.8%	30.3%	21.2%	22.0%	16.0%	17.2%	13.8%	14.2%
West Germany	4.7	8.0	6.4	8.2	6.5	5.2	9.3	4.7	8.2	6.3	10.3	14.7
United States	5.5	9.8	6.2	8.5	7.6	5.0	8.6	9.5	3.1	7.8	6.5	10.0
Netherlands	7.0	6.1	3.9	5.4	4.1	4.1	4.3	3.6	3.5	3.0	3.8	4.0
India	6.8	5.2	5.9	6.1	3.1	6.7	2.8	7.2	1.6	6.3	4.8	5.3
Japan	10.0	4.6	16.7	3.8	5.1	4.3	7.4	5.7	9.6	3.7	9.1	2.4
Hong Kong	12.0	6.7	1.8	6.4	1.9	7.2	1.4	7.5	1.2	5.9	1.3	5.6
Belgium	1.4	3.2	1.6	4.4	1.0	2.7	1.3	2.1	1.2	2.7	3.7	0.8
Italy	1.2	2.5	2.5	2.4	10.7	2.7	5.6	2.7	5.0	2.0	2.6	6.6
China	—	—	0.7	3.9	5.6	4.0	13.7	3.5	22.3	4.1	7.5	2.9
Other	14.0	18.0	21.1	20.4	25.7	27.8	24.4	31.6	28.4	41.2	36.7	33.3
TOTAL	100.2	99.9	99.9	100.1	100.1	100.0	100.0	100.1	100.1	100.2	100.1	99.8

Sources: Tanzania, *Statistical Abstract, 1966* (Dar es Salaam: Government Printer, 1968), p. 56, for 1961 imports, and p. 53, for 1961 imports; Tanzania, *Statistical Abstract, 1970* (Dar es Salaam: Government Printer, 1972), p. 79, for 1964 and 1967 imports, and p. 75, for 1964 and 1967 exports; Economist Intelligence Unit, *Quarterly Economic Review, Tanzania and Zambia* 3 (1971): appendix 2, for 1970 imports and exports; Bank of Tanzania, *Economic and Operations Report*, June 1974, p. 84, for 1973 imports, and p. 82, for 1973 exports; *ibid.*, June 1977, p. 72, for 1976 imports, and p. 70, for 1976 exports; Tanzania, *Monthly Statistical Bulletin* 22, 2 (June 1972): table 28, for 1970 exports; *ibid.*, 20, 1 (February 1970): table 22, for 1967 exports; *ibid.*, 22, 2 (June 1972): table 27, for 1970 imports.

of capitalist Kenya has been a feature of the pattern of trade since the colonial era, as indicated in Table III.16.

Thus Tanzania is tied closely to the world capitalist economy. Fluctuations in demands by Western countries for Tanzanian products determine both the prices that can be paid to peasants and the amounts of goods that may be purchased abroad. Along with the flow of goods come Western managers, technicians, and ideas. A substantial literature on the concomitant neocolonial ties has been produced,[27] and its basic conclusion is that in such a situation it is virtually impossible to implement policies that aim to establish self-reliant socialist states. Some of the subtle effects of these links upon the implementation of the ujamaa village policy will be noted in Chapters V and VI.

Tanzania, then, is a country with a population overwhelmingly rural, with limited economic differentiation, with significant ethnic diversity which has minimized potential conflict, with a history of migration, with a rapidly increasing African population, with only a small proportion of the land under cultivation, with private owner-

Table III.16

VALUE OF INTER-EAST AFRICAN TRADE:
SELECTED YEARS, 1961-1976

(In millions of shillings or dollars)

Year[a]		To Tanzania			From Tanzania		
		From Kenya	From Uganda	Total	To Kenya	To Uganda	Total
1961	Shs.	178.0	34.1	212.0	36.9	7.8	44.7
	$US	25.4	4.9	30.3	5.3	1.1	6.4
1964	Shs.	266.0	48.1	314.1	82.2	20.4	102.6
	$US	38.0	6.9	44.9	11.7	2.9	14.7
1967	Shs.	227.6	48.6	276.2	65.8	15.0	80.8
	$US	32.5	6.9	39.5	9.4	2.1	11.5
1970	Shs.	295.0	40.0	335.0	118.8	28.8	147.6
	$US	42.1	5.7	47.9	17.0	4.1	21.1
1973	Shs.	337.1	2.2	339.3	152.5	17.7	170.2
	$US	48.2	0.3	48.5	21.8	2.5	24.3
1976	Shs.	668.9	—	668.9	248.0	6.8	254.8
	$US	83.6	—	83.6	31.0	0.9	31.9

Sources: Tanzania, *Statistical Abstract, 1970* (Dar es Salaam: Government Printer, 1972), p. 88, for 1961 figures; Bank of Tanzania, *Economic Bulletin* 8, 3 (December 1976): 50, for 1964-1976 figures.

[a]Figures for 1961 through 1967 do not include Zanzibar.

ship of land the exception rather than the rule, with an agricultural sector that has become stagnant, with increasing economic domination and control by the government, and with continued dependence on the Western world. Most of these characteristics are common to other African countries. One of the unique features of Tanzania, however, has been the position and character of its political party and that party's role in policy implementation.

AGENTS OF IMPLEMENTATION: THE PARTY

The sole political party on mainland Tanzania until early 1977 was the Tanganyika African National Union (TANU). Its combination with the Afro-Shirazi party from the island of Zanzibar under the new name Chama cha Mapinduzi (Party of the Revolution) (CCM) has not fundamentally altered the characteristics that evolved over nearly a quarter century. By the mid-1970s TANU envisioned its role as fourfold: "(a) to set the national goal, (b) to organize and mobilize the masses, (c) to supervise the implementation of the Party's policy and (d) to assess the outcome of such implementation."[28] To perform these tasks, it has sought close links with the people. Indeed, the key to the success of any agent involved in policy implementation in a poor country is its relationship or linkage with the people. They are the ones whose compliance is sought. Aspects of the party through which the linkage may be examined include its size, structure, composition, recruitment, opposition, organization for implementation, and relationship to the government.

(1) Estimates of party membership range between 10 and 25 percent of the total population of the country. Formally, TANU sought to be a mass party. In the party's annual report for 1969, membership figures were given for eleven of the seventeen regions, totaling 1,272,028, or approximately 15 percent of the total population.[29] An estimate for 1970 by the party's secretary-general gave the membership as 3 million, or roughly 25 percent of the population.[30] Even when figures are cited, however, they often greatly exaggerate actual membership. For example, James R. Finucane found that the figure put forth for TANU membership in Mwanza town was more than four times the total population of the town.[31] During the early 1960s, restrictions on membership were gradually eliminated. Non-Africans were permitted to join in 1963 and civil servants the following year. In fact, membership was almost a prerequisite if one wanted to obtain a license, to have a court case heard, or needed services.

By the mid-1970s, however, the party became more selective. In late 1974 it decided to demand of the members compliance with the leadership code, which forbade, among other things, earning two or more salaries, associating "with the practices of capitalism or feudalism," and renting houses to others.[32] When alarm grew among members who were violating the principles in some small way, the President declared that the party was not concerned with minor infractions.[33]

Until the CCM was formed, reviews of membership lists and expulsions of those who failed to comply with membership requirements appear to have been rare. Yet once the CCM was established, more rigorous enforcement of leadership-code compliance and adherence to the party's creed was demanded. Some observers suggested that the party was undergoing a transformation into a vanguard party.[34]

(2) *The structural layers between the members and the central decision-makers are many.* The majority of TANU members are well insulated from the party's decision-makers at the center by means of an elaborate hierarchy of structures. These comprise the following:

> Central Committee
> National Executive Committee
> National Conference
>
> Regional working committee
> Regional executive committee
> Regional conference
>
> District working committee
> District executive committee
> District conference
>
> Branch executive committee
> Branch conference
> Sub-branch executive committee*
> Sub-branch conference*
>
> Cells

Important decisions in Tanzania have increasingly been made by the National Executive Committee (NEC), including those relating to the Arusha Declaration and to decentralization.[35] Neverthe-

*Eliminated when the CCM was formed.

less, Henry Bienen's observation made a decade ago that policy is actually initiated by a smaller group of individuals, led by the President, is still probably true.[36] The effect of the many layers of party structure between the membership and the decision-makers is that, despite the sincere intentions of the President and other TANU leaders, most members can do little to determine the actions of the party.

(3) *A high proportion of the members of most party structures are not directly elected.* The argument that democracy exists in the party because most organs are composed primarily of elected members is clearly an oversimplification of a complex issue. The system of selection of members of these various structures does not follow a single principle of representation. For example, those who may select members for the district executive committee include the members of the district conference, the National Assembly, the branch conference, the Central Committee, the President, the district chairman, sections of the party, affiliated organizations, and the electorate! Representation in most other TANU organs is similarly diverse, as can be seen in Appendix 1.

Minor changes in the selection of leaders at various levels were made when the CCM was formed. Yet the basic problem remained: the average party member had difficulty in making his voice heard in the important decision-making bodies of the party. Even when he has a chance to vote for TANU leaders, his choice is limited by candidate-review procedures.

(4) *Central leadership control of the party is enhanced by the method of election to TANU offices.* Candidates for the National Assembly, formally a standing committee of the National Conference, and other TANU offices must be approved by party organs at higher levels. By this means, the top leadership is able to impose criteria for recruitment to political office. This role was made quite clear by Pius Msekwa, vice-chairman of the electoral commission, when commenting on the party manifesto prepared for the 1975 National Assembly elections:

> It is as if the Party has said "here are job opportunities and here are the qualifications." The parliamentary aspirants are the candidates and interviewers are the voters. What the voters should look for is whether the candidates in their constituencies have the qualifications that have been pronounced by the Party.[37]

In each national election, candidates chosen by district conferences have been turned down by the NEC, as shown in Table III.17. Before the 1975 elections this power of the top leadership was rationalized on three grounds: "[1] the higher organs of the Party are more competent to look at national interests. ... [2] The higher organs of the Party have more access to deeper information on people than the lower organs of TANU. ... [3] Lower organs of the Party might be attracted more to local interests."[38] This, of course, is a peculiar declaration for a party which explicitly calls for more popular control. Control over candidacy has also been exercised by lower levels of the party. For the 1974 party elections, for example, the percentage of potential candidates reportedly rejected by regional working committees was substantial, as is illustrated in Table III.18. The sifting of candidates by higher levels of the party, then, is a power that has frequently been used. It is, however, a crude weapon—a defensive weapon. Demands for compliance by officials or party candidates constituted a less crude, more offensive weapon.

The election manifesto of 1975 called for candidates to sup-

Table III.17

NEC REJECTION OF DISTRICT-CONFERENCE CHOICES FOR
TANZANIAN NATIONAL ASSEMBLY CANDIDATES:
ELECTIONS OF 1965, 1970, AND 1975[a]

Year of Election	Number of Districts with Electoral Competition	Nominees Passed Over by Higher Party Organs		Districts Affected by Higher Party Organs' Actions	
		Number	Percent of Nominees Accepted	Number	Percent of Districts with Electoral Competition
1965	95	18	9.5%	16	16.8%
1970	114	47	20.6	31	27.2
1975	89	76	42.6	42	47.2

Sources: For 1965: Data derived from *One-Party Democracy*, ed. Lionel Cliffe (Nairobi: East African Publishing House, 1967), pp. 360-409; for 1970: Election Study Committee, *Socialism and Participation, Tanzania's 1970 National Elections* (Dar es Salaam: Tanzania Publishing House, 1974), pp. 379-437; for 1975: University of Dar es Salaam Election Study material.

[a]Number of districts with electoral competition excludes single-candidate districts and those for which no data are available; the number rejected includes those passed over when NEC chose candidates from the rank-order lists.

Table III.18

REJECTIONS OF DISTRICT-CHAIRMAN AND
NATIONAL-CONFERENCE CANDIDATES BY REGIONAL
WORKING COMMITTEES, MAINLAND TANZANIA: 1974

Region	Percent of Candidates for District Chairman Rejected	Percent of Candidates for National Conference Rejected
Mwanza	a	42%
Mara	53%	21
Shinyanga	56	18
Singida	69	54

Source: Daily News (Dar es Salaam), 18 March 1974, p. 4; 20 March 1974, p. 1;
22 March 1974, p. 1; and 17 March 1974, p. 5, respectively.

aNo information available.

port TANU's position on ujamaa villages: "As regards the Wananchi [citizens] living in the villages, the Party will continue to preach and to explain the advantages of people living together and working together for their common benefit."[39] Support for the ujamaa village policy was also sought through the requirement in both the 1970 and 1975 elections that candidates declare whether they lived in such villages or, if they did not, their reasons. Table III.19 summarizes the response in 1970 to the first question.

Helge Kjekshus, who analyzed the data, concluded that the nominating process actually "seems to have paid little attention to Ujamaa membership among the candidates."[40] He argued that "the large claim to village membership in many regions resulted from the candidates' verbal association with the villages rather than from any physical partaking in the villagization effort."[41] A sample of candidates for the 1975 election indicates that approximately 50 percent were living in ujamaa villages and slightly more than 50 percent of them won.[42] Here, too, the attention of candidates was at least drawn to a policy which the party sought to have implemented.

Although the central leadership's control of the party was enhanced through the candidate selection and the conduct of elections, some observers felt that low turnouts and "no" votes for the presi-

Table III.19

ISSUE OF UJAMAA-VILLAGE RESIDENCE
IN THE 1970 ELECTIONS

Respondents	Total Number	Number Resident in Ujamaa Villages	Percent
Potential Candidates	1,095	261	23.8%
Nominees	191	65	34.0
MPs	98	34	35.8

Source: Helge Kjekshus, "The Elected Elite: A Socio-Economic Profile of Candidates in Tanzania's Parliamentary Election, 1970," Research Report No. 29, The Scandinavian Institute of African Studies, Uppsala, 1975, p. 25.

dential candidate could be taken as indications of resistance to leadership actions. Bismarck Mwansasu accounted for the doubling of the "no" vote for the President between the 1970 and 1975 elections as an indication of popular reaction to the villagization aspect of the ujamaa village policy. He said:

> There are reports that during operation vijijini Government functionaries as well as Party leaders told peasants that they were being moved because the President had so ordered. Even the burning of houses was justified as an order of the President. Because officials decide to hide their activities behind the President, it is not surprising that he becomes the object of protest.[43]

Nevertheless, elections did provide an opportunity for the expression of some generalized popular sentiment toward party policies.

(5) *Despite the efforts of TANU to eliminate formal opposition to its policies, subtle forms of resistance have continued.* Opposition to TANU has taken several different forms. There has been open opposition at times in the National Assembly. For example, in 1968 a series of issues arose which involved Zanzibar, criticism of the West Lake RC for forcing people into ujamaa villages, and a revision of the interim constitution. Seven MPs were expelled from the party by the NEC as a consequence.[44] In 1973, when the National Assembly

blocked the income-tax bill by a vote of 66 to 46, the President vehemently attacked the action. He argued that "he could not agree that Tanzania's Parliament should be used for purposes of preventing the Government from taking measures designed to implement Tanu's policies of bringing about equality step by step." He declared that "the main reason the Bill was rejected appeared to be that it embraced the incomes of Members of Parliament." And he said he was "prepared to call an election on the issue."[45] Two weeks later the bill was reintroduced, and it passed both readings in a thirty-minute session.[46] Besides the fairly quick repression of opposition in the National Assembly, other instances of it were handled by detention orders. The reasons for detentions normally are not announced, but when the President released 157 detainees on Union Day in 1975, 96 were said to have been detained for currency violations and the rest for security reasons.[47] Perhaps the most sensational opposition was that which occurred between July 1968 and October 1969 and became public at the time of the subsequent treason trial. Apparently the security forces thought it would be dealt with under detention orders, but the "highest level" decided on a trial. The plot was mainly the work of Oscar Kambona, who was in self-exile in Britain. (He had been general secretary of TANU and had held several important ministerial responsibilities, including defense, before he left the country in 1968). It really never got anywhere, but involved a planned coup and implicated two leading politicians, Michael Kamaliza and Bibi Titi Mohamed, and several others. Both politicians were initially convicted of involvement. The explicit basis of opposition appeared to be the desire for an "opening up" of TANU and the "rescuing" of it from manipulation for personal gains. The key prosecution witness was the exiled Pan-Africanist Congress (PAC) leader Potlako Leballo, who was an intermediary among the conspirators. Every time he was given a document to deliver, he took it to the security people to have it photocopied before passing it on.[48] Constructive opposition has always been praised as an important practice within TANU, but what top leaders considered constructive was never clearly defined. More passive forms of resistance have involved "no" votes, as indicated above, and slowness in complying with implementation demands. The latter was particularly important in the implementation of the ujamaa village policy.

(6) *TANU established organs specifically for the purpose of overseeing the implementation of the ujamaa village policy*. At the time the President prepared "Socialism and Rural Development,"

there was within the youth affairs department of TANU an assistant secretary, N. J. Millinga, in charge of youth settlements and all other TANU Youth League (TYL) economic activities. By November 1968 he had become the secretary for ujamaa villages, a new department, responsible for the coordination of all ujamaa village programs. A few months later, assistant secretaries were appointed for "general administration and liaison with government ministries" and "planning and training of cadres." By January 1970 still another assistant secretary was appointed, charged with "visiting and reporting on the problems of ujamaa villages." Toward the end of that year the political education department had picked up the task of "political education in Ujamaa villages and liaison with the Ujamaa Village Department."[49] Thus the formal party bureaucracy in the headquarters gradually expanded to oversee policy implementation. With a staff of only four, however, and with thousands of villages and government officers involved, meaningful supervision was extremely difficult.

(7) *Party-government struggles for domination of the state have led to de jure supremacy of the party in policy formation but de facto domination of the government in policy implementation.* The links between the party and the government are normally forged by the party in an effort to attain its objective of overseeing the implementation of its policies. Many of the links are positions that fulfill dual functions, including regional and area commissioners and divisional and ward secretaries. The President of the republic is the president of the party. MPs are representatives of the people, members of a subcommittee of the TANU National Conference, and directly responsible for overseeing government action. The TANU chairmen at various levels serve on a range of committees that involve both party and government officials. The party constitution is a part of the state constitution. Such links between the party and the government appear to have provided more government leverage in the party than party leverage in the government.

The party budget increased substantially from a little over 4 million shillings in 1968 to 8.5 million shillings in 1971 and to 85.5 million shillings in 1975/76.[50] Data available in three TANU annual reports show that the government provided 95.0 percent of the expenditures in 1968, 95.5 percent in 1969, and 96.8 percent in 1971. It is quite apparent that the party is financially dependent on government resources. Since the mid-1960s, moreover, trained civil servants have been seconded to TANU headquarters to operate its bureaucracy. Hence the government influences the party not only indirectly through the dual functions of the many overlapping positions, but also directly through finance and personnel.

The power of the government has been recognized. In a government reshuffle in 1972 the President said, "In TANU theory, the National Executive Committee of TANU is more powerful than the Cabinet. . . . But our practice is different from this theory and policy of TANU."[51] And in a policy directive by the standing committee on parastatal organizations issued to limit the transfer of party branch chairmen and secretaries in national institutions, it was admitted that such transfers of party leaders by government institutions often had been made for reasons other than technical efficiency.[52] The aim of these transfers was to get rid of party leaders who gave managers trouble.

Attempts to require party membership of government servants have been abandoned. In mid-1971 it was found that only 300 of 1,000 civil servants in Bukoba were TANU members and, consequently, "several" were fired. It was claimed that "such people were enemies of the Party and the Government and as such it would be dangerous to keep them at a place where they had access to some government secrets."[53] Those responsible for the action were rebuked, however, by the President, who argued that it would be "a very serious mistake if we made TANU membership an essential qualification for securing employment." He felt that for membership in the party to be meaningful it had to be voluntary.[54] In September of 1971 the NEC decided to allow civil servants to run for office without giving up their positions. This was still another move that interlocked party and government.[55]

In an effort to counteract, at least formally, the trend to government dominance, the NEC decided in late 1974, at Musoma, to make party supremacy a part of the constitution. For several months afterwards, attempts were made to clarify what this meant. In an editorial in the government newspaper, the roles of the party, the state, and parliament were differentiated:

> The state in any land is an instrument of oppression. To equip it for this task, the state has in its control such instruments of oppression as the Police, Courts, Prisons, the Army and the Civil Service.
>
> . . . the parties cannot themselves perform the functions of the state already described herein, they would alienate themselves from the people. They would turn into instruments of oppres-

sion. It suffices for the parties to ensure that state power is used in the best interests of the people.

Parliament is the Party's watchdog over the state and the manner in which it deploys its instruments of oppression. Under Tanu's constitution, Parliament is a standing committee of the Biennial Conference, the supreme source of people's power.[56]

Perhaps the focus on instruments of oppression was a result of their importance, especially in 1974/75, in the implementation of the villagization effort. The distinction between a "doer" and a "watcher" suggests formal superiority of the latter but real superiority of the former. Nevertheless, emphasis on the supremacy of the party caused some concern among government officials and attempts to explain what it meant:

Party supremacy does not mean displacement of Government. Party supremacy does not mean that Government functionaries will be doing their daily jobs with Tanu leaders breathing down their necks. Tanu is too sacred, the Party is too supreme to do this kind of childish supervision. . . .

The Party gives these instruments the freedom to play their respective roles. All the Party does is to retain the supreme power to direct, call to order, criticise, correct, educate or even dismantle any of these instruments if they do not work in line with the policies of the Party. . . .

No Party leader therefore should interfere or involve himself in the day-to-day running of these instruments under the pretext of Party supremacy.[57]

Two months later the President was reported to have "issued a stern warning . . . [against] abusing power by interfering in the implementation of the day-to-day policies directed by the Party. . . . 'Implementation of all directives should be left to the Government alone,' he pointed out."[58] The clarifications, then, on the question of party supremacy appear to indicate to civil servants that in fact no change in their actual position was planned. Although policy formation was still to be reserved to the party, implementation was assigned primarily to the government.

AGENTS OF IMPLEMENTATION: THE GOVERNMENT

The government's role as the prime agent for the implementation of the ujamaa village policy has been affected by a number of institutional characteristics and experiences. Of particular importance are the degree of popular participation, the tendency toward structural instability, the predominance of administrative over political officers, the relative ineffectiveness of functional officers in promoting rural development, and the growth of "bureaucratization." Just as the average party member has limited influence on decision-making within the party, so the average citizen has little effect on decision-making by the government. In neither case does this situation appear to have been intentional.

(1) *Popular participation in decision-making has remained very limited*. Popular influence on government was sought through various local representative councils. In the period just before and just after independence, district councils were formed in every district. The new system did not, however, function as the central government wished. One writer referred to the situation as "democratic indigestion."[59] In January 1963 a local government service commission was established which appointed staff of the council, including the executive officer.[60] Nevertheless, there was often a split within the councils between central government representatives who wanted to allocate most resources to productive infrastructure and local representatives who wanted the resources to go to welfare services.[61] Control by the central government proved difficult. Powers over local education and health were taken from the councils in 1969 because of their inability to use them acceptably. Debts continued to pile up, so that by April 1971, as shown in Table III.20, many had to be "written off" by the National Assembly.

Because of their failure to function responsibly and effectively, the district councils were abolished when decentralization took place in 1972, and district development councils were established in their place. The district chairman of TANU automatically became the chairman and the district development director (DDD) the secretary. Although the President assigned to them the old task of representing the people at the district level, the difficulties persisted.

Associated with both the district council and the district development council were what were at first called district development committees and later district development and planning committees, which generally functioned as agents of the central government.[62] Initially, a committee of central government officials at district level was appointed to deal with the coordination of planning.[63] Early in 1963, the district development committee was made

Table III.20

DISTRICT-COUNCIL DEBTS "WRITTEN OFF,"
MAINLAND TANZANIA: APRIL 1971
(*in shillings*)

District	Amount	District	Amount
Dodma	10,748,356	Kilimanjaro	240,295
Mpwapwa	5,479,377	Shinyanga	222,036
Kondoa	4,968,322	Mbeya	181,858
Manyoni	1,670,038	Mbulu	140,400
Singida	1,585,995	Nachingwea	59,881
Iramba	1,381,800	Mwanza	55,947
Kilwa	797,845	Kilosa	45,800
Masai/Sonjo	657,731	Arusha	36,000
Bagamoyo	539,030	Meru	12,000
Pare	466,910	Morogoro	8,804
Handeni	465,320	Pangani	7,960
Chunya	250,712	Rufiji	3,358
Arush/Meru	249,031		
		TOTAL	30,275,537

Source: Nationalist (Dar es Salaam), 28 April 1971, p. 1.

a subcommittee of the district council. In principle, the members of this committee were mostly to be elected, but in fact it was composed predominantly of technical officers.[64] They were supposed to prepare annual development estimates and plans for submission to the district council.[65] With the creation of the district development council, the AC became its chairman and the DDD its secretary. The President identified it as "the executive arm of the District Development Council."[66] Nevertheless, the district development committees appear to have continued functioning as forums in which ministerial representatives or other central government officials might announce or explain proposals and decisions. In the words of one observer, those committees "served to win district cooperation for the *implementation* of decisions already made."[67]

The most important representative committees below the district level were the village development committees (VDCs), which had been created in 1962 to serve in channeling local enthusiasm into development projects. According to Stanley Dryden, they existed "first, to draw up plans for the development of village areas and, secondly, to mobilize whatever resources were available locally to implement those plans."[68] In 1964 the TANU committees for the area were amalgamated with the VDCs and the TANU chairman became the VDC chairman. Bienen observes that "This edict guaranteed neither that village splits would cease, nor that TANU committeemen would dominate."[69] The composition of the VDCs varied. Dryden points out that "at least half the numbers of a typical committee may be committee members or nominees of the local branch of TANU, the remainder being local teachers, cooperative society officials, civil servants and local government employees who happen to be stationed in the area."[70] The village executive officers were the secretaries, but complaints frequently arose about the lack of central government help for the committees.[71] The opposite complaint was voiced at other levels. Bienen estimated that there were 7,500 VDCs in 1963, a figure often repeated in the literature.[72] It was not until 1966 that the committees were given legal recognition.

The relationship of the VDCs to the district council was close. Their plans went to the district development/district development and planning committees, and their secretaries, the village executive officers, were directly responsible to the council's executive officer. Finucane observed in Mwanza that in "some instances the VDCs acted in effect as the Council's agents."[73] There was ambiguity, however, concerning what their function was supposed to be. According to one observer, "The role of the Village Development Committees is . . . a starting point for efforts to explain central decisions and to advance the implementation of central decisions."[74] In July 1969 they were abolished, and ward development committees took their place. Finucane observed, however, that "the most striking aspect of their first year was how little they differed from the old village committees." He noted:

The low number of officials who attended meetings, the localized nature of most of the activities, the predominance of a penetrative or downwards linkage in their connections with the national political system, the poor attendance of cell leaders at meetings, and the tendency for the economically better-off cell leaders to attend while their poorer associates stayed home—these were aspects of the VDC's which made them ineffective in performing as a channel for a "two-way flow of ideas between government and the people."[75]

With the 1972 administrative decentralization, the ward development committees were retained in essentially the same form.

Although a principal objective of the decentralization undertaking was to increase popular participation in government, most studies have found little evidence that it has worked. For example, A. T. Kundi found in the mid-1970s "that the decentralization measures proclaimed in 1972 have not so far succeeded in facilitating popular participation in decision-making."[76] R. M. Mayaya observed that "as far as Tanzania's decentralization is concerned . . . the newly established rural-government structure is not conducive to enhancing popular participation."[77] W. N. Lobulu found that "substantive decisions are made by the bureaucrats at the district headquarters rather than the people as stipulated in the decentralization blueprint."[78] A. P. Mosha concluded that "Popular participation does not appear to have increased as a result of the reorganization."[79]

What is obvious from this review of institutions that were assigned representative tasks is that, in the view of most observers, there has been almost universal failure. The councils either broke down and failed to function or became forums for informing people of central government decisions. The difficulty does not seem to be traceable to the conscious intention of those who created the structures to subvert them or to mislead the people. Rather, it seems to be a function of control of resources of knowledge, wealth, and perceived status, which has been so overbalanced in favor of the central government that the population at large has possessed insufficient countervailing force necessary for a real "say" in decision-making.

(2) *The continuous modification of the structure of administration has interfered with the establishment of stable patterns of participation.* Changes of administrative structures have been frequent. The basic forms found in the three main administrative phases at the region, district, and subdistrict levels are shown in Table III.21. Although there were only two major post-independence changes, those of 1962/63 and 1972, several minor alterations took place. For example, the ward became an administrative area in 1969 with its own ward executive officer and ward development committee in place of the village executive officer and the village development committee.[80] All these changes seem to have been the result of the belief that structures determine behavior: if behavior of a particular sort was not as wanted, the way to correct it was to change the structure. The frequent changes, therefore, indicate that desired behavior was not being obtained.

Table III.21

CHARACTERISTIC ADMINISTRATIVE FORMS BEFORE AND
SINCE TANZANIAN INDEPENDENCE

Colonial System (1960)	Early Independence System (1963)	Decentralization System (1972)
Provincial commissioner	Regional commissioner	Regional commissioner
	Administrative secretary	Regional development director
		Regional planning officer Regional personnel officer Regional financial officer
		Regional development committee
Functional officers	Functional officers	Functional officers
District commissioner	Area commissioner	Area commissioner
	Area secretary	District development director
		District planning officer District personnel officer District financial officer
	District council	District development council
	Executive officer	
Functional officers	Functional officers	Functional officers
Native authorities	Divisional executive officer	Divisional secretary
	Assistant divisional executive officer	Ward secretary
	Village executive officer	Ward development committee
	Village development committee	

Boundary changes usually resulted in the imposition of a new administrative structure on a new area; hence changes in the number of administrative units indicate structural changes. Table III.22 shows variations in the approximate number of units in the course of a fifteen-year period. The stability of the administrative unit

Table III.22

CHANGES IN NUMBER OF ADMINISTRATIVE UNITS,
MAINLAND TANZANIA: 1960-1975

Unit		1960	1965	1970	1975
Regions		9	17	17	20
Districts		54	60	61	96
Wards	Rural	--	1689	1544	1846
	Total	--	1799	1760	2154

Sources: The district and regional figures are available in Tanzania Government Directories. The ward figures for 1965 are from district-council constitutions in subsidiary legislation and can be taken as approximate; those for 1970 are from Government Notice No. 212, published July 31, 1970, and those for 1975 are from Government Notice No. 191, published September 12, 1975.

obviously is directly related to its size. In 1965, wards were simply electoral districts for district councilors. The great increase in the number of districts in 1975 resulted partly from decentralization, which involved the creation of districts out of towns as well as the division of other areas, and partly from the adjustment of district boundaries to conform with electoral-district boundaries. All these changes made it difficult for the rural population to become familiar with the pattern of operation of government leaders and institutions.

(3) *Politico-administrative officers tended to adopt the style and function of government officers.* Early in 1962, shortly after independence, the offices of regional and area commissioners were established as the principal representatives of the central government and as the party secretaries of their respective areas. Their functions were basically the same as had been those of the provincial and district commissioners, except for the removal of magisterial and

some local government powers.[81] Thus they were generally responsible for law and order, planned development, and the proper conduct of government business. It was hoped that these officers would, in fact, exercise supreme power in their areas because they represented both state and party power. By the late 1960s, however, Finucane found in Mwanza that they "were not able to significantly lessen the dominance of the bureaucracy."[82] He concluded that the "Commissioners for the most part . . . were agents of the hierarchy . . . attempting to mobilize the people to follow central directions."[83] The process of decentralization in 1972 was intended to give them the status of ministers vis-à-vis their regions, and they were expected "to devote a great deal of their time to political education for socialist development."[84] Although their position does not appear to have markedly changed, real variation exists among commissioners as to their influence. Many writers have given some of them credit for a key role in initiating the villagization operations in the first half of the 1970s.[85]

Decentralization also created positions at the divisional and ward level parallel to those of the commissioner—called the divisional and ward secretaries. They exercised dual party and government functions, but perhaps because there was no powerful administrative officer with countervailing power at those levels, their local significance was greater. The ward secretaries appear to have been given the major burden in villagization, much as had the native authorities during the colonial era.[86]

(4) *Administrative officers have generally dominated government structures at the regional and district levels.* When the regional- and area-commissioner structures were established, administrative positions—those of administrative and area secretary, respectively— were created to assist them. Several writers have noted that the positions were relatively powerful because they acted as the filter for communication to and from the commissioners.[87] With decentralization, in 1972, these officers were replaced by development directors at both levels. The new officers were to assume the function of chief executive officers and, according to the President, although they will "have real power and responsibility for management . . . they will be subject to final overall policy direction and control from Dar es Salaam."[88] The development directors were assigned three assistants—the district planning, financial, and personnel officers. These officials and the functional officers were responsible to the development director, a relationship paralleling the

relationship between officers in a ministry and its permanent secretary.[89]

Below the district level, administration was carried out during the colonial period by various ranks of native authorities. After 1962/63, when the offices of the chiefs were abolished, three new administrative levels came into existence—divisions, subdivisions (in some places), and villages. Appointments to the posts of divisional, assistant divisional, and village executive officers were made by a committee of the district council and all but the lowest were subject to the approval of the regional commissioner.[90] The functions of the officers were to stimulate development, supervise tax collection, and maintain law and order. Reportedly, several ex-chiefs and subchiefs were assigned the new positions, but loyalty to TANU was said to be a criterion with considerable weight.[91] By 1965 it was reported that the intention was to choose the two higher positions through the local government service commission. Although administrative officers at all levels had general responsibility for policy implementation, functional officers were charged with specific tasks.

(5) *The functional officers have had considerable difficulty in promoting rural development.* In each district and region are representatives of the functional ministries. Because of staffing problems, not every area had its full complement of officers, and reorganizations of ministries resulted in further instability. By the early 1970s, however, officers for health, education, natural resources, water, land development, public works, industries, agriculture, and cooperatives had been installed at most regional and district levels.[92] The instability of regional administrative structures and the number of administrative units have already been noted. Instability within the functional ministries was also considerable. Informal shifting of responsibility often occurred several months before formal transfer took place, causing difficulties in fixing exact dates. Table III.23, nevertheless, provides some indication of shifts of responsibility for four matters directly related to the implementation of the ujamaa village policy. The changes led to period phases of confusion and discontinuity of work. The effects were not as serious at lower levels where functional responsibility was more stable, but some demoralization was bound to occur.

The two functional ministries whose work in rural areas has been most vigorous are those of agriculture and cooperatives. The cooperative movement has been closely associated with the ujamaa

Table III.23
SHIFTS OF RESPONSIBILITIES AMONG TANZANIAN MINISTRIES

Agriculture	Cooperatives	Community or Rural Development	Settlement/ Ujamaa Villages
Ministry of Agriculture (by January 1962)	Ministry of Agriculture (by January 1962)	Ministry of Local Government (by January 1962)	Ministry of Lands, Settlement and Water Development (by August 1964)
Ministry of Agriculture, Forests, and Wildlife (by June 1964)	Ministry of Cooperative and Community Development (by December 1962)	Ministry of Cooperative and Community Development (by December 1962)	Ministry for Regional Administration and Rural Development (by May 1969)
Ministry of Agriculture and Cooperatives (by July 1967)	Ministry of Commerce and Cooperatives (by June 1964)	Ministry of Local Government and Rural Development (by July 1967)	Office of the Prime Minister and Second Vice President (by December 1973)
Ministry of Agriculture, Food and Cooperatives (by January 1969)	Ministry of Agriculture and Cooperatives (by July 1967)	Ministry of Regional Administration and Rural Development (by October 1968)	
Ministry of Agriculture and Cooperatives (by December 1970)	Ministry of Agriculture, Food and Cooperatives (by January 1969)	Office of the Prime Minister and Second Vice President (by December 1973)	
Ministry of Agriculture (by February 1972)	Ministry of Agriculture and Cooperatives (by December 1970)		
	Ministry of Agriculture (by February 1972)		
	Office of the Prime Minister and Second Vice President (by December 1973)		

Sources: Data for Tanganyika and Tanzania Government Directories, 1962-1974, and Government Notices 500 of 1962, 497 of 1964, 104 of 1966, 251 of 1967, 120 of 1969, 293 of 1970, 263 of 1971, 40 of 1972, and 10 of 1976. The earliest mentioned change was taken from the charts. Often changes occurred before they were officially announced.

village effort. By the late 1960s, the government's interests appear to have shifted from the promotion of cooperatives to their control because of concern over the role of traders and kulaks in the movement. According to Goran Hyden,

> At least three different measures aimed at breaking the power position of the traders and the kulaks in the cooperative union leadership can be identified: (a) the creation of regional cooperative unions all over the country; (b) increased control over recruitment of union staff; and (c) intervention in the election of committeemen in the unions. The previous mismanagement in the cooperative movement has been used as the excuse for these extensive reforms.[93]

In addition, marketing boards were established which continuously expanded their range of activity as exclusive buyers of crops from cooperatives. Critics argued that societies, unions, and boards did little to help the peasant improve his income. A study of marketing in Tanzania found that in Iringa the cost of selling a ton of maize in 1957/58, when marketing was handled by Indian traders, had been Shs. 130- ($19); in 1967/68, following the introduction of new marketing structures, this had risen to about Shs. 260- ($37). Of this sum the cooperative society took Shs. 55- ($8), the union took Shs. 51- ($7), and the national agricultural products board took Shs. 154- ($22).[94] As might be expected, peasants became dissatisfied.

In the early 1970s the marketing boards were transformed into crop authorities, and in 1974 these bodies were given the power to bypass the unions and buy directly from the primary societies. Although this eliminated one structure, it does not appear to have increased efficiency.[95] For one thing, it was costly for every board to go to each primary society to buy small quantities of the crop for which it was responsible. At the same time, the government was seeking to shift emphasis from marketing to producer cooperatives. Its efforts took the form of making the highest stage of development of an ujamaa village a multipurpose cooperative society. The Cooperative Societies Act under which these new cooperatives were registered soon proved unsuited to the kinds of activities envisioned for ujamaa villages. A new act, the Villages and Ujamaa Villages Act of 1975, was passed under which the villages were registered. These villages took over all the functions of the primary cooperative societies, which consequently were disbanded. Partly because of the abolition of these societies and partly because of mismanagement, all cooperative unions were disbanded in 1976.[96] For at least a decade prior to the demise of the primary societies and the unions, cooperative officers had met with considerable opposition from peasants who felt that the institutions were exploitative.

The other major group of functional officers directly related to the implementation of the ujamaa village policy is the agricultural officers, who have had more experience than any other functional officers in attempting to gain peasant compliance. Moreover, no other functional officers are as numerous as those working in agriculture. Table III.24 indicates the approximate number of persons served by each agricultural officer or assistant in several regions during the early 1970s. Except for the peculiarly large number of peasants served by each officer or assistant in Mtwara during 1972, a fairly uniform average of 5,000 is apparent.

The techniques used by these agents to gain peasant compli-

Table III.24

NUMBER OF INHABITANTS PER AGRICULTURAL OFFICER/ASSISTANT
IN MAINLAND TANZANIA: SELECTED REGIONS AND YEARS

Region	Number	Year	Region	Number	Year
Arusha	6019	1973	Tabora	5954	1972
Kigoma	4516	1973	Tanga	5372	1972
Mara	5027	1973	West Lake	3899	1972
Morogoro	6044	1973			
Singida	6889	1973	Kigoma	5430	1971
Tanga	4890	1973	Kilimanjaro	3143	1971
West Lake	4468	1973	Mbeya	6738	1971
			Singida	4816	1971
Kigoma	4623	1972	West Lake	7046	1971
Kilimanjaro	3437	1972			
Mtwara	10913	1972	Kigoma	5342	1970
Singida	4248	1972	West Lake	6098	1970

Source: Regional Annual Agricultural Reports.

ance have been the subject of study since the colonial era. N. V. Rounce divided such methods into two categories:

1. Educative methods
   (a) Routine touring by African staff
   (b) Annual meetings of chiefs and native authorities
   (c) Mass meetings
   (d) Demonstrations by advanced farmers, chiefs and leaders of society
   (e) Competitions
   (f) Education of the young African

2. Legislation

He suggested with regard to legislation that it was "becoming more and more clear . . . that in the absence of the economic stress of Western civilization, and the fiscal methods of inducing people almost unconsciously to carry out improvements, the African will have to be compelled to help himself."[97] Resort to legislation through the Native Authority Ordinance was common during the colonial period. Table III.25 shows the number of offenses against such orders over a twenty-year period.

Table III.25

OFFENSES AGAINST NATIVE-AUTHORITY ORDERS
IN TANGANYIKA: 1930-1950

Year	Number	Year	Number	Year	Number
1930	4,223	1937	9,328	1944	29,654
1931	4,372	1938	10,971	1945	31,374
1932	3,980	1939	14,379	1946	31,365
1933	3,458	1940	13,697	1947	28,850
1934	5,020	1941	13,737	1948	27,111
1935	6,876	1942	18,202	1949	25,848
1936	5,935	1943	30,161	1950	32,400

Source: Annual Reports of the Provincial Commissioners, appendices for the years indicated.

By-laws passed by the district councils or district development councils after independence were much like those passed in the pre-independence period. The core of such laws requiring cultivation is exemplified by that of Bagamoyo:

The Bagamoyo District Development Council (Cultivation of Agricultural Land) By-laws, 1975

Every resident who holds agricultural land in accordance with local customary law relating to land tenure shall, unless directed otherwise in writing by an authorized officer, cultivate and maintain an area of not less than one acre of cash crop or crops. . . .
Any person who contravenes or fails to comply with any of these By-laws shall be guilty of an offence and shall be liable on conviction to a fine not exceeding five hundred shillings or to imprisonment for a term not exceeding two months or to both such fine and imprisonment.[98]

Cultivation by-laws like this were passed in most of the district councils during the 1960s, as indicated in Table III.26. Paralleling the increasing number of by-laws has been an increase in the severity

Table III.26

ADOPTION OF CULTIVATION BY-LAWS IN MAINLAND TANZANIA: 1964-1969 and 1976

Year	Districts Passing By-laws	Cumulative Total	Year	Districts Passing By-laws	Cumulative Total
1964	7	7	1968	16	43
1965	7	14	1969	1	44
1966	1	15	1976	2	46[a]
1967	12	27			

Sources: Cited as by-laws in government notices published between 1964 and 1976 in subsidiary legislation, supplements to the Gazette.

[a]This figure covers only the first part of the year.

of penalties for noncompliance. The average penalties specified in by-laws passed in the course of a series of years is shown in Table III.27.

Table III.27

SEVERITY OF PUNISHMENT FOR VIOLATION OF CULTIVATION
BY-LAWS IN MAINLAND TANZANIA: 1964-1969 AND 1976

	Average Punishment	
Year	Fine (shillings)	Imprisonment (months)
1964	171.43	2.0
1965	192.86	2.0
1966	200.00	2.0
1967	295.83	3.6
1968	345.88	4.2
1969	500.00	6.0
1976	500.00	2.0

Sources: Cited as by-laws in government notices published between 1964 and 1976 in subsidiary legislation, supplements to the Gazette.

Although the by-laws were instituted to help agricultural officers achieve their objectives, many felt that they harmed the work of the officers more than they helped it. The task of enforcing the laws undermined their role as friendly advisors to the peasant. Apparently they wanted the laws, but not the designation of "authorized officer" for implementation purposes. Most considered that their major function was to employ what Rounce called "educative methods." What these involved is indicated by the standard form of their reports, shown in Table III.28. Emphasis on these countable means of extension may have distracted attention from more effective tools. At any rate, R. Hulls found in Mwanza that they made virtually no contribution.[99] In 1975 the President declared that if all such officers were removed, production would be unaffected.[100] Part of the problem with both agricultural and cooperative officers was their independence of local control.

(6) *Increasingly, observers are blaming "bureaucratization" for the difficulties government and party face when seeking to*

Table III.28

STANDARD FORM OF REPORT ON EXTENSION METHODS,
MINISTRY OF AGRICULTURE, MAINLAND TANZANIA:
1960s AND 1970s[a]

Method	Form
A. Spoken word	1. Meetings and discussion groups (a) TYL, (b) VDCs, (c) Divisional Development Committees/ still included in the 1970s, though disbanded in the 1960s/, (d) DDCs, (e) Agricultural sessions, (f) Women's clubs, (g) Farmers clubs or associations, (h) Primary cooperative societies, (i) Cooperative unions, (j) Traders' associations and/or chambers of commerce.
	2. Farm visits
	3. Office calls
	4. Broadcasts
B. Visual aids	1. Film shows
	2. Slide shows
	3. Charts
	4. Posters
	5. Photographs
	6. Farmers' day
	7. Demonstration of mechanized aids
C. Written word	1. Articles for press
	2. Leaflets and circulars
	3. Sales of *Ukulima wa Kisasa* (*Modern Farming*), a newspaper

[a]This form can be found, for example, as an appendix to the Regional Agricultural Reports for Mbeya, 1966, and Kigoma, 1971.

implement policies requiring the active compliance of the people.
The most salient characteristic of Tanzania as it has evolved in the first decade and a half since independence is the growing predominance of government. Rival bodies have been reduced in power, absorbed, or suppressed. At the same time, this process has often resulted in eliminating links with the people. There is a tendency in much of the literature to assume that the substitution of bureaucratic for democratic principles automatically leads to popular alienation, and that such alienation brings resistance to government

efforts to gain popular compliance. The growth of bureaucracy and its consequences have been viewed in differing ways.

The best-known class interpretation of the evolution of Tanzania is that of Shivji, who suggests that, as in the case of the Soviet Union, a "bureaucratic bourgeoisie" is emerging. He argues that it is increasingly separating itself from the petty bourgeoisie which was the dominant group following independence. Its growing domination, he argues, does not bode well for the implementation of a policy aimed at improving the lives of the bulk of the population. He defines the composition of the "bureaucratic bourgeoisie" in terms of specific occupations in three general sectors:

Politico-administrative: political heads of government ministries and departments (central and local) and their top civil servants; heads and top functionaries in the judiciary, police and security; and the top leadership of the party.

Economic: heads and higher functionaries of parastatals, public corporations, and other quasi-economic, either state-run or state-supervised institutions (cooperatives, marketing boards, higher educational institutions included).

Military: top military officers (majors, colonels, captains, and lieutenants).[101]

It should be noted that Shivji does not confine membership solely to those identified with the government, but also includes the top leadership of the party.

Phil Raikes has argued that "the ruling 'bureaucratic bourgeosie' entrenches itself increasingly with every year." Actions taken by bureaucrats, however, do not appear always to follow from their self-interest. He refers to their "self-mystification" as manifest in the villagization operations, which, though they may "entrench the bureaucracy more deeply as the master of Tanzania," do not necessarily "contribute to [the bureaucracy's] . . . economic well-being."[102] Although he holds that inconsistencies may exist in bureaucratic behavior (i. e., actions sometimes do not seem to follow from self-interest), bureaucratic dominance is increasingly a fact.

Finucane maintains that such a situation differs little from that which prevailed during the colonial period and observes that "the bureaucrats themselves are industrious, responsive to government's wishes, and well-intentioned in their efforts. But the basic, familiar pattern remains—an elite, ensconced in a state bureaucracy, trying with varying degrees of detachment to convince the masses to change their ways."[103] In his view, moreover, the small elite is not really interested in "convincing" the masses: "A concomitant of the bureaucratic approach to development in Tanzania was that the small elite, mostly concentrated in government bureaucracy, was satisfied with the maintenance of their relatively better-off socio-economic position while the peasant masses continued to be uninvolved in the application of more productive technologies."[104] Others, such as Gerhard Tschannerl, insist that the problem is not so much lack of interest on the part of the government officials as it is the subversion of the self-reliance necessary for real development. Tschannerl argues that "under the dominant ideology of the state, that is, the ideology of the bureaucratic bourgeoisie as opposed to proletarian ideology, the client relationship will necessarily continue to be the principal mode of interaction. There is consequently no room for genuine self-help by the peasants."[105]

H. U. E. Thoden Van Velzen and other writers appear to contend that the problem is really one of an alliance between the rural bureaucracy and the kulaks, which means that policy implementation is always bent to favor these two groups.[106] Thus, it is impossible to implement without distortion even policies whose potential is mass development. In the early 1970s von Freyhold took a somewhat different position. She concluded that the opposition of the "proto-kulaks" to the ujamaa village policy had a greater chance of being overcome in Tanzania than elsewhere because of the progressive ideology guiding government functionaries. At that time she saw antagonism, rather than alliance, as characterizing the relationship between the kulak and government agents.[107] By the mid-1970s, however, her ideas had changed substantially and she concluded that the functionaries had, in fact, become the chief barrier to implementation.[108]

CONCLUSIONS

These social, economic, political, and administrative factors had an important influence on the formation and implementation of the ujamaa village policy. The growing power of the government vis-à-vis that of other institutions was manifested in diverse ways. The government's role in the economy was increasing rapidly. The tendency of politico-administrative officials to become associated more with administration than with politics enhanced the position of the government. The designation by the party of the government as the principal agent for policy implementation gave the latter legitimacy in exercising power. The dependence of the party on government finance and government manpower to sustain its operations increased its dependence. One way the party might reassert its dominance was through the initiation of a major party policy.

Rural transformation had posed a perennial problem since independence. The functional officers responsible for rural development had not had much success. Agricultural production per capita had been stagnant for many years. And by 1967 the cooperative movement was faltering. The need for more radical and innovative action was apparent to many.

Structural changes in the administration had been one of the principal methods of solving rural-development problems and almost all other types as well. Two major and numerous minor changes in the structure of regional administration took place in the past decade and a half, and there were frequent changes in administrative boundaries. Moreover, responsibility for rural undertakings was continually reshuffled among ministries. Such changes were ostensible signs of activity, but they frequently brought more confusion than efficiency. Consequently, a need for more than the structural reform of administration became apparent.

Popular participation in party and government decision-making had remained minimal despite considerable efforts by both institutions to elicit such participation. Decision-making has become more centralized within the top levels of the party, and numerous structural layers hinder access to it. The basis of recruitment to most party organs makes officials more responsible to other party bodies than to party members. Even where members have direct choices, party officials limit the range of candidates they might pick. Government attempts to build viable representative councils have repeatedly met with failure. Decentralization efforts have not noticeably increased popular participation. Yet there appears to be a relationship between the legitimacy of a government, the ease with which some kinds of policies may be implemented, and the degree of popular participation in decision-making. Some leaders, therefore, favored action that might facilitate the participation of the rural population with the aim of counteracting the spread of bureaucratization.

Several characteristics of rural Tanzania enhanced the possibility of the successful implementation of a socialist policy. Economic differentiation had not proceeded to the point where a rich peasant class or a landlord class could thwart major restructuring of rural areas, though in some local areas resistance to or distortion of the policy—or both—was possible. Perhaps because many ethnic groups existed in Tanzania, tribalism was not as divisive a factor as it had been in other countries. Land scarcity was a problem in only a few parts of the country; hence new villages might be established without depriving people of their means of livelihood. Much of the peasantry had a tradition of shifting cultivation, so that the movement of homesteads was not as serious a problem as in other countries. Private traders who might be displaced were mostly of Asian origin, a fact that would make their ouster easier than if they had been indigenous. Therefore, a villagization/communalization policy had a greater chance of success in rural Tanzania than in many other countries.

All these factors—the party's need to assert its dominance, the persistence of rural underdevelopment, the failure of administrative structural change to bring rural transformation, the desire for popular participation as a counterweight to the growing power of the bureaucracy, and the presence of rural conditions that might facilitate the introduction of a socialist policy—contributed to the President's decision that a bold policy was called for to change radically the direction of Tanzania's drift.

Chapter IV

THE POLICY: UJAMAA VILLAGES

The announcement of the curtailment of the village settlement scheme by the prime minister, Rashidi Kawawa, in April 1966 did not signify the end of government-encouraged settlement. Existing settlements that had a chance of being economically viable were to continue. What was involved was a shift of support to less capital-intensive efforts. Several such settlements had been started in various parts of the country in the period just before and after independence by local TANU Youth League branches. Perhaps the most successful was that at Litowa, which gave rise to several others and formed the basis of the Ruvuma Development Association in Songea district.[1] The RDA villages became the new model for settlement, and it was this idea that was picked up and carried forward in the ujamaa village policy.

The basic policy was first outlined by President Nyerere in "Socialism and Rural Development" in September and endorsed by the thirteenth biennial conference of TANU in October 1967.[2] This was his second "post-Arusha" policy paper seeking to indicate how the socialist goals announced in the Arusha Declaration could be achieved. Although the President and others expanded, reinterpreted, and modified the tenets in subsequent years, this document continues to be basic to an understanding of the policy.

The Swahili title of the paper is *"Ujamaa Vijijini,"* which literally translated means "Socialism in the Villages" rather than "Socialism and Rural Development." The Swahili notion of putting socialism into villages is more representative of what the policy came to imply than the English notion of creating socialist villages that would facilitate rural development. Perhaps partly for this reason, the President, even when speaking or writing in English, sometimes uses the Swahili expression to refer to the policy. Also, he sometimes treats it as a group of policies rather than a single policy. Thus, he refers to "ujamaa policies in rural areas," "the policy of ujamaa vijijini," "policies of ujamaa vijijini," and "the ujamaa village policy." For the sake of consistency, the last is used in this study.

In Chapter I, policy was defined as a plan outlining the means and ends of action undertaken by a government. It is a vision of the path of development. It can also be described as "a hypothesis containing initial conditions and predicted consequences."[3] Expressed as a hypothesis, the ujamaa village policy can be summarized as follows: "If the party and government apply resources, then peasants can be brought to live and work together for the good of all in ujamaa villages." Stated thus, the policy appears broad and vague. The "resources" of the party and government are not specified and the meaning of "to live and work together for the good of all" is left unspecified. The "if" clause deals with the means and the "then" clause deals with the ends of policy. Interpretations and modifications of both have been extensive over the years since 1967.

ENDS

The objectives of the policy are divisible into two levels: first, the central aim is the creation of ujamaa villages; second, however, ujamaa villages are seen as vehicles for achieving broader goals. Many of the difficulties faced in the implementation of the policy stem from the assumed interrelationship between these two levels. The dominant view has been that the ujamaa village is a sufficient condition for the broader goals, whereas the subordinate view holds that the ujamaa village is only one of several necessary conditions. Ambiguity on the issue is a feature common to both the initial formulation of the policy and to subsequent modifications.

President Nyerere in "Socialism and Rural Development" stated quite specifically that ujamaa villages are sufficient conditions for development: "We shall achieve the goals we in this country have set ourselves if the basis of Tanzanian life consists of rural *economic and social communities where people live and work together for the good of all.*"[4] In the same paper, he appears to hedge this assertion by suggesting that additional conditions such as a better marketing apparatus, harder work, and a democratic system of local government are also necessary for development.[5] In fact, however, he implies that these conditions would somehow be fulfilled by the mere creation of the ujamaa village. The element of ambiguity recurs, however, in many other speeches and writings.

It is probable that emphasis on the idea that the creation of ujamaa villages implied the attainment of other goals was partly a tactic of implementation. An ujamaa village was much more attractive if it meant the achievement of a wide range of aspirations than if it meant only living and working together. Nevertheless, the equation of the two in the policy objectives posed some serious problems. Peasants were discouraged when, after they joined what was said to be an ujamaa village, the good life did not automatically follow. Confusion then arose over whether such villages should or should not be called ujamaa villages. And insufficient attention was paid to the requirements for the achievement of the broader goals.

Despite the early equation of the two policy objectives—the creation of ujamaa villages and their goals—separate examination is useful.

UJAMAA VILLAGES

President Nyerere has been fairly consistent in describing the essence of an ujamaa village. He uses such expressions as "economic and social communities where people live and work together for the good of all" and "a place where people live together and work together for the benefit of all its participants."[6] The consistent association of the words living and working together in all the President's writings suggests that a causal relationship may exist between the two. At times the President appears to imply that living together is likely to lead to working together and at other times that working together is likely to lead to living together. Seldom, however, does he treat either as sufficient for the other. In fact, he uses the two variables to distinguish types of rural conditions, as shown in Table IV.1. The ujamaa village is thus the conjunction and only the conjunction of living *and* working together. Although living together may lead to working together, the reverse is also possible. The conjunction is not a necessary one, and many other forms of rural life are found in its absence.

Table IV.1

FORMS OF RURAL LIVING AND WORKING TOGETHER
IN MAINLAND TANZANIA

| | | Living | |
		Together	Apart
Working	Together	Ujamaa village	Traditional homestead
	Apart	Village	Direction of current trend

The lack of clear definition of both living and working together gave rise to implementation problems. There were two primary questions concerning the concept of living together. One was "How close would people have to be to be considered as living together?" The other was "How many people must there be in such an area for the people to be considered as living together?" The former question was crucial in several areas, for its answer determined whether or not movement would be required for the implementation of policy. The President was vague on the issue in "Socialism and Rural Development." He specifically suggested a number of ways in which people in the Kilimanjaro area might work together that did not necessarily require moving together, but also implied that movement would probably be necessary to create a communal farm.[7] In most of the densely populated parts of the country the policy was interpreted to allow scattered dwellings if there was no unused land between households. At the other extreme were areas in which the policy was interpreted to mean the construction of contiguous houses in straight lines separated only by a roadway. The latter question was also an important issue because it determined whether small villages would have to be moved or whether they would not. "Socialism and Rural Development" provided a guideline. The President said that an ujamaa village would be a group of people "large enough to take account of modern methods and the twentieth-century needs of man."[8] Such a guideline was, obviously, open to considerable variation in interpretation. In the same paper he gave an example of a village with forty members.[9] Many different figures have been proposed by the President as well as by others. For example, the deputy secretary-general of the TYL envisioned thousands of members in mid-1973; a few months later the President said that 500 families were an ideal number for Kasulu district; and the Villages and Ujamaa Villages Act of 1975 specified a minimum of 250 families.[10] The lack of criteria to define what living together meant in the vision of an ujamaa village consequently both posed problems and provided implementers with room for maneuver. Much the same is true of the idea of working together.

Working together was defined in the policy in broad terms. The President noted in "Socialism and Rural Development" that the "extent of the private activities may well vary from one village to another, but . . . all must play a fair part in the life of the community from which they all benefit."[11] The notion of playing "a fair part in the life of the community" is itself a broad conception of working together. It might involve many different types of activities. For example, Nyerere suggested working on a small industrial or "service" project, a communal poultry unit, tannery or workshop, a jointly owned truck, or an irrigation project.[12] In fact, no boundary on the type of activity required was specified, provided it benefited the group.

On the basis of the President's outline, other statements defining the ujamaa village policy have been made. For example, the Cooperative Union of Tanzania has interpreted it as follows: "An Ujamaa village is made up of a group of people who have willingly joined together in order to carry out their activities which will bring about change of their own lives together."[13] A standard village constitution in Iringa Region defines it as "a village started by peasants and/or workers on their own free will and doing their economic and developmental activities together in cooperative socialist ways for the common good and under the guidance and with the aid of TANU."[14] In a report from an ujamaa village in Kigoma Region an ujamaa village member is defined as one who

> declares immediately that he will no longer be exploited or exploit. He has given up the tendency of working for others or making others work for him. He has abided by the Arusha Declaration Code and he shall follow them by action immediately. If he agrees to that he automatically belongs to the Wajamaa and then owns everything he has found in the possession of the Wajamaa.[15]

The Villages and Ujamaa Villages Act of 1975 defines the policy as one in which "a substantial portion of the economic activities of the village are being undertaken and carried out on a communal basis."[16] Each definition is an attempt to interpret more fully the President's conception of an ujamaa village as a place where people live and work together for the good of all.

What an ujamaa village should be had been spelled out by the government in terms of a set of criteria which regional and district officials have been called upon to apply in selecting annually the best ujamaa village in each region since 1970. The leaders of the winning villages are then presented with prizes for their villages on July 7, Saba Saba Day (the celebration of the founding of TANU). Two features of these lists of criteria should be noted initially. First, only the topics considered important are explicitly cited, and what is "good" or "bad" with regard to the topics is left to the determination of the person who applies them. Second, almost never is a system of weighting assigned to the topics to permit consistent valuation, even if there were common agreement on what was "good" and "bad."

In 1972 the government published a list of topics, given below, which should be used to identify "best villages":

(1) How the ujamaa activities of the village are carried out, and their quality.
(2) Good example of leadership, cooperation, and development for other villages.
(3) Efforts of the villagers in acquiring essential services such as permanent houses, godowns for preserving their crops, and so on.
(4) Economic plans of the villages and the effort taken to implement these plans.
(5) The self-reliance activities undertaken.
(6) Good use of capital and of available expertise.
(7) General development of the village.[17]

These criteria were elaborated and broadened by the commissioner of rural development in a 1973 guide to the selection of the best village. The major additions to the criteria cited above are the level of political consciousness and the system of income distribution:

(1) Political consciousness and the economic and political principles observed in the village:
  (a) What is the committee structure in the village?
  (b) How are the meetings of the various committees carried out?
  (c) How well have villagers participated in national campaigns?
  (d) Do the villagers put more effort into individual or communal activities?
  (e) How many groups such as the UWT and the TYL exist in the village?
(2) Economic planning in the village:
  (a) Who does the planning?
  (b) How are the villagers incorporated into the plan?
(3) Implementation of village plans:
  (a) How are the village activities carried out?
  (b) How well are individual and communal activities carried out?
  (c) How is the productivity of each person measured?

(4) Self-help activities to obtain necessary social services:
 (a) How many self-help activities exist and what is the estimated cost of each?
 (b) How successful have these activities been and what is the
 reason for their success/failure?
 (c) What self-help plans do they have for the future?
(5) Use and care of village finance and equipment:
 (a) How are forests used?
 (b) How is the land used?
 (c) How are communal buildings such as stores used and cared
 for?
(6) Understanding and cooperation between the villagers and
 others:
 (a) What is the degree of understanding and cooperation
 among villagers, between villagers and leaders and among
 the leaders themselves?
 (b) What is the degree of cooperation between the villagers
 and the party and government workers of the region,
 district, division, and ward?
(7) Distribution of income:
 (a) How is communal income used?
 (b) If there are houses built, who built them, and how are they
 allocated to the villagers?
 (c) If there is a harvest, what criteria are used in distributing
 it?[18]

The regional ujamaa and cooperative officer in Kigoma took
these criteria and interpreted them for application to his region in
both 1973 and 1974. Each year his interpretation was sent to district
officers along with that from the commissioner cited above. The
major addition was a set of criteria pertaining to the role the village
played in the movement of people which had brought nearly everyone in the region into villages by the end of 1974:

(1) Village leadership:
 (a) Existing committees and work procedures.
 (b) Initiative and understanding shown in carrying out their
 responsibilities.
 (c) Their social and economic plans in uplifting the well
 being of the villagers.
(2) The activity of moving into villages:
 (a) The number of villagers in the village at that time.
 (b) The number and quality of houses built by the villagers.

96

(c) The villagers' efforts in the making of their village environment.

(3) Socialist activities:
  (a) Farming—acreage, the use of fertilizers, care of the farm, their crops, forest clearing, etc.
  (b) Trade—shops, small industries, fishing, etc.
  (c) Various cultural activities.
(4) Awareness of the policy of socialism and self-reliance:
  (a) Aid received and how spent.
  (b) Understanding of the meaning of exploitation and how to eliminate it.
  (c) Problems encountered and how they were solved.[19]

In 1975 a slightly different set of criteria was applied to identify the best village in Pare district. The criteria included:

(1) Village organization, its committees, and how they function.
(2) Development planning and its implementation.
(3) Emphasis on communal vs. individual work.
(4) Efforts to get necessary services, and other economic matters such as the village income and how it is distributed.[20]

Many other lists concerning the nature of the best village were prepared and distributed, but this selection is sufficient to make several points concerning the concept of an ujamaa village as reflected in the policy. First, topics considered indispensable to the ujamaa village cover a broad range. Most lists, but not all, include good planning, leadership, consciousness, effort, and development. Second, the way the criteria are specified gives great scope for differing interpretations at different levels and among districts. Thus, an ujamaa village is almost, though not quite, a mere subjective assessment by officials of what they conceive "good" to mean. Third, there are changes in criteria in the course of time. The Kigoma addition of "moving together" is a case in point. This temporal variation appears related to the kind of problem that local officials appear to feel it is most important to overcome.

Another definition/description of what the policy envisions for an ujamaa village can be gleaned from the constitutions of the villages. As one officer put it, a village constitution is "a teacher of Ujamaa and its creed." A standard constitution widely used as a model for villages which became cooperative societies before 1975 groups the major features under the following nine headings:

(1) *Membership*: Any worker or peasant 16 or over who "agrees to comply with the leadership, objectives, and rules of the village can apply for membership" to the village committee. If accepted he then serves a probationary period of at least six months. Formal resignation, expulsion or simply leaving the village will terminate membership. Only members of the village can continue to live in the area of the village.

(2) *Land*: All the land is controlled by the village, but it can allocate small plots to individuals.

(3) *Assets*: The village income may include money derived from contributions, fees, loans, savings, etc. This should be used to form a development fund, for economic development purposes, and a service fund, for the provision of social services and welfare activities.

(4) *Implementation of Economic Plans*: Villages should make annual and five-year plans. The village should be divided into work groups each with an elected leader who, wherever possible, should assign piece-work tasks. At the end of each day he will inspect the work and record the member's contribution. Members must follow work directives, work hard, and care for village property. If work discipline is broken, the village committee should warn him. If he still does not comply, "he can have some of his work days deducted, be given a punishment, be relieved of any leadership post if he happens to have one, or be expelled from the village." Prizes for individual or group excellence in work should be set.

(5) *Income Distribution*: Money from crop sales should be used to pay debts, taxes, village expenses, depreciation of assets, cultural and educational activities, compulsory saving, planned commercial business expenses, and wages for skilled workers, and what remains should be distributed. Payments should be calculated and made annually.

(6) *Political Activities*: The village will form a TANU branch or sub-branch. The village committee will be the same as the TANU committee of the village. Political education will be conducted to increase political consciousness and interest to work communally for the common good. Delegations may be sent to other villages for the exchange of experiences. Democratic principles and procedures should be followed.

(7) *Culture and Social Welfare*: The sick, old, and pregnant shall

be looked after. Education, cultural activities, sports, cleanliness, good houses, nursery schools, etc., will be encouraged, and precautions against famine will be taken.

(8) *Organization*: The highest body will be the village conference or meeting of all members. It will elect the village committee, chairman, assistant chairman, secretary, and treasurer. It receives and approves all reports, plans, admissions, expulsions, etc. It meets at least four times a year. Election of village leaders should be by secret ballot, but other votes should be by hand. The village committee will consist of the chairman, vice-chairman, secretary, treasurer, and six to ten members elected by the conference. The village committee will run the day-to-day affairs of the village. It meets at least once a month.

(9) *Leadership*: The chairman will serve three years, but can be reelected. He will be the TANU chairman in the village. The secretary will also be the TANU secretary. He is also "the chief executive officer of the village."[21]

What the constitution does is spell out in greater detail the meaning of living and working together for the good of all. This model was circulated by the ujamaa and cooperative officers. Its stress on organizational structure and procedure was partly a consequence of that fact and partly of the purpose to which it was to be put.

Even greater diversity of government-recognized villages arose with the major operations, especially in 1974 and 1975, to move people into villages. A new terminology was developed to distinguish these villages from those established earlier and called ujamaa villages. Development villages (*vijiji vya maendeleo*) and permanent villages (*vijiji vya kudumu*) were used as designations. Nevertheless, officials in regions which had had earlier operations often continued to apply the term ujamaa villages to all government-recognized villages. The confusion was merely a manifestation of the substantial diversity of interpretations of what an ujamaa village was. Attempts to regularize the terminology were made in several regions. In Iringa Region, for example, the ujamaa and cooperative officer wrote to his district officers as follows:

It should be remembered that the President of the United Republic of Tanzania has already stopped speaking of permanent (kudumu) or development (maendeleo) villages. Instead, we are identifying villages according to the development of the villages themselves. And the system used is as follows:

1. The normal village which has not started cooperation or ujamaa should simply be referred to as a "village."
2. The village which has been registered as a cooperative should be referred to as a "cooperative village."
3. The village which does all its activities on an ujamaa basis should be referred to as an "ujamaa village."[22]

Two months later the Villages and Ujamaa Villages (Registration, Designation and Administration) Act, 1975 (No. 21 of 1975) was passed; it identified only two types of villages and sought to set uniform standards for the country as a whole. The idea of uniform standards was contrary to the original thinking of Nyerere in "Socialism and Rural Development." He left the ujamaa village a concept with a wide range of possible meanings.[23] For eight years, as we have seen, various meanings were given to the term. The reason for this vague specification of characteristics is the same as for the absence of national legislation on the subject for so many years. One observer commented on the governmental attitude toward legislation in 1971 as follows:

> The prevailing view in the Ujamaa villages Division of the Ministry of Regional Administration and Rural Development (Maendeleo) is that there is no urgency for legislation to incorporate ujamaa villages, for such legislation would inevitably introduce bureaucratic rules and rigidity which would inhibit development. Moreover, it is recognized that as most villages are ujamaa only on paper without any viable economic programme and clear thought as to their objects, incorporation is not yet a priority issue.[24]

However, more and more legal cases grew out of the establishment of ujamaa villages, and confusion increasingly arose over just what these entities were and what they were not. Finally, at the sixteenth biennial conference of TANU (1973), the President stated that a law was being prepared.[25] It was not presented to the National Assembly, however, until mid-1975.

The Villages and Ujamaa Villages Act established two categories: Villages and ujamaa villages. The principal characteristics of a Village (capitalized below to indicate its special legal designation) are as follows:

Form of settlement:
It contains a minimum of 250 families living in a defined area.

Organization:
    (a) Members—It has a Village assembly (formerly a village conference or meeting) consisting of all residents at least 18 years old.
    (b) Leaders—It has a Village council (formerly the village committee or executive committee) elected by the assembly.

Leadership:
It is led by a chairman and a secretary, who are also the chairman and secretary of the TANU (CCM) branch, if there is one. If there is none, the council elects such officers from among its members.

Control of land:
Land is under the control of the Village council.

Control of other property:
Livestock and small tools are individually owned, but major machinery and buildings are collectively owned.

Cooperative status:
It is a corporate body that functions as if it were a multipurpose cooperative society.[26]

Another way of identifying the traits of Villages is to examine the criteria on which formal designation was based. Applications required information as to the number of families resident, the number of people able to work, the occupation of most villagers, the total land allocated to the Village, the major economic activity of the Village, and the social and economic facilities available to the villagers. The distinction between a Village and an ujamaa village is not major. When all the criteria of a Village have been met and, according to the act, where "a substantial portion of the economic activities of the village are being undertaken and carried out on a communal basis," the Village may apply to become an ujamaa village.[27] The criteria required in an application for such a designation include the same as those for Village designation, together with an indication of the skills of the villagers, the major communal activities, the proportion of communal activities relative to individual activities, the degree of self-reliance, and the number of members of TANU in the Village. In neither case is the "correct answer" to the questions on the form indicated, a situation that is likely to lead to differing interpretations. Nevertheless, designation as an ujamaa village eventually requires the assent of the responsible minister.

What the Villages and Ujamaa Villages Act did was twofold: it identified communal production as the distinguishing feature of an ujamaa village, and it made what had been considered the highest form of an ujamaa village—the multipurpose cooperative—a precondition to designation as simply a Village. At a minimum, it provided a meaning for living and working together which had nationwide applicability.

GOALS OF UJAMAA VILLAGES

The President has equated the goals of socialism in rural areas with the goals of ujamaa villages. In "Socialism and Rural Development" he stated that they were "a society in which all members have equal rights and equal opportunities; in which all live at peace with his neighbours without suffering or imposing injustice, being exploited, or exploiting, and in which all have a gradually increasing basic level of material welfare before any individual lives in luxury."[28] He has also cited dignity, education, fraternity, the end of individualistic attitudes and the drift to towns, security, and technological advance. These defined the good socialist life in Nyerere's view.

The Arusha Declaration is perhaps the foremost statement of Tanzanian aspirations. It was prepared by President Nyerere and submitted to the TANU National Executive Committee at the end of January 1967. After some modification it was published as a party document on 5 February 1967. The first section restated the TANU creed, which is contained in the party constitution. That creed specifies the key values expected of TANU members. Its publication with the Arusha Declaration suggests that those are also the goals defining Tanzanian socialism. It states that TANU believes:

(a) That all human beings are equal;
(b) That every individual has a right to dignity and respect;
(c) That every citizen is an integral part of the nation and has the right to take an equal part in Government at local, regional, and national level;
(d) That every citizen has the right to freedom of expression, of movement, of religious belief and of association within the context of the law;
(e) That every individual has the right to receive from society protection of his life and of property held according to law;

(f) That every individual has the right to receive a just return for his labour;

(g) That all citizens together possess all the natural resources of the country in trust for their descendants;

(h) That in order to ensure economic justice the state must have effective control over the principal means of production; and

(i) That it is the responsibility of the state to intervene actively in the economic life of the nation so as to ensure the well being of all citizens, and so as to prevent the exploitation of one person by another or one group by another, and so as to prevent the accumulation of wealth to an extent which is inconsistent with the existence of a classless society.[29]

The second section of the declaration defines the policy of socialism in terms of the absence of exploitation, peasant and worker control of the major means of production and exchange, and the existence of democracy.[30] The juxtaposition of the TANU creed and the policy of socialism suggests that the Arusha Declaration sought merely to emphasize and elaborate certain aspects of existing TANU policy (e.g., points c, f, and h of the creed). The ujamaa village might therefore be interpreted as merely a new technique to achieve an old desire. However, there have been other interpretations of the goals of ujamaa villages.

Political education officers have served to propagate the objectives of ujamaa villages in many forums. A detailed exposition by an officer working in the Ministry of Agriculture is contained in the booklet "Siasa ya Tanu Katika Kilimo" ("The Policy of TANU in Agriculture"). He said, in essence, that the "goals of ujamaa villages are like those of the Arusha Declaration. They center on Man; to permit every Tanzanian to have a better life." He went on to cite ten basic goals:

(1) To enable citizens to work together so that they can produce more.

(2) To enable villagers to work intelligently and to use modern implements, thereby producing more and better crops.

(3) To enable the people to plan their work.

(4) To enable villagers to apportion work according to the ability of the individual, the importance of the work, the seasons of the year, and the needs of the village.

(5) To enable the villagers to obtain necessary services such as water, a hospital, schools, shops, a market, etc.

(6) To enable the people to understand the country's ideology and thereby increase their freedom.
(7) To consolidate and perpetuate democracy.
(8) To give the people security of life.
(9) To defend the people.
(10) To restore to the people their humanity and self-respect.[31]

He insisted that all these goals can and will be achieved through the agency of the ujamaa village—that productivity, planning, division of labor, services, ideology, democracy, security, defense, and dignity can all follow from the ujamaa village.

The goals of ujamaa villages are also specified in village constitutions, which usually cite numerous general and specific objectives. In the case of the model constitution referred to earlier these are:

(1) To enable villagers to uplift their standard of living by:
    (a) Inculcating the spirit of hating all kinds of exploitation and instead building and maintaining the spirit of working cooperatively for the good of all members.
    (b) Giving every villager an opportunity to work which gives him a just return, because work is the right and responsibility of every human being.
    (c) Expanding the economy of the village by starting ujamaa farms, ujamaa shops, various ujamaa industries, ujamaa trade, and any other ujamaa activities, provided they are for the benefit of the village.
    (d) Selling the crops or other goods produced in the village.
    (e) Buying and/or building and maintaining buildings, offices, industries, machines, and other equipment necessary for village development.
    (f) Cooperating with other ujamaa villages or state corporations in trade activities so that no conflicts arise with the village leadership and the TANU creed and objectives.
    (g) Giving the villagers an opportunity to obtain education, medical care, and other necessities for the life and well being of man.
    (h) Setting an example to other citizens who have not joined so that they may like the ujamaa way of living together and working together for the common good.
    (i) Accomplishing these aims or any one of them, provided they do not contradict the TANU creed and objectives.

(2) To give security of life to the villagers by:
   (a) Strengthening and consolidating the socialist spirit of brotherly love and respect.
   (b) Planning and incorporating all members into socialist work and distributing income according to the work done.
   (c) Saving money in the bank or elsewhere for future use.
   (d) Taking care of the aged, widows, orphans, and those who meet with misfortune.
   (e) Lending money or sponsoring credit to villagers.[32]

At this level it is apparent that the goals of ujamaa villages are not necessarily assumed to be the spontaneous consequence of the existence of the villages themselves. It is evident that the village recognizes, or the ujamaa and cooperative officers recognize, that the good life requires effort and attention to achieve its potentialities.

Finally, the Villages and Ujamaa Villages Act specified three objectives for ujamaa villages:

(1) To build a society in which all members have equal rights and opportunities and in which all members have a gradually increasing basic level of material welfare before any individual lives in luxury.
(2) To develop new socialist relations of production based on communal land utilization, communal ownership of the means of production, socialist organization of labour and application of the principle of tying income to efficiency to eliminate every form of exploitation in collective production and to allow residents of ujamaa villages to develop their activity and creative initiative to the full.
(3) To promote a spirit of self-reliance in social and economic activities such as by building schools, dispensaries, and the like.[33]

In the specification of goals over a period of time, there are trends that appear to indicate increasing appreciation of difficulties. Initially, broad goals were declared which were implicitly identified as the consequence of ujamaa village life. The assumption that attainment of the goals followed automatically appears to have been diluted by experience. That experience is partly reflected in goals specified by those more closely tied to the actual implementation— for example, the political education officers and the framers of the village constitutions. Generally, the goals identify a good life for any human being. The socialist aspect is the idea that the goals would be more readily attained through group effort. Experience with group effort, however, has resulted in the course of time in some changes concerning organization and remuneration. The village constitution calls for small work groups—rather than the whole village, as implied initially by the President—to be the organizational form of communal work. And the Villages and Ujamaa Villages Act calls for tying income to efficiency, which indicates a realization that working together does not inevitably mean hard or productive work.

MEANS

The policy outline of the means to achieve these ends is really the policy outline of the implementation process. As has been noted, the basic task is to cause people to live and work together in ujamaa villages, and this requires an alteration of peasant behavior.

TECHNIQUES

The President has stated many times that ujamaa villages must be established by persuasion, and has frequently argued against the use of both force and inducement. As we shall see, however, he has provided loopholes, so that all three techniques had a place in his vision.

In "Socialism and Rural Development" the President remarked that "socialist communities can not be established by compulsion."[34] In Circular No. 1 he said that the establishment of ujamaa villages "cannot be done by force."[35] In "Freedom and Development" he asserted, "An Ujamaa village is a voluntary association of people who decide of their own free will to live together and work together."[36] On numerous other occasions as well he expressed the view that force must not be used to create ujamaa villages.

The President's view was echoed by many others. For example, in 1972 a writer in the *Daily News* (the government newspaper) declared that "the use of force is absurd and, in Tanzania, out of the question. Coercion dehumanises man and has the effect of alienating the people from the revolution."[37] In early 1973 the Mbeya regional TANU executive secretary commented that "if TANU and Government leaders use force to implement development programmes they will confuse and frustrate the people and impede development."[38] Later that year, the deputy secretary-general of the TYL said to a group of Swedes visiting Dar es Salaam that "I want to assure you that the Party has never had any intention of forcing people into Ujamaa villages."[39] Such statements indicate that the ethic of "persuasion and not force" had permeated many leaders in Tanzania.

President Nyerere never ruled out force, however, as a technique for gaining compliance with some government directives. In "Socialism and Rural Development" he explicitly stated that forced cultivation may be both necessary and effective,[40] and in "Freedom and Development" he wrote of the utility of force in some type of activities: "You can build pyramids and magnificent roads, you can achieve expanded acreages of cultivation, and increases in the quantity of goods produced in your factories. All these things, and many more, can be achieved through the use of force."[41] However, the limits on the utility of compulsion, the President argued, were contained in the proverb "You can drive a donkey to water, but you cannot make it drink." He contended that force could "only achieve short-term material goals."[42] The question arose as to whether an aspect of the ujamaa village policy might be classified as a "short-term material goal," the ethic of persuasion being retained for other aspects.

According to a former TANU national executive secretary:

> The President suggested to the NEC in 1972 that it is possible to separate the aspect of "living together" from that of "working together on a communal farm," and that these two could be tackled in different stages. He recommended that efforts should first of all be concentrated on getting people to live together, and once they live together they will themselves see the benefits of cooperation for their common good. The NEC discussed and accepted the President's submission, and directed that it should be implemented throughout the country.[43]

The impact of this decision on the technique to be used to induce compliance with the policy was not immediately obvious. At the sixteenth biennial conference of TANU in 1973, however, the President was a little more explicit. He said that "development has its own law and one law is the collection of people. People who have collected in one place can do certain things. They must succeed."[44] Referring not to the initiation of the ujamaa village policy, but to his 1962 inaugural speech, noted in Chapter II, which urged villagization, he said:

> The question of living in villages has been emphasized for eleven years. . . . I am talking of living in villages; I am not talking of

Ujamaa. . . . To be an Mjamaa is not something compulsory. . . .
I am talking of living in villages. . . .

My duty is to see to it that the policy of the party is carried
out; living together is the party's policy; it is your policy; you have
said it yourself; the National Executive Committee has declared
that we are no longer saying that moving into villages is for one
region but it is for the whole nation. Now my duty and my com-
rades' duty is to implement it.[45]

He even went so far as to imply that if delegates wanted a chance for
reelection in the TANU elections coming up the following year,
they would be well advised to implement the new policy.[46]

A few months later the President went further toward advocat-
ing force for getting people to move together. On 6 November 1973,
at Endabashi village in Mbulu district, he made a crucial declaration:
it was now an order for everyone to live in villages, and all had to
move by the end of 1976.[47] In the 1972 NEC meeting and in the
1973 biennial conference, the President made it clear that there was
no change in his view that force should not be used to create ujamaa
villages.[48] What he did was to remove the "living together" aspect
from the ujamaa village policy. Such hair-splitting, however, in an
attempt to show consistency in the mode of gaining compliance was
not widely understood. Considerable confusion followed.

Although the English-language government newspaper, the *Daily
News*, initially reported that the President had called for all rural inhabitants to move into *villages*, the Swahili-language party newspaper,
Uhuru, reported that he had called for them to move into *ujamaa
villages*. Two days after the announcement, *Uhuru* published an editorial which further confused the distinction the President was making:

Six years have now passed since the party officially announced
the policy of living together in Ujamaa villages. . . . In all this time,
the party has used the method of persuasion to get the people to
move into Ujamaa villages so as to hasten development. Yet very
many people still prefer the traditional way of life in which they
live individually. . . . Mwalimu Nyerere at Mbulu recently . . .
declared . . . that in three years time every rural citizen should be
living in an Ujamaa village. . . . Those who were reluctant to join
Ujamaa villages have been given enough time and their fear can no
longer be tolerated. . . . The issue of living in Ujamaa villages is
now an ORDER of the party.[49]

The same day, the *Daily News* in an editorial did likewise. It declared:

Those who have been told about the policy but have not understood it, those who have been educated about it but are still reluctant and those who have heard about it but are still consciously or unconsciously opposed to it must be made to live with their fellow peasants in communal villages where they will have an even better chance of grasping the advantages of socialist living.

It would be an unsocialist and retrogressive gesture if all such elements were to be left behind in backwardness or if they were delayed getting even the most elementary social amenities simply because at present they do not understand what socialism is all about.

Mwalimu's call is to say the least a call to arms.[50]

The internal confusion was paralleled by external puzzlement. When asked in one interview about force in villagization, Nyerere replied: "It's partly compulsory . . . so is vaccination. For 12 years we have been arguing, arguing. Now we have to deal with the problem of inertia (people refusing to move)."[51] In another he stated: "We have not abandoned Ujamaa and we are not forcing Ujamaa. We decided to quicken the programme." But he argued that living in villages "has nothing to do with Ujamaa."[52] He denied that force was used in creating ujamaa villages: "How can you compel people to go into Ujamaa, to share their labour and so on? We think it's a jolly good thing . . . but socialism is a matter of conviction. And you can't convince by law."[53] Nyerere's explanation about the shift in tactics is obviously an important development in the policy. It suggests that other segments of the policy may, if possible, be split off similarly and treated as susceptible to compulsion.

The government report to the seventeenth biennial conference in 1975, however, summarized the situation and reaffirmed the necessity of using noncompulsory techniques:

The villagisation means that we are already implementing the "living together" aspect of our Ujamaa policy. We have a long way to go before we can claim that the "working together for the good of all" aspects of Ujamaa are also operative. . . . You can compel people to live in villages, but a decision to work in cooperation with others must be made entirely voluntarily. The way forward to Ujamaa living after villagisation requires political education, and economic example.[54]

The third alternative technique between persuasion and compulsion identified in Chapter I was inducement—the offering of incentives. The initial policy opposed incentives. In "Freedom and Development" the President stated that it was "important that the people should not be persuaded to start an Ujamaa village by promises of the things which will be given to them if they do so."[55] In his paper "To Plan Is to Choose," he declared that "it would be absurd and very wrong for TANU or Government officers to persuade people to start or to join an Ujamaa village through promises of outside help."[56] "Help" was nevertheless very appropriate. In the latter paper, where he deplored incentives, he said:

> Ujamaa villages and groups of villages will be given priority in the services of . . . trained people, as well as in the location of new schools, dispensaries, local water supplies, and so on. Groups of people working together in socialist or cooperative units must also get priority in the allocation of regional development funds. In other words, all Government activities in the rural areas will be directed towards helping the sound, economic development of socialist rural production and socialist living.[57]

The "help" was to be given after the decision was made to join or establish an ujamaa village. This was supposed to distinguish it from an incentive, which is a promise of future help. Presidential Circular No. 1 stresses the necessity of help:

> Once a group of people have decided to move their houses and/or to farm together so as to live and work as a community, it is essential that TANU and the officers of Maendeleo should be at hand to ensure that the maximum facilities are made available— for example, the land, water, credit for a communal plough, and so on.[58]

For the "help" not to function as an incentive, however, it would have to be kept a secret from the villagers, and such a situation is unlikely. Consequently, although the policy opposed the use of incentives, it called for their use in another guise.

What is apparent in this discussion of techniques is that the idea of persuasion being the sole technique of getting people to live and work together was modified through two major mechanisms. First, the policy was split into two parts, and force was said to be permissible to get people to live together, because that was not really ujamaa. Second, "help" was given which was actually a substitute for and basically the same thing as incentives. The policy, then, "covered over" the use of force and incentives but did not exclude them.

Some observers have noted that the emphasis on different techniques can be used to divide the implementation process. Thus, the period from 1967 to 1969 was considered the phase of persuasion, from 1969 to 1972 that of inducement, and from 1972 to 1976 that of compulsion.[59] There is some reality to such a division, but it should not obscure the fact that there was continuing ambiguity over what was the most appropriate means for implementation.

STAGES

It was envisaged that the procedures for implementing the policy would be carried out by stages. Different agents proposed different stages in the implementation process, but staged development was an important framework of implementation. The proposals differed according to the major criterion or criteria used to divide the process.

The first model was proposed by the President in "Socialism and Rural Development." He used the extent of communal farming as his primary criterion and proposed three stages: first, moving together; second, starting a communal plot; and, third, relying wholly on the communal plot for livelihood.[60]

An expert in the rural development division noted stages based on economic-viability criteria. He identified the first stage as "a formative one, when the village . . . has not yet attained social and economic viability"; the second stage "is reached when the community has gained experience of living and working as a unit, has a workable constitution and has become economically viable"; and the third stage is the one in which "the village becomes a full-fledged multi-purpose cooperative society and has adequate security to attract commercial credit from any source. . . ."[61]

Another suggestion, made by a Dodoma regional commissioner, was that stages be based not on the extent of communal farming activities alone but on the basis of all communal activities. Thus, like Nyerere, he identified stage one as occurring when people agreed to live together in an ujamaa village; stage two occurred when a producers' cooperative society was formed; and stage three was reached when those engaged in the communal farm and the producers' cooperative began to engage in other joint activities such as a shop, a flour mill, and so on.[62]

In a paper circulated in Kondoa the criterion used was primarily political consciousness: the formation stage was that in which farmers decided to cooperate; stage two was attained when the members "understood well the meaning of living and working together for the benefit of all, they have a village constitution known to all and engage in some village economic activity"; and the last stage was reached when the villagers "show symptoms of economic success and have matured politically" and all activities are done on a cooperative basis.[63]

Iringa Region established a four-stage plan for implementation that seemed primarily based on organizational criteria. At stage one, people decide to join together in some productive activity and prepare a list of their names; at stage two, communal and self-help activities have started, building of houses in one place has begun, and the village has a constitution and a committee; at stage three, the constitution and development plans are implemented further; and at stage four, all is run well and application is made to become a registered producer cooperative.[64]

In an editorial in the government newspaper the stages of implementation were identified with the two major aspects of the policy: stage one meant coming together and stage two meant working together.[65] The 1975 Villages and Ujamaa Villages Act identifies only two stages, which, like Nyerere's initial idea, were distinguished according to the degree of communal activity undertaken.

The attempts to identify stages in the implementation process are almost endless. The criteria of division appear to be determined by the particular concern of the observer—e.g., those concerned with finance use the principle of economic viability whereas those concerned with political education use that of political consciousness. Stages indicate the direction of progress sought. Clearly, there were many different views about the direction the ujamaa village policy should take.

AGENTS

Tanzania has envisaged the use of a great variety of agents in the implementation of the policy. In "Socialism and Rural Development," Nyerere foresaw villages started by a TANU cell leader, an agricultural officer, the community development officer, a primary school teacher, a sheikh or padre, or any Tanzanian who understands the objectives.[66] He has often maintained, however, that TANU bore the main responsibility for mobilizing people. In Presidential

Circular No. 1 he said: "TANU has a prime—not exclusive—responsibility. Theirs is the job of mobilising the people, arousing their enthusiasm, helping them to discuss the ideas, and then, with Maendeleo, helping them to move from talk to action."[67] In his speech to the sixteenth biennial conference of TANU he reiterated the party's primary responsibility in the implementation of such policies.[68] In fact, the President appears to have had in mind a kind of division of labor among agents. Although anyone might be instrumental in initiation, TANU was to take the lead in persuading people to join ujamaa villages. Once this was accomplished, other government agencies were to step in and provide all possible "help" toward assuring the success of the committed. As will be seen, with the shift to compulsory villagization, government officials assumed a more central role than that the President appeared to have intended.

DIVERSITY OF ENDS AND MEANS

The policy specification of both ends and means contained immense diversity, part of which was deliberate. The President recognized the existence of diverse conditions and the need for the development of independent decision-making by the rural inhabitants. In "Socialism and Rural Development," he stated: "It is obvious . . . that with the variations in potential in soils and in social customs, it would be absurd to set down one pattern of progress or one plan which must be followed by everyone."[69] He made a similar point in Presidential Circular No. 1:

Whether the first step taken is that of living together or working together, of collective ownership or mutual help, or any one of a hundred other alternatives, is irrelevant. It will not only differ between regions and districts, but perhaps also even between villages within one subdistrict, for it will depend upon the local people's wishes.[70]

And in his "Ten Years After Independence" address he said:

We have no blueprint which tells us all the answers to questions about how such villages should be run and should operate. Indeed, different types of land, different climates, different peoples and different crops mean that there should not be a single model; for an Ujamaa village will only succeed when it takes all these things into account in its organization and practice.[71]

In addition to the many different conditions with which the policy had to deal, diversity was caused by the President's habit of posing questions without providing answers. This is perhaps one reason he is known as Mwalimu (teacher). His objective, however, has often been to break the villagers' dependence on leaders for advice. An interesting case in point was his discussion in January 1968 of how communal work should be remunerated:

> Is it enough . . . to rely upon every member understanding the benefit to himself of everyone putting forward his maximum effort? Is it enough to rely upon social sanctions as a discipline against those who slack, with expulsion as the only final weapon against them? Or would such groups be advised to work out some system of division according to the amount of work done, or the number of hours spent on the communal projects? If you do this, are you breaking the socialist principle of equality—for it will lead to some differences in income between the members? And if you do not do it, are you allowing the poor workers, or the lazy ones, to exploit the others? But again, if you do advocate payment by work done, what about those people who work to the best of their ability, but who are sick, or weak, or just not very capable?[72]

When decisions were left to villagers to make, it was evident that uniformity could not and should not be expected, but the resulting diversity also posed problems. The purpose of the policy—and its essential nature—was to map out goals and the processes for achieving them. Obviously some diversity is acceptable, but if it becomes too great, the whole *raison d'etre* of policy is subverted.

Two major efforts have been made to reduce the diversity, one by the party and one by the government. In 1969, the Central Committee of TANU declared the Ruvuma Development Association a prohibited organization and "took over" all ujamaa villages. The action was explained in the party newspaper as not "a kind of physical take-over at the expense of the freedom to organise on the part of the residents of these villages," but rather a step prompted by "the danger that if matters continued as they were we would have had a mushrooming of 'ujamaa' villages representing at the most extreme, every shade of the 'idea' of socialism."[73] The controversy that arose over the nature of the real objectives of the Central Committee's action probably will never be resolved. The party's claim, however, that greater uniformity in the implementation of the ujamaa village policy was desired is probably at least a part of the stimulus for its action. Much of the diversity we have observed above was subsequent to 1969, hence the move does not appear to have had much practical effect. The Villages and Ujamaa Villages Act of 1975 provided more uniform guidelines for implementing the ujamaa village policy. Gross variation is being limited. Even that act, however, deals primarily with establishing uniformity only for the policy ends, the form of ujamaa villages, and not for the policy means, the techniques used in their creation and/or evolution. Strong pressures remain in Tanzania for the maintenance of the diversity of means and ends which has characterized the policy's evolution.

CONCLUSIONS

The ujamaa village policy—i.e., the outline of ends and means—paralleled previous policies examined in Chapter II above and took into account the Tanzanian socioeconomic situation and agents of implementation described in Chapter III. It sought the settlement of peasants in villages, a goal of both concentrations and village settlements, and it aimed at general development, also an objective of the latter. Although initially it emphasized the technique of persuasion, the policy evolved to include the other two major methods—inducement and compulsion—described in Chapter I.

The changes in permissible means of implementation suggest that the party and government faced a dilemma similar to that faced by the colonial government when it attempted to implement policies requiring the contribution of labor—i.e., it had to use compulsion or fail to achieve policy objectives. The central organs of the party and government appear to have concluded that, if a choice was necessary, compulsion was the lesser of two evils. The ujamaa village policy, however, implied the delegation of responsibility for deciding the technique to regions, so that differences in population density, ethnic composition, economic conditions, land availability, and so on could be taken into account. Nyerere's formulation of the policy showed sensitivity to popular aspirations, yet the diversity of interpretations did not assure general peasant acceptance of the policy. Chapters V and VI will deal with the process of implementation.

Chapter V

LIVING TOGETHER:
THE MOVEMENT OF PEOPLE INTO VILLAGES

When the ujamaa village policy was initiated in 1967, less than 5 percent of the rural population lived in villages.[1] Of the remaining 95 percent, a few peasants lived in relatively close proximity to each other, but most lived at widely scattered points throughout the countryside. To implement the policy it was possible, without any movement of people, simply to reidentify traditional villages or to draw boundaries around areas of relatively dense population and to call them ujamaa villages. That was not generally the case, however. In most areas, the population was so dispersed or the existing villages were so small that it was necessary to move people.

By the end of 1976, virtually the entire rural population had been moved into villages. The magnitude of the operation is indicated graphically in Figure 1, but success was of course not a foregone conclusion. The question to which this chapter is addressed is: "How were compliance techniques successfully employed to motivate peasants to move into villages?"

Motives for a particular type of behavior are often too varied and complex to be clearly determined. Early in the implementation effort, A.O. Ellman suggested that possible motives for joining villages included "the bait of getting services," "pressure . . . on farmers," and "the belief that cooperative ujamaa organisation offers the farmers the best chance of improving their standard of living."[2] These approximate inducement, compulsion, and persuasion respectively. P. Raikes has distinguished five kinds of villages by the motive for their formation or the method by which they were formed— i.e., those started through self-initiation, "sign-painting," material inducement, coercion, and kulak opportunism.[3] In terms of the three implementation techniques, the first of these motives/methods is most closely related to persuasion, the third to inducement, and the fourth to compulsion. The second motive/method involved no movement, and the fifth appears to have been a reaction to both promised incentives and threatened sanctions. Much more complex than the motives discerned by Ellman and Raikes are those expressed

116

by the peasants. In a survey conducted by the author in four regions, the following reasons were given for joining villages:

"I had no choice but to follow the decision of my husband." [Madege]

"I heard that people who did not move would be moved." [Zashe]

"My children advised me that I should go by telling me that the life would be good." [Kidabaga]

"I wanted to follow the call of the President to live in ujamaa villages." [Heru Juu].

Figure 1

PERCENTAGE OF RURAL POPULATION LIVING IN GOVERNMENT-RECOGNIZED VILLAGES/UJAMAA VILLAGES: 1967-1977

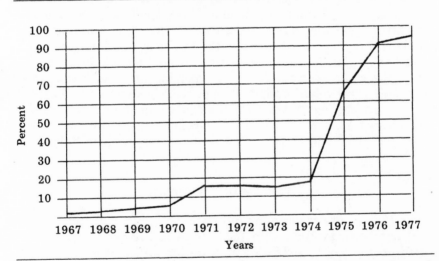

Sources: Rural population figures are based on figures from Tanzania, *Quarterly Statistical Bulletin* 26, 1 (June 1975): table 1. Figures for village populations vary substantially from source to source. For early 1969: A.O. Ellman, "Progress and Prospects in Ujamaa Development in Tanzania" (paper delivered at EAAES conference, Dar es Salaam, 1970), p. 4; for end of 1969: *Nationalist* (Dar es Salaam), 8 May 1971, p. 4; for 1970-74: "Sehemu ya Mipango na Utafiti Kikundi cha Takwimu, Ofisi ya Waziri Mkuu na Makamu wa Pili wa Rais," *Maendeleo ya Vijiji vya Ujamaa* (Dar es Salaam: NPC, June 1974), table 2.1; for 1975: Francis F. Lyimo, "Problems and Prospects of Ujamaa Development in Moshi District" (M.A. dissertation, University of Dar es Salaam, 1975), p. 11; for 1976: *Daily News* (Dar es Salaam), 8 September 1976; for 1977: *ibid.*, 28 December 1977, p. 1.

"I was just brought, without being told why." [Mpinga]

"I was afraid I would be called an enemy of ujamaa and get into trouble if I didn't move." [Kifura]

"I followed the advice of the elders." [Kitowo]

"I thought I would get a lot of maize." [Wambi]

"I thought that if we lived and worked together we would get a lot of money." [Kitowo]

"The ten-cell leader advised me to join." [Kitowo]

"I saw it was a good thing to live together because the government gives us aid." [Usakami]

Although a mixture of techniques is usually responsible for motivating peasants, the party/government shifted its emphasis from persuasion to inducement to compulsion as implementation progressed. Persuasion was stressed as the key after the publication of "Socialism and Rural Development" in 1967, incentives became important following Presidential Circular No. 1 in 1969, and force became a legitimate means after the President's announcement of a deadline in 1973. The introduction of new techniques in each of these three phases was additive, for when incentives were introduced, persuasion was retained, and when compulsion was introduced, both persuasion and incentives continued to be employed. Nevertheless, the character of each phase was determined chiefly by the nature of the new technique. The most widely employed technique was persuasion.

THE USE OF PERSUASION

The use of persuasion to motivate the rural population certainly did not begin in 1967 with the ujamaa village policy. It had been used extensively by extension staff during the colonial period. Hans Ruthenberg's reference to "persistent persuasion" as the key mechanism in the late 1950s for bringing about agricultural change has already been noted.[4] During the early post-independence period it remained the most important tool at the disposal of party and government officials in rural areas. Persuasion differs from both inducement and compulsion, for it does not involve the introduction of any *certain* reward for compliance or penalty for noncompliance, as noted in Chapter I. Its aim is to change the cost/benefit valuation of those affected without the addition from the outside of something to "sweeten" compliance or "sour" noncompliance.

The technique of persuasion can be divided into four components. First, there are those who persuade (the sources of the persuasive message). Second, there is information which is transmitted (the message conveyed). Third, there are the means by which the message is sent (the medium of communication). Fourth, there are the people who are to be persuaded (the object of persuasion). The source, message, medium, and object serve as useful foci in the examination of the role of persuasion in the implementation of the ujamaa village policy.

SOURCE

The most important source of the message calling for people to move into villages was certainly the President. He persuaded peasants to join the villages and leaders to help implement the policy. His writings were basic. Presidential Circular No. 1 of 1969, which dealt with the implementation of the ujamaa village policy, stated:

> The first necessity is the education and training of TANU and Government leaders in the ideology, purpose, and methods of establishing ujamaa villages. The basic text on which this training will be based is the policy statement *Ujamaa vijijini*, supplemented by the other writings included in *Essays on Socialism* and the introductions of *Freedom and Unity* and *Freedom and Socialism*.[5]

The President was very successful in enlisting a great variety of agents to pass the message to the peasants. The prime minister, the first vice-president, ministers, regional commissioners, area commissioners, the UWT chairman, TANU officials, and many others toured the regions exhorting people to move into ujamaa villages. In fact, there was hardly an organization or group in the country that was not in some way enlisted. These included schools, the cooperative movement, the National Service, the NUTA, the TYL, the National Development Corporation, the Christian Council of Tanzania, the National Muslim Council, the Catholic church, and even the chief justice, magistrates, and Lions Club members. The number of groups actively engaged in persuasion appears to have grown geometrically through the second phase of implementation. In the third phase, however, when compulsion became important, nongovernmental groups seem to have become less active. Apparently, there was uneasiness about associating themselves with the use of force.

The effort of the President to enlist widely varying sources was not without its critics. Henry Mapolu called the use of so many agents "perhaps the weakest link in the ujamaa villages programme," and argued that *close* supervision, organization, and general direction were requisites to success.[6] Mapolu's pessimism about the possibility of constructing ujamaa villages according to Nyerere's initial model has been borne out, but his implicit argument that the more the persuaders, the fewer the persuaded has not been confirmed.

MESSAGE

The messages conveyed two ideas. First, they implied that there was a high probability that benefits would accompany the mere act of living together. Second, they suggested that there was a slight possibility that government assistance would be received or government penalties would be avoided should people move into villages. The external incentives and sanctions involved in persuasion were only a "possibility" as contrasted with their "imminent likelihood" in inducement and compulsion. In reality, the line between the two is indefinite. The complex mixture of internally and externally derived benefits which was supposed to arise from living together is exemplified by the following messages:

A. *Relative improvement due to internally generated benefits derived from the act of living together:*

Prime minister: "Living together is the first step in bringing development and battling the enemies of poverty, ignorance, and disease."[7]

Chairwoman of UWT: "The way to get rid of degradation was to cooperate together in the work of ujamaa villages."[8]

Regional commissioner (Mara): "The only short-cut towards development was through people living together in villages and working hard."[9]

Prime minister: "Living separated from one another was the great enemy of development and the perpetuator of poverty."[10]

Prime minister: "The reason so many had not progressed was because they worked individually and not in ujamaa villages."[11]

Regional chairman of TANU (Mbeya): "Those who oppose ujamaa will regret it when they see those who accepted gaining a high standard of living."[12]

President: "People who refused to join ujamaa villages were retarding their own progress together with that of the country as a whole."[13]

Prime minister: "The people of Kilimanjaro should not fear their farms being put together for that was not the only form of ujamaa."[14]

B. *Relative improvement due to externally attached incentives or sanctions to the act of living together:*

Area commissioner (Mpanda): "TANU and the government had decided the only way to obtain rapid development was to live in ujamaa villages because in that way different necessities, such as water, schools, dispensaries, could be provided."[15]

Minister for health: "If people lived together, it would be easy for the government to provide the necessities of health and education."[16]

C. *Combination of A and B:*

First vice-president: "Living together makes possible rapid development and the provision of necessary services."[17]

District chairman of TANU (Iringa rural): "To live in ujamaa villages would not bring poverty but equality, quick development, and assistance."[18]

Similar messages were repeated innumerable times in many different forums from one end of the country to the other.

MEDIUM

Although the spoken word remained the most frequently used medium of persuasion, it was the subject of considerable criticism. It was said to have resulted in "false promises" and "exaggeration." The President, conscious of this problem, warned that all "exaggeration endangers credibility, and habitual exaggeration kills it. TANU and its Government must remain credible—at least to our people."[19] In fact, an editorial in the government newspaper in 1975 went so far as to argue that the spoken word could never serve as the medium for rapid rural transformation:

Correct ideas come from social practice. . . . It follows that there can be no such thing as a revolution by exhortation. There can even be no such thing as a revolution by mere ideas or belief. . . .

Leaders who merely talk, very soon degenerate into liars, misleading the people in every way.[20]

"Social practice" as an alternative medium to the spoken word was increasingly emphasized as words seemed to lose their impact.

Leadership behavior became an important channel for conveying the message that people should live in ujamaa villages. An example is the 1970 elections to the National Assembly, referred to in Chapter III. In late 1969, the party newspaper, under the heading "New Election Qualification," reported that the TANU national executive secretary, Pius Msekwa,

> said that there was an Ujamaa village in every district and since the task of the party is the construction of socialism in the rural areas through Ujamaa villages candidates who will have nothing to do with these villages will not be considered for election.
>
> It is possible for everybody to join an Ujamaa village even for people who are salaried employees and are living in urban centres. . . . All they have to do is to identify themselves with one in the same manner as they are identified with a village from where they come.[21]

Later the same month the Central Committee declared that it would not tolerate any TANU leader who refused to live in an ujamaa village.[22] Although the decision was not enforced, it served as a means of urging compliance. Other cases occurred at district and regional levels. Arguing that it would be difficult to persuade people to live in ujamaa villages unless the leadership lived in them, the executive committee of TANU in Morogoro Region resolved in 1972 "that any TANU cadre who resides within the area of an ujamaa village must agree to be a member of the village."[23] To assure rapid development of ujamaa villages, it was decided at the annual meeting of TANU in Mpanda district that by June 1975 half the workers of every branch of TANU should be living in ujamaa villages.[24] And the regional executive committee of TANU in Kigoma decided to take away the leadership position of anyone who lived in an area where he could join an ujamaa village but who did not join such a village.[25] In these ways "social practice" became a medium for persuading people to join.

OBJECT

The targets of persuasive messages were both those who were

to implement the policy and those who were to move into villages. A great deal of time was spent on the former. At each of the recent biennial conferences of TANU, the President has called upon delegates to implement the ujamaa village policy. At the fifteenth biennial conference delegates were urged to hold seminars "in order to achieve great strides in arousing the people's political consciousness."[26] Such seminars played an important part in persuading TANU, government, and village leaders, but did not affect the scattered peasantry. The following examples are characteristic of seminars held throughout the implementation period:

(1) At a month-long seminar in Manyoni district, the AC called on a group of teachers to assist the implementation of the ujamaa village policy and "plant the seeds of ujamaa in the hearts of their students."[27]

(2) At a seminar in Lindi Region, speakers called on doctors, medical assistants, and nurses to cooperate more in the work of initiating ujamaa villages.[28]

(3) At a meeting in Dar es Salaam, the commissioner of ujamaa villages and cooperative development urged TYL branch leaders to encourage all schools to identify themselves with ujamaa villages so as to prepare the youths for a future life in them.[29]

(4) At a two-day seminar in Bukoba, TANU, government, and religious leaders were "called upon to stamp out enemies of the campaign to move to ujamaa villages." In addition, they were urged "to show an example to the people by being the first to move to the new villages."[30]

Because a mass meeting is much more difficult to hold where people live in scattered homesteads, it follows naturally that leaders on tours of regions would tend to address those already living together. This is precisely what happened. The samples of messages previously cited were delivered to villagers, schoolchildren, or townspeople—none of whom were targets necessary for successful implementation.[31]

Persuasion did have some success. While it was the dominant technique, roughly 5 percent of the rural population moved into ujamaa villages. During the early years of implementation, much of the time devoted to it by officials of TANU and the government was a kind of investment. Other leaders were taught the value of the policy and were prepared to persuade the peasantry, yet even when such leaders visited rural areas to urge compliance, their targets were often those who were already resident in villages. Moreover, some peasants who were reached were skeptical about the messages and saw a discrepancy between the words and the deeds of those urging movement into the villages. J. Rald described the reaction of many peasants in West Lake Region to persuasion:

> Years [of] long experience with colonial officers, missionaries, modern extension workers, and party officials have taught the village community the best way to deal with innovations. That is the "ndiyo bwana" attitude: an attitude of acceptance and understanding even enthusiasm (if the speech is really good)—*and then doing nothing.* If it comes to clash with the innovators the village community can always fall back on an attitude of ignorance and "we did not really understand."[32]

By 1969 many leaders considered that the rate of movement into ujamaa villages was too low. As a result, they turned to the more rational use of inducements as a solution.

THE ADDITION OF INDUCEMENTS

The President's emphasis in "Socialism and Rural Development" on persuasion was a reflection of his aversion to both compulsion and inducement, his attitude toward the latter being based not only on moral but also on practical grounds. Despite the government's growing control of the economy, the resources that it could use as incentives were limited. Furthermore, experience with the village settlement scheme had indicated that incentives could undermine the morale of villagers. These considerations did not bar a more rational use of aid that was being provided to rural areas at the time. It was realized, too, that individual material incentives were only one form of incentive that might be applied.

Incentives can be categorized according to various criteria, including the source (governmental or nongovernmental), the degree of success (effective or ineffective), the time frame within which benefits or disabilities would be experienced (rapidly or slowly), the substantive character (material or moral), or the recipient (collective or selective). The last two criteria are probably the most widely used in the literature.[33] The material vs. moral categories are sometimes referred to as the material vs. nonmaterial dichotomy. The distinction is basically between objects that can be seen directly and those that must be detected indirectly. A collective incentive has been defined as "any good such that, if any person Xi in a group X1, . . . ,

Xi, . . . , Xn consumes it, it cannot feasibly be withheld from the others in that group."[34] A selective or private incentive can be defined as one that can be withheld from other members of the group.

Some writers suggest that there is similarity between the moral and the collective categories and between the material and the selective categories.[35] Their argument is that in a socialist country, collective or moral incentives, or both, are appropriate whereas selective or material incentives, or both, are inappropriate. In fact, there has been virtually no criticism in Tanzania of collective-moral incentives. Most complaints against the use of incentives are against the use of selective-material ones.

Inasmuch as the government had been providing aid to rural areas prior to 1969, the apparent changes that year were really just a rationalization of ongoing assistance. Such aid was simply linked more closely with ujamaa villages and a higher proportion of it was provided in the form of collective goods. The character of such inducement becomes apparent when the four categories of incentives derived from the collective/selective and moral/material dichotomies are examined.

COLLECTIVE, NONMATERIAL INCENTIVES

Most collective, nonmaterial incentives involve the association of the status of a person, position, or institution with an ujamaa village. As a consequence, peasants may be drawn to the village. Four sources of transferred status were foreign leaders, national leaders, local persons of importance, and major institutions.

1. *Foreign Leader Association.* Almost every foreign leader who visits Tanzania is shown an ujamaa village. Status is transferred by their presence and by their encouragement and praise of the villagers. For example, when President Tolbert of Liberia visited Tanzania in 1973 for the Saba Saba celebrations, he was shown some ujamaa villages. He praised the villagers and urged that they continue to work hard to further the policy of ujamaa.[36] Status was thus transferred, and villagers were encouraged. This was typical of the numerous foreign visits to ujamaa villages mentioned in Chapter I, which accorded status and importance to life in those villages.

2. *National Leader Association.* Another means of transferring status to ujamaa villages has been the association of national leaders

with them. Contact was made through (1) visits to villages, (2) work in them, and (3) residence in them. The association of those leaders with villages has differed in the duration of contact and the consequent impact of the status transfer. The many regional tours of the President, the prime minister, ministers, commissioners, TANU chairmen, and others to encourage people to join villages have already been mentioned. Such tours involve not only persuasion, but also the incentive of attaching importance to ujamaa village life. Often, on their tours, leaders join in the work of the villages, thereby conferring additional status. One exuberant writer described in the following way the President's influence during the initiation of the government effort to establish ujamaa villages in Dodoma:

> Starting from dawn, the President worked tirelessly hand in hand for several weeks with peasants. . . . Most of the peasants I have met, a year later now, testify that Mwalimu's energetic participation in Operation Dodoma greatly inspired them and following his example they were all-out to create their own promised land.[37]

The forms of other leaders' participation are almost limitless, and include help in harvesting crops, building houses, digging trenches for water supplies, and many other tasks.[38]

We have already noted the attempts to induce leaders of the party and government to live in ujamaa villages. Their presence is another way in which national leaders associate status with living in villages. Perhaps the President's recurrent visits to Butiama ujamaa village, often to take a break from the work of state, exemplify best the status transferred to villages by national leaders through their residence in them. Butiama assumed the character of a "vacation White House."

3. Local People Association. A number of other groups and individuals have shown their interest in, and given status and importance to, ujamaa villages by visiting and working in them. Sometimes leaders from other parts of the country made informational visits. Ujamaa village leaders from Kondoa district visited Upper Kitete village in Arusha Region for that purpose,[39] and leaders from Mwanza Region went to both Dodoma and Kigoma to examine the successful operations conducted in those regions.[40] Sometimes leaders from other parts of the country have paid working visits, often in connection with seminars being held near ujamaa villages. A group of Mara Region leaders, after a seminar, helped a Musoma district ujamaa village;[41] chairmen of branches of the Afro-Shirazi Youth

League, after a seminar, lived and worked in ujamaa villages in Ruvuma;[42] and primary-school teachers attending a month's seminar on socialism and self-reliance went out and planted corn with ujamaa villagers in Iringa.[43] Full-time students from local schools occasionally participated in the work of ujamaa villages. Pupils from three Tabora schools, for instance, went to nearby ujamaa villages to help harvest tobacco for a day,[44] and the children from Msalato secondary school in Dodoma helped with grape production at various villages in the district.[45] Sumbawanga schoolchildren joined TANU and government leaders in helping to weed a field in an ujamaa village.[46] Examples of such assistance are innumerable. The working visits of these citizens were an expression of solidarity with, and encouragement to, those moving into ujamaa villages.

4. Institutional Association. Several institutions have associated themselves closely with ujamaa villages, the most important of them being the party/government. Although the President has been closely linked with the policy from the start, he has sought to transfer some of that association to the party. "Socialism and Rural Development" thus became a party document, and in his speech to the sixteenth biennial conference in 1973, previously referred to, the President declared that "living together is the party's policy, it is your policy, you have said it yourself."[47] The party/government effort to give status to those building ujamaa villages is exemplified by the selection of the best village from each region each year, as described in Chapter IV. The presentation of awards was made at what formerly was the biggest national celebration, Saba Saba Day. One reporter described the event in these words:

> Among the highlights of the Saba Saba celebrations was the presentation of awards to the best Ujamaa villages. . . . The presentation was made by the President against the background of loud applause and after details of the achievements at production by the villages were read out to the rally. . . . The awards were a recognition by the nation of the increasingly crucial role which Ujamaa villages will play in the transformation of the rural economy.[48]

COLLECTIVE, MATERIAL INCENTIVES

Despite the ideological aversion to material incentives, their variety and cost certainly exceeded those of any other type. Ostensibly, the aid was *not* to lure people into the villages, but to help them succeed in their efforts once they decided to join. Most were collective incentives, such as the provision of water, land, productive equipment, building materials, small industries, price preferences, and such goods as radios. Although no summary records are available to indicate the proportion of the total funds allocated to rural areas that went to ujamaa villages, it is generally recognized that by 1970 it was high. Among the types of aid that functioned as collective, material incentives are the following:

1. Water. The provision of water to ujamaa villages was used as a lure to draw peasants into them. For example, during a visit to Shinyanga the minister for water development and power told the people that his ministry "was in a better position to give them clean water if they lived together in Ujamaa villages."[49] Millions of shillings were spent on bringing water to ujamaa villages in regions such as Dodoma, Tabora, Coast, Morogoro, Masasi, Lindi, and Mbeya.[50] This incentive was especially strong in the vast areas of the countryside where water had been difficult to obtain.

2. Land. In the small areas of Tanzania where shortage of land was a problem, provision of it served as an incentive for ujamaa village settlement. For example, in 1973 the regional commissioner of Lindi ordered the acquisition of 66,000 acres of sisal and rice farmland that had been farmed by an Asian who had left. He turned it over to a group of peasants with the warning "that the farms should be run on Ujamaa principles. He said that only people who would live and work together would be allowed to use the land. There would be no room for those who liked to perpetuate capitalism."[51] The regional commissioner for Arusha once promised peasants that if they would stop working for capitalist farmers, those farms would have to close down, and if they closed down, he would give the peasants the land to start ujamaa villages.[52] Almost all the early villages in Moshi district were formed as a consequence of land being made available to those who would establish ujamaa villages. Image ujamaa village in Iringa and others in other districts were established on farms of expatriate settlers who had left the country.

3. Agricultural/Veterinary Production Supplies and Equipment. Large quantities of goods to facilitate production have been supplied to ujamaa villages, including seeds, fertilizer, insecticides, tractors, storage sheds, milling machines, cattle, bees, chickens, cattle dips, hand tools, guns, trees, fishing equipment, and plows. When villagers in Tanga received a paddy combine harvester, the regional commissioner "reminded them that it was only through the Ujamaa way of life that such facilities could be obtained from the Government."[53] The regional commissioner of Tabora, in urging a group of peasants in Mpanda to move to villages, promised that "the Government was ready to assist them with modern beehives if they joined Ujamaa villages."[54] Instances of such material assistance have been manifold.

4. Small-Scale Industries. The government effort to encourage small-scale industries in ujamaa villages is part of the effort to induce people to live together. Many such industries have been established. For example, inhabitants of an Mpwapwa ujamaa village, with the support of the rural-development division, built a small factory employing carpenters and iron workers, which was opened by the President in March 1972.[55] By mid-1973, ten ujamaa villages in Nzega were reported to have started small-scale industries in masonry, carpentry, and blacksmithing.[56] And in early 1974 it was reported that ujamaa villages in Moshi district had already begun to engage in carpentry, sawmilling, bee and pig keeping, shoemaking, and blacksmithing.[57]

5. Schools. Nearly all ujamaa villages have, or will soon have, schools. Although there have been instances where movement to an ujamaa village involved movement from an area where there was a school to one where there was none, the reverse was usually the case. Most often, then, schools served to lure people to villages. The normal procedure was for the villagers to contribute their labor and for the government, in return, to contribute roofing materials, cement, beams, nails, and other equipment. It would also promise to staff the school.

6. Dispensaries. Much like the lure of a school, that of a dispensary was strong. Usually the government supplied building materials and the villagers labor. Then the government stocked the dispensary and paid the medical assistant who ran it. Considerable sums were spent on construction and supply alone. The ministry of health estimated that in Operation Dodoma it would spend Shs. 3,462,000 on aid for the construction of dispensaries, provision of first-aid kits, and training of village medical helpers in ujamaa villages in one year.[58]

7. *Loans.* The provision of credit to African smallholders dates back to the establishment of the Local Development Loan Fund in 1947. It was transformed into the African Productivity Loan Fund in 1955, the African Credit Agency in 1961, the National Development Credit Agency in 1964, and finally the Tanzania Rural Development Bank (TRDB) in 1971. The evolution of the credit institutions is closely related to changes in the attitude of the government regarding where material incentives should be applied. Until the formation of the National Development Credit Agency in 1964, most loans went to individual farmers. Between 1963 and 1967, however, the proportion of loans going to cooperatives increased from 20 percent to 87 percent.[59] After the formation of the TRDB, loans to individuals constituted only 6.5 percent of the amount loaned in 1971/72 and less than 0.1 percent in 1972/73. At the same time, loans to ujamaa villages increased from 13.7 percent to 19 percent.[60]

Accessibility to loans thus became associated with membership first in a cooperative and then in an ujamaa village. The cooperatives generally passed the loans on to members—in other words, they became individual incentives. The ujamaa villages, on the other hand, used them primarily for village projects, and thus they became collective incentives. Nevertheless, the long-term effect of loans on villages was often harmful. In 1971 the prime minister cautioned ujamaa villages about contracting loans before they had become economically viable. Two years later he complained that "people should not treat Ujamaa villages just as a means of acquiring loans. Some people grouped themselves for the sake of getting loans using 'ujamaa' as a pretext."[61] This was partly a response to the mass registration of ujamaa villages in Iringa district as cooperative societies solely to become eligible for loans without regard to their actual internal development. Notwithstanding the long-term problems caused by loans to ujamaa villages, their short-term function was to encourage membership.

8. *Economic Preferences.* Economic preferences were another lure to draw the peasants into ujamaa villages. These took the form of cheaper licenses to grow specialized crops, free seedlings to start orchards, or reduced marketing fees. In Mbeya Region, for example, the Tanganyika Pyrethrum Board resolved to give licenses without charge to pyrethrum-growing ujamaa villages, whereas individuals would continue to pay Shs. 50 ($7).[62] In Mtwara Region 40,000 coconut seedlings and 17,760 orange, lemon, and tangerine seedlings

were distributed to ujamaa villages free, but individuals had to pay Shs. -/50 ($0.07) for each.[63] And the Iringa Farmers Cooperative Union resolved to charge a produce cess of one cent for every kilogram of maize bought from the ujamaa villages and two cents per kilogram for maize bought from individual farmers. It was stated at the time that "this step is aimed at discouraging those who still engage in individual farming. It will also enable the Union to give more assistance to Ujamaa villages and provide them with services such as fertilizers, seed and transport."[64]

9. *Other Benefits.* The accessibility of ujamaa villages to party and government officials led to various other benefits which brought more people into them. For example, radios were provided to ujamaa villages to facilitate adult-education classes,[65] electric generators were distributed to some ujamaa villages as a prelude to electrification,[66] and famine relief was channelled through ujamaa villages.[67]

The warnings against the use of material incentives stressed their expense to both the government and eventually the peasants, the detrimental effect they might have on self-reliance, and their interference with the task of politicization. A correspondent noted in the party newspaper that previous rural-development efforts failed because they were "too expensive and the initiative came from above and thus the peasants expected too much from the government."[68] Ellman, who was involved with the government in the ujamaa villages effort, has noted that too much material aid may prevent villagers from standing on their own two feet, may hinder attempts to socialize people to accept collective values, may delay the initiation of ujamaa villages elsewhere until similar incentives are given, and may place heavy economic burdens on members for repair and upkeep of machinery.[69] President Nyerere warned TANU district chairmen and secretaries at a seminar that "You don't impress a suffering people by telling them to sit idle waiting for bulldozers, tractors, water and other things from the Government."[70] Despite these cautions, material incentives continued to be used extensively.

INDIVIDUAL, NONMATERIAL INCENTIVES

Just as collective, nonmaterial incentives involve the transfer of status as an inducement to live and work in ujamaa villages, so do individual, nonmaterial incentives. The difference is that in the former case everyone in the village shares the transferred status, but in the latter case only select individuals do so. The incentives include the status given to those who hold government or party positions, who lead the village, who go to seminars, or who are recognized as exemplary converts. The fact that both the party and the President linked the maintenance of party position to moving into ujamaa villages has already been noted. In this way, an incentive to join villages was created.

Leaders within the ujamaa villages were also given status for their work over and above that given to other members. Frances R. Hill noted, for instance, in her study of Dodoma, that "Ujamaa offered different incentives to local leaders and ordinary members of Ujamaa villages. Leaders joined or even promoted Ujamaa villages to maintain their position as communal cadres, to maintain their contact with government on which part of their prestige and influence depended. . . . Their followers had no hopes for prestige."[71]

Status was always transferred by visits of national and foreign leaders more to village leaders than to village members, and village leaders benefited disproportionately from village success. For example, leaders of the best villages were brought to the Saba Saba celebrations to receive the praise of the government and the people for the efforts of the village. Moreover, in 1974, they were treated to a trip to China. Participation as a leader in the village therefore permitted one to receive disproportionate benefits, among which status was important.

Status was also accorded selectively to those individuals from ujamaa villages who were chosen for seminars. Seminars were held both to teach skills such as bookkeeping, health care, carpentry, and masonry, as well as more effective techniques for farming, fishing, etc., and to instill ideological awareness. One observer points out that the two were interrelated, for "without political education the whole training would be inadequate."[72] The incentive function of the seminars, though, was the status they conferred on those who attended them.

A final form of individual, nonmaterial incentives is the publicity and status accorded those who gave up their former ways as capitalists and became good socialists in ujamaa villages. For example, publicity was given to a man named Tumaini, who, before he reformed, had many investments in Lindi district, including boats, big cashew farms, and herds of cattle. It was reported that "realizing the benefits of Ujamaa life, he voluntarily abandoned capitalism to turn to Ujamaa life."[73] Consequently, he acquired status and became symbolic of a good Tanzanian.

INDIVIDUAL, MATERIAL INCENTIVES

Individual, material incentives were of limited significance because they would hinder the attainment of a major objective of the ujamaa village policy, which was to substitute communal property and work for individual property and work. Yet few collective goods are shared equally, even though no one can be denied a portion. To the extent that such goods are unequally shared, a form of individual material incentives exists. Furthermore, leaders of some villages did receive allowances and other material rewards that were not provided to everyone who joined.

All four types of incentives appear to have had an impact. There was an initial rise in village membership of about 10 percent between 1970 and 1971. The increase leveled off, however, and an actual decline in the proportion of the rural population in ujamaa villages occurred between 1972 and 1973. This came despite the initiation of a few operations in Dodoma and elsewhere that involved the use of force. By 1973, only 15 percent of the rural population had responded positively. It was this situation that led the President to urge the separation of villagization from the ujamaa village policy and the general application of force where necessary.

THE ADDITION OF FORCE

The most notable success in the movement of people into villages took place in what were called "operations." Operations involved the planned application of persuasion and inducement, to which was added compulsion. Compulsion was defined above as the imminent likelihood of the introduction of a sanction—in other words, something bringing pain or loss. The pain or loss varied over a wide range of intensities, but never reached levels reported in Soviet collectivization of the late 1920s and early 1930s or in the recent Kampuchean rural transformation.

The party and government justified all the early operations in terms of the urgent need to alleviate some extraordinary problem that was affecting the people concerned. (This was much the same justification for the use of force as was invoked by the colonial government in Circular No. 40 of 1934, discussed in Chapter II.) The first operation took place in the Rufiji valley following disastrous floods in 1968, with the objective of moving people to ujamaa villages on higher ground. Operation Dodoma, which followed in 1971, aimed at moving people into villages so that famine relief could more easily be supplied. Operation Kigoma, initiated in 1972, sought to overcome the particularly serious problem of underdevelopment that afflicted that region. Operation Chunya, which began the same year, was to overcome the "tumor of famine."[74] Such justification was not used when the operations became "national" following the President's declaration at the end of 1973 of the deadline for everyone to move into villages.

The early operations usually resulted from suggestions by the President or the prime minister while they toured the affected areas. Apparently, local officials wanted the approval of the party/government leaders before they undertook a task that might involve the use of force. Operation Kigoma took place after a presidential visit in March 1971 during which Nyerere ordered arrangements to be made for resettlement.[75] The operation in Mwanza began after the President's call in 1973 to transform primary cooperative societies into ujamaa villages.[76] The Ruvuma operation likewise was said to have followed a call by the President when he toured the region in June 1973.[77] After the prime minister called for the people of Tabora to move into villages early in 1974, the operation ensued.[78] Much greater local initiative was evident subsequent to the President's order that movement be completed by the end of 1976.

Finally, the operations have tended to follow a chronology linked to a number of factors. It has been pointed out, somewhat facetiously, that the higher the proportion of government officials from an area, the later the area underwent an operation. For example, Kilimanjaro Region supplied a high proportion of civil servants and it was one of the last to be affected, whereas Kigoma Region supplied relatively few civil servants and was one of the first affected. Although the relationship exists, the suggestion that it is a causal one is probably spurious. More reasonable are explanations related to the wealth of the affected areas. The poorest regions, such as Dodoma and Kigoma, were among the first affected, and the wealthiest, such as West Lake and Kilimanjaro, were among the last. Even within regions and districts the same trend was apparent. Hill suggests that this was because of a deliberate policy of risking as little production loss as possible.[79] Many officials feared that the disruption caused by villagization would bring at least a temporary decline in production. The relationship may also be associated with the greater readiness of peasants from poorer areas to move their residences, as shown in Chapter III. The less the resistance expected, the less the hesitancy to undertake an operation.

THE OPERATIONS

Planning for the operations was primarily a regional concern. According to the district development director (DDD) in Shinyanga, "neither TANU nor Government at the national level gave any Guidelines for the implementation of the Operation villages programme. The implementation strategy was virtually left to each Region and likewise, to each District to formulate."[80] That does not mean that there was no coordination. In fact, each area sought to make use of the experiences of other areas in its planning. Thus, before Kigoma started, regional officials sent a team to Dodoma to study the operation there.[81] For the same reason, Kilimanjaro sent a team to Mwanza.[82] Not all areas exchanged teams, however. In neither Bariadi nor Shinyanga did this occur, because the regional development director (RDD) of Shinyanga Region "was of the firm view that each district possessed its peculiar socio-cultural and ecological characteristics which necessitated special methods and strategy for resettlement."[83] Nevertheless, general similarities in the plans are obvious. Most divided the operation into a set of stages, and most established a timetable for the completion of each stage. They also designated specific tasks to individual officers or groups of officers.

In general, planning was initiated at the regional level and decentralized to the district and then to the divisional or ward level. Von Freyhold has suggested that in the major operations the ward level was the key.[84] For planning, however, the divisional level was often used. In Dodoma Region, phase one was directed by a presidential team with ten regional leaders led by the TANU regional chairman.[85] In Kigoma Region there was likewise a presidential team, under which were teams in each of the three districts led by the district TANU chairman and comprising other important officials and individuals.[86] Elsewhere, such as in Mwanza, planning took place chiefly at the district level. The most usual form involved the establishment at that level of two committees, one political and the other economic. This was the case in both Mwanza and Pare districts; in Iringa Region, social committees were established as well. The political or political education committee was composed of TANU and cooperative leaders, police, and judiciary members. Its function—to present to the peasants the reasons for the operations—was essentially reflected in its title. The economic committee comprised the planning officer and agricultural, veterinary, and other functional officers. Its purpose was to plan layout of the village and the infrastructure that would have to be built.[87] As members of these district committees pursued their work, ward, division, and ten-cell leaders were co-opted. Decentralization of responsibility for planning was common. For example, in the Coast Region the divisional secretaries were asked to decide how to implement the movement order and to report back to the district level.[88] In Mwanza Region the ward development committees, with the help of "expert advice," were given the task of choosing village sites; planning of the movement was entrusted to the divisional secretaries;[89] in Dodoma Region the divisional level was assigned the task of preparing lists of those who were to be moved where and when;[90] in Pare district the ward development committees were asked to pick the area for settlement;[91] and in Iringa Region the ward secretaries were specifically told the dates by which they had to finish measuring plots, building houses, and moving.[92] The complexity and lack of uniformity across the country are striking.

The timetables set in the planning phase are fair guides to the way in which implementation proceeded. During the rainy season, data were compiled about where people were living, politicization was initiated, and the location of the new villages was determined. During the dry season, plots were measured, temporary houses were put up, and the movement of people was planned. Shortly before the rainy season was to start, the people were moved. In several cases, the schedule was not maintained, with the result that planting was late and harvests the following year were small. The first phase of the operation in the Coast Region involved three steps:

(1) October-December 1972: Census and collection of statistics
(2) January-June 1973: Planning and surveying
(3) July-August: Moving[93]

The plan for Shinyanga district called for:

(1) February-April 1974: Politicization and WDC selection of sites
(2) April: Approval of site locations
(3) May-July: Plots assigned to individuals and building started
(4) August: Seminar for leaders on mechanics of movement
(5) 17 August-22 September: Movement of the people[94]

In Iringa Region the schedule was:

(1) Prior to 15 June 1974: Measurement of plots
(2) Prior to September: Building of houses on plots
(3) October to November: Moving[95]

And in Pare district the plan called for:

(1) January-February 1975: Collection of statistics on people and livestock
(2) March-April: Politicization
(3) May-June: Choice of village location and house plots
(4) July-August: Preparation of temporary houses
(5) October-December: Moving[96]

The timetables show what were thought to be the major tasks and the length of time each was expected to take, and were the core of the plans. As such, they were mainly responsible for a major criticism of implementation, in that they exemplified the mechanical approach adopted by the bureaucracy to the task of gaining peasant compliance.

In some areas the actual movement was carefully organized. For example, in Shinyanga district each division was assigned a team (this meant seven teams) to oversee the process. Each was led by a senior officer and included the divisional and ward secretaries concerned.[97] A similar form of organization was used in Maswa district, where each of the four divisions was assigned a team. The senior officials who headed them were the district TANU chairman, secretary, and executive secretary and the district development director. They worked closely with the divisional and ward secretaries and ten-cell leaders.[98] In fact, movement appears generally to have been supervised at the divisional level by an individual or a team of officials from the district level. The procedures for the actual movement differed from area to area. Most commonly, the operation involved a large number of trucks which picked up people and goods and took them to the new villages. It was estimated that in the first phase of Operation Dodoma, more than 300 were used,[99] and for several years afterwards there was a graveyard of trucks (many from China) near the railway station in Dodoma town. A frequent complaint of those managing the operations was the lack of available transport. In the early operations, it was often borrowed from neighboring regions, but this was impossible in the 1974/75 exercises. Trucks were also rented from private individuals and borrowed from marketing boards and cooperative societies. The general procedure may be illustrated by what took place in Kahama. According to an observer: "The usual practice was to take a few militia or policemen, junior officials in a lorry which went around the town and anyone without any particular activity was taken."[100] With this manpower they then went to the assigned area and began the task of moving people and their belongings. There was usually a hurry, and according to available reports, the property was often mishandled. In other areas, where transport by truck was not available, people used bicycles, ox and donkey carts, tractors, and their own backs and heads. The procedure, it is clear, was not altogether different from the movement into concentrations described in Chapter II.

FORCE IN THE OPERATIONS

Although the operations differed from previous efforts because they involved the use of force, neither persuasion nor inducement was abandoned. The role of both of the latter, however, changed to become merely a support for the former. The function of persuasion can be illustrated by several cases. At the start of the operations in Iringa, meetings were held with peasants from the areas to be affected in order to explain the program; in Tabora, during 1973 and the first quarter of 1974, there was a TANU and government campaign to educate people on the advantages of living together; in Mbeya district, leaders went to all wards to tell people of the importance of moving into villages; in Kilimanjaro, leadership seminars were followed by "open rallies . . . especially for the purpose of educating the masses on the advantages of living together";[101] in Kondoa, ward and cell leaders were instructed to tell the peasants about the operations "because we want the aim to be known to everyone so that people may show a need to move";[102] in Maswa, they sought "to educate people" about the move;[103] and similar approaches preceded the operations almost everywhere. Nevertheless, the message also indicated a deadline for the move and the imminent likelihood of sanctions should compliance not follow. In fact, the function of this "persuasion" was generally to "soften up" resistance to the move. It did not need to convince, for the fact that people would be moved whether they liked it or not was made quite clear to all.

The function of inducement similarly changed. No longer did the value of an incentive have to overcome the perceived cost of the move. It might reduce the perceived cost, but even if this did not occur, it did not really matter. For example, in Kilimanjaro the same message as in previous years was conveyed: leaders reportedly "outlined the advantages of living together and the problems faced by people living individually, especially in regard to social services, such as the possibility of getting fresh drinking water, hospital, school, etc."[104] To disentangle the three techniques employed in the operation is not easy. It is probable that persuasion and inducement affected more people during the operations than previously had been the case, principally because more were contacted. Nevertheless, the massive influx into villages was unmistakably due to the addition of force.

The form and extent of compulsion used to move people into villages has been the subject of greater controversy both within and outside the country than any other aspect of the ujamaa village policy. As was pointed out in Chapter IV, in order to avoid a conflict with early strictures against the use of force, the operations were considered a part of villagization, something that was said to stem not from the ujamaa village policy but from the President's 1962 inaugural address. That claim served to blur the reality. All of the early operations in Rufiji, Dodoma, and Kigoma were accepted as part of the ujamaa village policy, and movement into villages was the first or second stage in the President's own outline of the policy. To assert that force did not figure in the ujamaa village policy may provide some intellectual continuity, but it is not consistent with reality. The Western press picked up stories of the operations and equated them with horrors they associated with collectivization in the Soviet Union. The local press virtually ignored the use of force; administrators did not talk about it; word of it was passed from one individual to another. Gradually, however, evidence of its intensive use in some areas is being built up, partly by Tanzanian critics of the behavior of the bureaucracy.

Anyone who traveled widely in the countryside in the mid-1970s could see remains of homes that were abandoned and made unusable in the operations, and even some towns that were similarly affected. For example, the operation in Kondoa district in late 1974 and early 1975 left the town of Mondo a series of houses and shops without roofs, windows, doors, or their fittings, so that it resembled a ghost town in the Wild West. Even the MP's house on the outskirts was destroyed while he was away. The aim was to get people to move farther down into the valley. Two- or three-storey buildings south of Kondoa on the Great North Road were also destroyed and appear much like some of the ruins of Kilwa or Gedi. In the ten other districts in which the author worked in 1975 and in many other areas through which he passed, there were no cases as obvious as those in Kondoa, but reports indicate that that area's experience was not unique.

Early in 1975 an article appeared in the TYL magazine, *Maji*

Maji, which strongly criticized those responsible for the Mara operation. The author, R.R. Matengo, observed that

> The officials decided that people should move immediately and
> so the police, TPDF, National Service and Militiamen were mobil-
> ised to move the people. People were ill-treated, harassed, pun-
> ished in the name of TANU; under socialism and those who
> question it were told; "this is Nyerere's order," usually followed
> with a hysteric rebuke "wewe ni mpinzani mkubwa wa TANU na
> Rais" [you are a major hindrance to TANU and the President].
> This is the paradox of democracy; it makes TANU alienated from
> the peasants.[105]

He specifically focused on Ichungu division:

> Many peasants in Ichungu were taken by surprise to see armed
> militiamen, climbing on top of their houses, taking away the
> thatch, in some cases the iron-sheets were torn off, doors and
> windows removed or smashed into pieces, houses pulled down in
> some cases.
> While the operation was going on the leaders failed to even
> control the militiamen, or give them proper guidance. At Pemba
> and Kyoruba Villages some Militiamen looted the property of
> the peasants.[106]

His observations were supported by Kemal Mustafa, who studied
the same region a few months later and who, in addition, stated
that estimates he heard of the number of peasants who died as a
result of the operation ranged from a handful to over 100.[107]
Violence was also reported in Sengerema district by a student
at the University of Dar es Salaam: "In many areas . . . forcing became inevitable. People moved unwillingly. Militiamen, TPDF men
and FFU ordered the people to move. Some houses were put under
fire, and some property destroyed in the fear that people might
return back. Obviously the use of force reflects that people were
reluctant to move."[108]
A similar situation was reported by a student in the Kalinzi
area during Operation Kigoma:

> Force and brutality was used. The police were the ones empow-
> ered together with some government officials. For example at
> Katanazuza in Kalinzi . . . the police had to take charge physical-
> ly. In some areas where peasants refused to pack their belongings
> and board the Operation lorries and trucks, their houses were

destroyed through burning or pulling them down. House destruction was witnessed in Nyange village. It became a routine order of the day. And the peasants had unconditionally to shift. It was a forceful villagization in some villages particularly the heavily populated Kalinzi.[109]

The operation in Maswa also was reported to have involved violence:

According to the people themselves they said force, violence, intimidation and coercion was in full swing to every family which had not yet shifted up to that given time. . . . They said much food and other property was destroyed by fire that was burnt purposely by the officials in the district during the shifting process; this included the burning of their cattle sheds which caused some of their animals to run away to the forests where they were feasted by wild animals.[110]

A student described the application of force during the operation in Biharamulo district in the following words:

All houses were burnt down first in Nyarubungo Division. The Ward Chairman would give an order for the house to be burnt down, then a police constable or a militiaman with a gun would light a match-box and then the owner of the house was told to set fire on his house and this was done on every house in the area! This is what one of the affected told me. . . . The house with a corrugated iron roof and the two main doors were broken down . . . by the police constable or militiaman. This was done to every person who had not wanted to move to the village. . . . It was on 24 May 1975 that the actual burning in Nyarubungo and the nearby areas [took place].[111]

Fire was also used in Kahama district against those who were reluctant to move: "If he/she was . . . obstinate the house was set on fire or it was destroyed. Commonly, it was only the door and windows which were removed. In the new 'village' the family was dumped on their plot and that was that."[112]

The use of force in the Chunya operation was described as follows:

After some time the natives found themselves confronted by lorries and officials from the District. At that time they were compelled to pack their provisions in the lorries before them. Those who proved to be stubborn had their houses knocked down by the lorries, thus they were compelled to pack whether or not they wanted to.[113]

In Kisarawe district, according to Simeon Mesaki, the operation involved force where necessary:

There was no notice whatsoever and people were taken unawares, seeing convoys of lorries, Land Rovers and officials ordering them to demolish their houses before it was done for them. Many refused and it was [because of] their obstinacy that the civil servants did their job. They started with the roofs and then the doors and windows then the whole house was demolished to the amazement and anger of the former dwellers. Some threatened the "invaders" with snakes and witchcraft but to no avail. They were put into lorries to new sites together with their belongings.[114]

The DDD of Shinyanga district observed that the "fire weapon" had to be used in some cases to prevent people from returning to their old homes.[115]

These reports from various parts of the country concerning the use of force are generally provided by those especially concerned with the persons affected. The use of force on stubborn peasants is acknowledged only reluctantly by officials, as in the case of the Shinyanga DDD. The immediate agents of force were said to have included not only civil servants but all the other official agents of compulsion—i.e., the police, TPDF, National Service, and militiamen. The form reported was chiefly one of violence to property. Houses were burned, roofs ripped off, and doors and windows removed, and personal belongings sometimes were damaged when loaded into trucks. Reports of the use of physical force against individuals are few compared with those of physical damage to property.

The effect of force on those not directly involved was considerable. The Central Province PC's argument decades before, noted in Chapter II, that only those punished should be considered forced is inappropriate. Force has been defined above as the imminent likelihood of a sanction, and there is no better way of making the likelihood of a sanction seem imminent than to impose it on some individuals.

Mesaki noted that in Kisarawe district, after some destruction, the people who saw it or heard about it moved quickly. He said, "On seeing that it was not a joke, the majority of the peasants decided to give up passive resistance, and instead began to remove their belongings from the houses and waited for the vehicles to transport them to the approved areas."[116] In fact, he asserts that the leaders deliberately started with the most difficult area in order to set an example for the rest. In Shinyanga it was reported that "news from Geita and Maswa Districts, bordering Shinyanga District reached the District that people's houses were being put on fire indiscriminately, sometimes with food and goods inside them. So the people decided not to wait for Government help lest a similar catastrophe happened to them as well."[117] After the initial violence in Mara, people in other areas reportedly "rushed in panic to build temporary accommodations in unplanned village sites."[118] Thus even a limited use of force "educated" people in widely spread areas so that they understood the imminent likelihood of sanctions should they fail to move.

Resistance to the operations took many forms. It was reported that during the "politicization" drives that preceded movement there was not only the "ndiyo bwana" form of resistance but also active opposition. When one of the touring groups, led by the MP for Kisarawe Bara, M. Zavalla Pazi, reached Msanga in Kisarawe district, he was confronted by a spokesman who declared:

I stand here as a man who does not fear anybody and these are my words. We have built Msanga since time immemorial and are living as socialists. . . . And I tell you this independence we have today was demanded first by my grandfather who died in the hands of the Germans. . . . We got our independence peacefully but now you want to embarrass us by demolishing our houses so that instead we go to the bushes, leaving our prosperity behind. . . . I say I and my brothers of Msanga are not moving . . . and we do not want anything about socialism or living together. . . . Therefore honourable M.P. I say and I am asking you to tell your bosses that Juma Mwenegoha and all my brothers in Msanga do not want socialism neither living together.[119]

Reports of direct confrontation of this sort are not numerous. Usually, peasants tried to hide, flee, use witchcraft, appeal to officials, bribe, or engage in other more indirect forms of resistance. In Kigoma district, for example, it was reported that

some peasants accordingly had to resist against the operation. Nyantole villagers whom the DPO [District Planning Officer] dubbed as very stubborn, sent a village delegation (4 family heads) to Dar es Salaam to appeal at the Prime Minister's office against villagisation. . . . They were frustratingly returned back home, and in the final analysis they had no alternative, they had to shift.[120]

Others avoided compliance by hiding or fleeing: "Other peasants resorted to delaying tactics. During the day they would 'abandon' their houses and go into hiding and at dusk when the evictors had gone, would then return to their 'abandoned' houses. Other peasants fled to neighbouring regions such as Tabora (at Kaliua) and Rukwa (at Mpanda)."[121] Some peasants temporarily complied and then "infiltrated" back to their former villages. Before the operation in Shinyanga district, officials had to contend with what the DDD called "refugees in one country"—that is, large numbers of people who had fled neighboring districts to avoid compliance with the policy directive.[122]

Pressures were put on officials by distraught peasants to resist implementation. In Kigoma district, it was said, some peasants "went to the extent of harassing their TANU village leaders, accusing them of masterminding the operations."[123] Mesaki observed in Kisarawe that a rumor was circulating that "there are councillors and other notable . . . persons in the villages who were bribed by the government so as to organize the operations in the villages."[124] Although the rumor may well have had no foundation in fact, it indicates the bitterness that developed against some local leaders. Active resistance to the movement of people by leaders was uncommon, but several did not participate in the operations. For example, it was reported that in Maswa

> The former member of parliament . . . kept away during the shifting process, he did not cooperate with the District officials in shifting people. . . . When I talked with him I learnt that he did not participate because he feared that he would miss the votes during the next elections [i.e., those of late 1975]; and he also said that because many people were against shifting, he argued that he was a true representative of the people, and because of that, he found it useless to involve himself in the process.[125]

In Shinyanga, the DDD found several leaders, including the MP, who withdrew from the effort because of peasant discontent with the policy.[126]

Among the peasants expected to be in the forefront of resistance were those with the most wealth, the kulaks, but in reality their role in the resistance has been an ambiguous one. What appears to have been the normal trend was for initial kulak resistance to the idea of ujamaa villages to be transformed under pressure into kulak cooperation in efforts to determine the location of the villages and then into kulak support for the movement. This reaction was a rational one, given the alternatives available. For example, von Freyhold observed in the early "unofficial" operations in Tanga Region in the late 1960s that

> Once those who lived by the road realized that they would have to join an ujamaa village if they wanted to live in peace—and that a larger settlement might even be advantageous to those who were running any kind of business—the struggle centered around the question of where the village was to be.[127]

The effect of coercion, in von Freyhold's view, was that it "convinced many of the protokulaks [more wealthy peasants] that it was in their interest to pretend commitment to ujamaa."[128] Raikes, as we have noted, observed that "in recent years there has begun to emerge another mode of 'ujamaa' development as some far-sighted rich farmers have learned that they can turn ujamaa to their own advantage." He continues:

> Groups of wealthy farmers have formed "ujamaa villages" which are closer in nature to joint stock companies, by dint of which they have been able to get hold of land previously used for other people or purposes. This particular mode of development seems to have been mainly characteristic of highland and contiguous lowland areas, but there seem to be related processes at work elsewhere, with Ujamaa acting in these cases mainly as a means to get credit and government grants of machinery.[129]

The generally more prosperous peasants of Rungwe and Kilimanjaro have resisted successfully all attempts at carrying on operations to move people into concentrated villages. In fact, the solution in those areas has been to draw lines around them and call each a village. The kulaks, moreover, are often credited with considerable resistance in the early 1970s in the Ismani division of Iringa district and in the Usangu division of Mbeya district.[130] Some kulaks believed that movement of people was not in their interests and resisted it, but others considered that such movement was in their interests and accepted it.

ASSESSMENT OF THE OPERATIONS

The costs of each of the operations in monetary terms are difficult to assess. Budgets were prepared for many of them, but often excluded a number of the ongoing expenditures of ministries that were diverted to support the movement of peasants. Costs of infrastructure provided in the villages after the move are often mixed with costs of the move itself. Nevertheless, some data that permit rough approximations are available.

1. Dodoma. Hill notes that "official figures indicate that the Government spent Shillings 18 million on the first seven months of Operation Dodoma and allocated Shillings 38.6 million for the second year. Dodoma thus received in nineteen months an amount equivalent to three-fourths of its total five-year allocation under the Second Five-Year Plan."[131] This averages out as Shs. 430 ($61) per family or Shs. 82 ($12) per person for the first phase and Shs. 1,220 ($174) per family or Shs. 232 ($33) per person for the second phase.[132] Subsequent phases presumably amounted to less, but data are lacking. A sectoral breakdown of expenses for phase two of Operation Dodoma indicates that the greatest expenditures were those for agriculture, as shown in Table V.1.

Table V.1

OPERATION DODOMA—SECOND PHASE:
ESTIMATED SECTORAL EXPENDITURES

Sector	Percent
Agriculture	32.9%
Water	23.8
Education	21.1
Housing	12.8
Health	8.4
Community development	1.1

Source: Calculated from data in *Daily News* (Dar es Salaam), 13 June 1977, p. 3.

2. *Kigoma*. One estimate for the cost of the first phase of Operation Kigoma was Shs. 22 million,[133] which means an expenditure of Shs. 2,513 ($359) per family.[134] Other figures for all three phases in Kibondo district indicate an expenditure of Shs. 9,229,604, which works out as Shs. 341 ($49) per family moved.[135] In both the Dodoma and Kigoma operations the main expenditures were those by the ministries for development. Moving costs in Kibondo district for the three years of Operation Kigoma have been estimated at only Shs. 21 ($3) per family; the breakdown is shown in Table V.2. A sectoral breakdown of expenses for the three phases of the Kigoma operation indicates that most funds were allocated to water supplies, as indicated in Table V.3.

3. *Others*. The estimated cost of moving a family in a few other areas is available. In Iringa Region in 1975 the cost was about Shs. 1,437 ($205) per family.[136] In Tabora Region in 1974 it was about Shs. 145 ($21) per family.[137] And in Mpanda district in 1975 the estimated cost was Shs. 275 ($39) per family.[138] In Shinyanga a per-person cost estimate for 1974 was only one shilling ($0.14).[139] At the other extreme was a per-person cost estimate for Manyoni

Table V.2

ESTIMATED MOVING COSTS OF OPERATION KIGOMA
(KIBONDO DISTRICT): 1972/73-1974/75

Item	Cost
Fuel for vehicles	Shs. 275,000 ($39,286)
Maintenance of vehicles	Shs. 170,000 ($24,286)
Salaries for drivers of vehicles	Shs. 107,000 ($15,286)
Allowances for drivers of vehicles	Shs. 15,000 ($2,143)
Hire of vehicles	Shs. 5,000 ($714)
TOTAL	Shs. 572,000 ($81,714)

Source: R.H. Rugemarila, "The Economic Impact of Operation Kigoma" (Department of Rural Development, Mzumbe, Morogoro, 1976; mimeo), pp. 136 and 137.

Table V.3

SECTORAL EXPENDITURES OF OPERATION KIGOMA
(KIBONDO DISTRICT): 1972/73-1974/75

Sector	Percent of Total
Water	31.0 %
Agriculture	16.2
Movement and roads	14.0
Education	11.0
Health	9.6
Tsetse clearing	4.0
Training	3.0
Veterinary	2.1
Land planning	0.5
Beehives and equipment	0.2
Fisheries	0.1
Miscellaneous	9.7

Source: See Table V.2.

district in 1973 of Shs. 219 ($31).[140] The costs in terms of non-monetary expenditures of time and labor were, of course, many times these figures.

The bureaucracy accepted the challenge of implementation via operations given it by the President—in both the earlier and later operations—partly because it had no choice and partly because of the competitive challenge. Mesaki illustrates administrative reaction in his study of the Kisarawe district operation by quoting a letter from the RDD to the DDDs: "I want to emphasize that the act of demolishing and erecting a new place is not an interesting experience, moving involves disruption of life using coercion (nguvu) and physical energy and material."[141] The RDD's discomfort in regard to the operation was further illustrated at the start of the second phase when he said: "I won't allow civil servants to be tied down to the operation for more than three months when projects and especially agriculture and other routine activities are lagging behind."[142] The DDD in Shinyanga contended that the apparent intensity of response of bureaucrats to a project which clearly increased their workload could be ascribed in part to competition. He said:

There was the competitive attitude (particularly of Region to Region) with all its political overtones. Here was a moment for self-aggrandisement by proving ability to mobilise a rural population wholesale. Reports were being received from Mara Region that they were about to complete their Operation when we had not started at all. Top Party officials were heralding and positively reinforcing the achievements of resettlement in Geita District. Who would, in such circumstances, have wished to lag behind? Political leaders, therefore, called for quick measures being taken to complete the resettlement exercise in a short time.[143]

There was thus a dual aspect to the operations so far as the civil servants involved were concerned. Rapid success would mean commendation and, perhaps, promotion, but it would also require turning attention from other important tasks to which they were assigned and for which they had responsibility.

The reaction of the peasantry is not easy to assess. The most apparent trend is that people appear to be considerably more happy with living in the new villages than they were with moving into them. This is not true in all cases, of course, nor is it necessarily going to continue. It may well be a consequence of the immediate relief felt when peasants found that many of the bad things they had heard about ujamaa villages before they moved were not experienced. Various problems, however, prevented the positive peasant reaction from being universal.

The perspective of an individual affects his assessment of a problem. One that would seem major to a bureaucrat could be minor to a peasant, and vice versa. Then, too, something that is a problem in one region may not be in another. In Mwanza Region there were shortages of survey personnel; some leaders feared loss of position if they encouraged the move; there was poor siting of villages, which made them subject to floods, and insufficient land, especially around the houses; and too many families were placed in some villages.[144] In Rukwa Region there were transport problems and difficulties caused by rumors that cattle would be nationalized.[145] In Tabora Region, opponents apparently burned the houses of cell leaders; there were problems of what to do with the large cattle population, and water supply difficulties arose.[146] Lack of water was reported to be one of the most serious problems in Iringa Region.[147] Mbeya district was troubled with the usual shortage of transport, poor siting of villages along roads, thefts and loss of crops in the move, disputes over land rights, and problems in regard to settling cattle herders.[148] In Shinyanga, the authorities had to deal with old people without families and single women living alone, make sure that cultivation was started in the new villages, and remedy the inadequacy of water supplies. Moreover, there was a breakdown of the ten-cell units as a result of the move; villages were situated far from crops already under cultivation; and disputes arose over land rights in the areas of settlement.[149] The Shinyanga DDD also noted that some villages were merely long rows of houses along roads where peasants had been "dumped" during the operations.[150] In Kigoma district, domestic animals died in trucks, pots were broken in transport, food was lost, crops were abandoned, hunger faced many of the settlers, and some people were deposited under trees or along roads where self-sustaining villages were not possible.[151] Reference has already been made to the corruption involved in the siting of villages; villagers also complained that "sometimes people's properties were being taken by . . . the officials."[152] In Kondoa, lack of coordination caused difficulties:

> It sometimes happens that after an area has been surveyed and accepted by experts and a village started, another leader, a councillor, a TANU chairman, agricultural officer, TANU secretary, development officer, ward executive officer or even a cell leader starts another village in an unsurveyed area near the already started village. Sometimes he convinces people to leave the surveyed village and move to this new unsurveyed area. This is a mistake on the side of the leader though the aim may be quite good. This brings misunderstandings among leaders and even among the people themselves.[153]

Some of these mistakes had to be corrected in rectification campaigns in 1975 and 1976.

CONCLUSIONS

Despite these many obstacles, the operations were very successful and accounted for the movement of about 75 percent of the rural population into villages. Ten years after the initiation of the ujamaa village policy, over 90 percent of the peasantry had resettled in villages. What accounts for this success?

Persuasion alone did not lead to the mass influx of people into villages that the party and government desired. As already noted, in the first couple of years only about 5 percent of the population moved into villages. At the end of 1973, Raikes reflected on the use of political education and mobilization and concluded that it

> turned out not to be possible. There were not enough trained political cadres at any level. Nor, since TANU is a mass party, were local political leaders altogether clear about the aims of ujamaa. The majority of potential policy implementers in the rural areas were various government officials, not only in numbers, but in terms of access to funds for policy action . . . and perhaps most importantly, the interpenetration of government and party in Tanzania has had some success in its desired goal of politicizing administrators, but it has also led to the adoption of bureaucratic styles by political leaders.[154]

Raikes therefore concludes that the party was not strong enough to carry out the policy using the technique of persuasion and that the government approach was not attuned to the successful use of this technique. Both conclusions are corroborated by the data presented in Chapter III. The peasantry also had grown somewhat skeptical of the persuasion of functional officers because of its inappropriateness in the past. As a result, the message to the rural population may not have been as clear as leaders assumed. Rather than improve the technique and its application, they grew impatient and decided that attention should be devoted to other techniques.

When the message was "sweetened" by incentives, an additional 10 percent of the rural population entered ujamaa villages. It is impossible to ascertain what proportion of the increase was due to inducement and what proportion could be ascribed to improvements in persuasion. By 1972 a plateau had been reached, and persuasion and inducement no longer were drawing many people into villages. In simple terms, those peasants who felt that the benefits of joining outweighed the costs had joined, whereas those who felt that the costs of joining outweighed the benefits had not done so. The latter constituted the vast majority.

The addition of force changed the balance. It added a cost to noncompliance which peasants, living a relatively marginal existence, could not easily bear. The response was similar to that which occurred during the British efforts to establish concentrations. Most peasants complied. Although the use of force in the operations appears to have been the key to altering peasant cost/benefit assessments of moving, it was accompanied by renewed efforts to persuade and to demonstrate the benefits of incentives. For various reasons, the party and government leaders were able to carry out the operations without significant opposition: the policy had potential benefits which many peasants perceived; the kulaks were weak at the national level, and many concluded that they might actually benefit from the villages; and the cooperative movement, the labor movement, and all other significant organized groups had been incorporated into the party or government. Once the villages were created, however, they had to be made productive socialist communities if the policy were to be fully implemented. As will be shown in Chapter VI, that task has presented a much more formidable challenge than village resettlement.

Chapter VI

WORKING TOGETHER: COLLECTIVE WORK IN THE VILLAGES

Interpretations of the significance of villagization were not uniform. Many observers argued, especially in the early years of implementation, that it was a sufficient condition for the good life. Others contended, especially in later years, that it was only a necessary condition. The trend away from the former and toward the latter interpretation was a result of rapidly growing practical experience with the villages. In 1971 the editor of the party newspaper asserted: "It is quite clear that merely living together in ujamaa villages without the peasants working together . . . is as good as not having moved into the Ujamaa village at all."[1] And in 1975, at the seventeenth biennial conference of TANU, the President emphatically stated that "living in villages is only a beginning. The people in the villages have to work together to get the benefits of living together."[2] What Nyerere was really asking was that "ujamaa" be rejoined to "village" in order to attain the promised good life.

Interpretations of the meaning of working together were likewise not uniform. The President's view of the "ujamaa" aspect of an ujamaa village stressed communal farming. He said that the second stage of development toward an ujamaa village was reached when "a group of people start a small communal plot . . . on which they work co-operatively, sharing the proceeds at harvest time according to the work they each have done." He defined the third stage as being reached when villagers devoted virtually all their effort to the communal farm.[3] Nyerere's vision of "ujamaa" was not identical with that of participants in collective agriculture who were questioned in a four-region survey carried out in 1975. For that survey, four regions differing in wealth, geographical location, ethnic composition, education, and historical experience were chosen. Two random samples were selected: the first was of villages with communal agriculture in each of the regions, and the second, of villagers participating in communal agriculture within the sample of villages. (Details of the survey will be found in Appendix 2.)

153

Table VI.1

PERCEPTIONS OF THE MEANING OF "UJAMAA" BY PARTICIPANTS
IN COMMUNAL AGRICULTURE (FOUR-REGION SURVEY):
TANZANIA, 1975

Region	Definition				
	Live Together	Farm Together	Share Product with Each Other	Cooperate or Work with Each Other	Other
Dodoma (N = 378)	166 [29.6%]	39 [7.0%]	9 [1.6%]	280 [50.0%]	66 [11.8%]
Iringa (N = 435)	223 [33.5%]	173 [26.0%]	17 [2.6%]	181 [27.2%]	71 [10.7%]
Kigoma (N = 191)	76 [29.5%]	21 [8.1%]	11 [4.3%]	113 [43.8%]	37 [14.3%]
Kilimanjaro (N = 81)	27 [20.0%]	8 [5.9%]	12 [8.9%]	68 [50.4%]	20 [14.8%]

N = Number of respondents. Percentages are percent of total responses.

As Table VI.1 shows, approximately 30 percent of the responses identified ujamaa with merely living together, implying that villagization was a sufficient condition for the good life. Only about 10 percent identified ujamaa with farming together and only 5 percent with sharing the proceeds of joint work. Inasmuch as these were the principal emphases in Nyerere's conceptualization, the data suggest that popular perceptions deviated from the policy objectives. Roughly 50 percent of the responses identified ujamaa with some other form of cooperative endeavor. Such responses included "cooperating with others," "joining others," and "helping others"— types of cooperative behavior much closer to what Samuel S. Mushi called ujima than to what Nyerere called ujamaa.[4] The discrepancy is often cited as proof of the failure of party and government officials to politicize the peasantry or of peasant "ignorance." A more likely explanation is that the villagers' behavior was a defense mechanism:

they defined ujamaa more in terms of what they wanted than in terms of what they knew advocates of the policy wanted. They could thus satisfy outside demands that they strive for ujamaa, but reinterpret the goal to maximize benefits and minimize costs. Their behavior was similar to the old "ndiyo bwana" approach of peasants to official demands.

For the sake of simplicity, ujamaa activities can be grouped under two headings—agricultural and nonagricultural undertakings. Agricultural activities center on communal farming; nonagricultural activities involve such work as building schools or keeping shops. As will be seen, the success attained in implementing the former has declined, whereas that realized in promoting the latter has increased.

The reluctance of villagers to participate in communal agriculture has been extensively documented. S. O. Odede reported that a sample of ujamaa villages studied in the Tanga area indicated that villagers spent at least three-fourths of their productive labor on private plots.[5] Audun Sandberg noted that, with few exceptions, all attempts at communal farming in ujamaa villages in the Rufiji area had failed.[6] L. J. Mshana reported that the response to communal farming in Kigoma Region was similarly poor.[7] J. Bugengo found that even in the President's own ujamaa village, Butiama, the communal sector had made little contribution.[8]

The limited success of communal agriculture is confirmed by data from the four-region survey. First, as shown in Table VI.2, the percentage of the population participating is small and the duration of that participation is relatively short. Moreover, a day's work normally lasts only five or six hours, from about 8:00 A.M. to 1:00 or 2:00 P.M. Second, the income distributed to actual participants is quite small (see Table VI.3). Even these small incomes are probably exaggerated, because the less-developed villages had no clerks to keep records and were therefore not included. Nevertheless, data from a larger sample collected by the Iringa district ujamaa and cooperative office, given in Table VI.4, suggest that the survey results for the Iringa area are reasonable. Moreover, these figures provide a comparison indicating a continual decline in income per participant from 1971 through 1973. In none of the four regions did the GDP/capita exceed 2.5 percent of the average regional GDP/capita derived from agriculture, herding, fishing, and forestry for the 1973/74 crop year.[9]

Greater success has been realized in nonagricultural communal activities. Villagers have joined together to build schools, dispensaries, water-supply facilities, and shops. By the mid-1970s, school

Table VI.2
PERCENTAGE OF ADULTS PARTICIPATING IN AND AVERAGE
DURATION OF PARTICIPATION IN COMMUNAL FARMING/FISHING
IN 1974 (FOUR-REGION SURVEY): TANZANIA, 1975[a]

Region	Percentage of Adult Population in Region Participating	Percentage of Adult Population in Ujamaa Villages Participating	Average Duration of Participation per Adult in in Region (days)	Average Duration of Participation per Adult in Ujamaa Village (days)
Dodoma (N = 9)	13.6%	22.7%	2.1	3.5
Iringa (N = 19)	10.7	48.5	5.9	26.4
Kigoma (N = 8)	1.9	8.9	1.1	5.3
Kilimanjaro (N = 5)	0.2	54.5	0.2	58.6

[a]Table is based on the calculation of village-level means.
N = Number of villages surveyed.

Table VI.3
AVERAGE INCOME DISTRIBUTED FROM COMMUNAL
FARMING/FISHING ACTIVITIES IN 1974
(FOUR-REGION SURVEY): 1975

Region	Income Distribution per Village[a]	Income Average per Participant
Dodoma (N = 6)	Shs. 1,008/- ($144)	Shs. 5/05 ($.72)
Iringa (N = 15)	Shs. 10,202/- ($1457)	Shs. 65/61 ($9.37)
Kigoma (N = 7)	Shs. 1,536/- ($219)	Shs. 3/87 ($.55)
Kilimanjaro (N = 1)	Shs. 8,998/- ($1285)	Shs. 109/76 ($15.68)

[a]Rounded off to nearest shilling or dollar.
N = Number of villages surveyed.

Table VI.4

AVERAGE ANNUAL INCOME DISTRIBUTED FROM COMMUNAL
FARMING ACTIVITIES IN IRINGA DISTRICT:
TANZANIA, 1971-1973

Year	Average Village Income[a]	Average Annual Income per Participant
1971 (N = 19)	Shs. 18,230/- ($2,604)	Shs. 168/80 ($24.11)
1972 (N = 36)	Shs. 17,660/- ($2,523)	Shs. 66/89 ($9.56)
1973 (N = 34)	Shs. 12,936/- ($1,848)	Shs. 60/17 ($8.60)

Sources: Documents, "Orodha ya Vijiji vya Ujamaa Vilivyogawano Mapato
Yao," 25 January 1974, and "Hesabu za Mgawano wa Vijiji vya
Ujamaa," 21 May 1974; DCO: Iringa.

[a]No income from fishing activities included. Rounded off to nearest shilling
or dollar.

N = Number of villages.

construction was the most common form of such work carried out in
ujamaa villages, indicated in Table VI.5. In September 1976 it was
estimated that about one in every three ujamaa villages had a cooperative or an ujamaa shop.[10] Thus, while the communal agricultural
production aspect of "working together" has not been very successfully implemented, progress has been made in encouraging other
forms of collective enterprise.

The motivations behind peasant participation in communal
agriculture, like those behind peasant movement into villages, were
complex and varied. Among the reasons given by participants in the
four-region survey for liking or not liking communal agriculture
were the following:

"Because it is the law of the party and the leaders of the village."

"Because everything we produce from the communal farm we
we sell instead of dividing it for food which we need."

"Because I get a little money."

"Because it is very time-consuming and not very profitable."

Table VI.5

COMMUNAL NONFARMING/FISHING ACTIVITIES
(FOUR-REGION SURVEY): TANZANIA, 1975

	Number of Villages Engaged in:						
	School-Related Building	House-Building	Road Work	Water-Supply Work	Health-Facility Work	Shop Construction	Brick-making
Dodoma (N = 19)	15 [79%]	5 [26%]	11 [58%]	10 [52%]	6 [32%]	6 [31%]	12 [63%]
Iringa (N = 22)	17 [77%]	1 [5%]	11 [50%]	3 [14%]	6 [27%]	1 [5%]	4 [18%]
Kigoma (N = 10)	9 [90%]	1 [10%]	3 [30%]	2 [20%]	4 [40%]	9 [90%]	4 [40%]
Kilimanjaro (N = 5)	1 [20%]	--	--	1 [20%]	--	--	--

N = Number of villages surveyed.

"Because we don't get much profit."

"Because the government said we should participate."

"Because we don't get so tired and can cultivate more land than we can alone."

"Because I have faith that socialism will bring a profit."

"Because when I am sick I get credit for days without working."

"Because I am afraid of the steps they might take against me should I not participate."

"Because the leaders steal the product and build houses of corrugated iron."

"Because it is the law of mankind that we cultivate together in order to produce a greater harvest."[11]

The reasons given by peasants for participating can be categorized into seven groups: (1) the expectation of material benefits, (2) the advantages to be expected from mutual self-help, (3) the fact that others joined the effort, (4) the expectation of government assistance, (5) the feeling that it was an obligation, (6) the insistence of party and government officials, and (7) the application, or the imminent likelihood of the application, of force. Table VI.6 indicates that the expectation of material benefits was the principal motive:

Table VI.6

REASONS GIVEN BY VILLAGERS FOR PARTICIPATING IN
COMMUNAL FARMING/FISHING (FOUR-REGION SURVEY):
TANZANIA, 1975

	Reason						
Region	Material Benefits	Benefits from Mutual Self-help	Others Joined	Govern- ment Assist- ance	Obli- gation	Insistence of Party or Govern- ment Officials	Forced
Dodoma (N = 378)	164 [42.2%]	44 [11.3%]	26 [6.7%]	6 [1.5%]	126 [32.4%]	20 [5.1%]	3 [0.8%]
Iringa (N = 438)	232 [49.8%]	71 [15.2%]	33 [7.1%]	37 [7.9%]	49 [10.5%]	38 [8.2%]	6 [1.3%]
Kigoma (N = 191)	96 [58.5%]	32 [19.5%]	10 [6.1%]	3 [1.8%]	20 [12.2%]	1 [0.6%]	2 [1.2%]
Kilimanjaro (N = 81)	39 [40.6%]	35 [36.5%]	4 [4.2%]	6 [6.3%]	8 [8.3%]	4 [4.2%]	--

N = Number of respondents.

Although peasants hesitated to admit that their participation was the consequence of "sticks" rather than "carrots," compulsion is implicit in 12 percent (in Kilimanjaro) to 40 percent (in Dodoma) of the reasons given. That is, participation resulted from a sense of "obligation," from being "told," or from being "forced." Yet, as previously noted, the President has emphatically declared that compulsion is inappropriate in bringing about this sort of ujamaa activity.

The use of compliance techniques to get people to work together can be distinguished on several grounds from the use of such techniques to get them to live together: (1) there was no national effort to introduce communal agriculture that sanctioned the use of compulsion as employed in the villagization operations; (2) there was no pattern of staged introduction of compliance techniques similar to those applied in the three phases of the villagization effort; and (3) there was much greater local responsibility for determining the manner in which persuasion, inducement, and compulsion would be employed.

APPLICATION OF PERSUASION

Many of the calls for people to join ujamaa villages included messages urging them to work together once villages had been established. As villages developed, however, village leadership assumed an ever-larger share of responsibility for encouraging people to participate in communal work. The role of both external and internal leadership in persuasion was sometimes complicated by poor rapport between leaders and peasants. In one instance this led to the killing of a regional commissioner.

Dr. Wilbert Klerruu, the regional commissioner of Iringa in 1971, was actively engaged in implementing the ujamaa village policy two years before the President made settlement in villages a requirement of all peasants. He was killed on Christmas Day that year at Makungugu ujamaa village by Saidi Abdullah Mwamwindi, a wealthy peasant cultivator. The incident became a symbol. Klerruu was seen as "the country's first martyr in building and defending Ujamaa."[12] The reality, however, is somewhat different from the myth. It indicates an approach to persuasion that critics claimed was widespread and counterproductive. Two months before, peasants in the area had been required to give up their private holdings and join the village at Makungugu. Although some decided to leave the area rather than comply, Mwamwindi and his wives and relatives joined the village. The villagers decided that everyone in the village would be permitted to farm some land privately. Mwamwindi was tractoring a portion of land which the village had assigned to him when Klerruu drove by the village. The regional commissioner stopped his car, apparently thinking that Mwamwindi was cultivating land privately which was supposed to be farmed communally, and rebuked the peasant for his action. After many weeks of testimony, the judge hearing the case reconstructed what happened as follows:

> The deceased met the accused at his shamba [farm plot] and addressed him, "Simama [Stop]. Why are you cultivating here?" The accused replied that he was ploughing the shamba that had

been allotted him by his fellow villagers as his individual shamba. The deceased retorted, "It is a lie, Shenzi [barbarian]. Stop ploughing, this land belongs to the Ujamaa village. Step down. Remove your tractor and don't cultivate here again." The accused felt reluctant to step down from his tractor but finally stepped down. The accused ask, "Are you going to include this area which has been given to us by yourself?" The deceased retorted "Lazima [Of course]." The accused asked, "What is all this my brother?" The deceased retorted, "Shut up your mouth. . . . I have told you and you will not listen." The accused retorted, "What did you tell me?" Then the deceased used some words of abuse in English. The accused caught only the words "Bloody fool." . . . and then the deceased poked the accused with his walking stick. It might not have hurt the accused in the sense of causing him any physical pain but it was all part of the insulting behavior.[13]

Mwamwindi walked back to his house, followed by Klerruu, took a gun, and shot the regional commissioner. He got help from his son to load Klerruu's body into the RC's car, took it to the Iringa police station, and turned himself in. The judge rejected an insanity defense and a defense based on a claim that Klerruu had insulted the graveyard of his ancestors as they walked to Mwamwindi's house. Despite the fact that two of the four assessors said that the provocation justified the killing, the judge disagreed. It is noteworthy that the model leader's behavior involved, according to the judge, the abuse of a peasant, the failure to work through the chairman and/or secretary of the village, and a kind of arrogance that Nyerere has frequently attacked.

Criticisms of leadership efforts to persuade have been many. The government has attacked "armchair" leadership and leadership by "warnings."[14] An editorial in the government newspaper criticized leaders who "go to Ujamaa villages to be honoured guests and talk down to the peasants."[15] As mentioned earlier, one of the most publicized verbal attacks on the work of extension officers was that made by the President in Mwanza in late 1975. It was reported that "There was deafening applause when Mwalimu said that even if he was to sack all agricultural officers, agricultural production in Tanzania would in no way be affected."[16] An agricultural officer responded a couple of months later, indicating the difficult position in which such leaders found themselves. He observed that under colonialism their function was to "tell" peasants; following independence this was changed to "advise" peasants; but since 1973 no direction regarding their role had been given. He suggested that a major part of the problem was that there were too many masters, including crop authorities, the ministry of agriculture, the regional development directors, and ward executive officers. He argued that the district agricultural officers really no longer had any power over the village agricultural officers.[17]

At the village level, government and party officials often placed the blame for implementation problems on village leaders. Villagers frequently criticized their immediate leaders as well. In Ihomasa ujamaa village in Iringa, a student found "members calling their leaders exploiters and leaders calling members ignorant and unreasonable."[18] Such criticisms were not always warranted.

Indeed, there has been a tendency to attribute low rates of turnout, whether they be for communal agriculture or nonagricultural work, automatically to the failure of leaders. The many contributory factors that may make the leader's task virtually impossible are sometimes ignored. Low returns from work, alternative obligations, and the like undermine even the most skilled persuader. The credibility of a leader could be weakened much more rapidly by the failure of communal production, which might become evident at the end of the first crop year, than by the failure of village life to bring improvements, which might not be expected for several years. Despite all the problems with leadership, thousands of peasants were persuaded to participate in both agricultural and nonagricultural work on a communal basis. Thousands of others, however, were disappointed by the results.

APPLICATION OF INDUCEMENT

The many forms of "aid" given to the villages were directed not only at facilitating resettlement but also at getting people to work together. Most externally supplied assistance was in the form of collective goods or services which could not be denied members, whether or not they participated in communal projects. Nevertheless, the promise of help should villagers try to build schools, of medicines should dispensaries be built, of pipes to bring water should trenches be dug was important in stimulating participation in nonagricultural communal work. Although fertilizers, insecticides, and other forms of outside assistance were provided to communal farms, the major source of incentives for participation was to be the crop produced.

In the four-region survey a direct relationship was found to exist between the degree of participation and the amount of remuneration—that, the higher the level of peasant participation in communal production, the higher the rate of payment to participants. As shown in Table VI.7, in all four regions the average rate of pay per day to participants was higher for the villages with more active participants than for those with less active ones, and except for Kigoma Region, the average income per participant was higher in villages with more active participants. These findings generally confirm the hypothesis stated. For both Dodoma and Kigoma Regions, however, the average value of production per day worked was higher for the villages with less active participants. What happened was that a larger proportion of those communal incomes was absorbed by the village rather than returned to the participants themselves. The effectiveness of a remuneration system is affected also by the size of the work group and the method used for determining what constitutes a day's work.

The organization of communal work has varied at different times from village to village. In certain villages, all of their members turned out for preparing the soil, planting, or weeding, and in some, village leaders headed sections of the village which undertook various farming operations. For example, in Butiama ujamaa village the membership was divided into three platoons headed by the chairman, the secretary, and the treasurer, respectively.[19] Others divide the village into smaller brigades, each of which is assigned a task. In Iringa Region, the model village constitution in 1974 called for such a division. At Magulilwa ujamaa village in Iringa, the following teams or brigades were established:

Mapinduzi (Revolution)
Jamhuri (Republic)
Mwongozo (The Guidelines)
Kazi (Work)
Chapakazi (Work Hard)
Msichoke (Don't Tire)
Ujamaa (Socialism)
Muungano (Union)
Kilimo cha Kufa na Kupona (Life and Death Agriculture)
Bega kwa Bega (Shoulder to Shoulder)

Several of these names have political significance: Mapinduzi is a reference to the Zanzibar revolution; Mwongozo refers to the TANU guidelines adopted in 1972; Kilimo cha Kufa na Kupona was a campaign initiated by the party to encourage agricultural production. The tendency in organization toward progressively smaller groups is

Table VI.7
RELATIONSHIP BETWEEN PARTICIPATION AND COMMUNAL PRODUCTION/INCOME
(FOUR-REGION SURVEY): TANZANIA, 1975[a]

Region	Degree of Participation[a]	Average Mean Workdays per Participant	Average Mean Number of Participants per Family	Average Mean Income per Participant	Average Mean Income to Village per Day Worked	Average Mean Income Paid per Day Worked
Dodoma	More active	19.80 (N=4)	1.25 (N=4)	Shs. 11/67 [$1.63] (N=3)	Shs. -/61 [$.09] (N=3)	Shs. -/56 [$.08] (N=4)
	Less active	7.60 (N=4)	1.26 (N=4)	Shs. 9/72 [$1.36] (N=3)	Shs. -/74 [$.10] (N=3)	Shs. -/48 [$.07] (N=4)
Iringa	More active	79.15 (N=9)	1.01 (N=9)	Shs. 278/23 [$38.95] (N=7)	Shs. 2/69 [$.38] (N=7)	Shs. 1/32 [$.18] (N=9)
	Less active	32.68 (N=9)	0.83 (N=9)	Shs. 21/68 [$3.04] (N=8)	Shs. 1/07 [$.15] (N=8)	Shs. 1/06 [$.15] (N=9)
Kigoma	More active	99.54 (N=3)	0.54 (N=3)	Shs. 41/44 [$5.80] (N=3)	Shs. -/35 [$.05] (N=3)	Shs. -/23 [$.03] (N=3)
	Less active	28.25 (N=3)	0.18 (N=3)	Shs. 54/61 [$7.65] (N=2)	Shs. 1/59 [$.22] (N=2)	Shs. -/20 [$.03] (N=2)
Kilimanjaro	More active	159.00 (N=2)	1.00 (N=1)	Shs. 602/44 [$84.34] (N=2)	Shs. 3/79 [$.53] (N=2)	Shs. 3/50 [$.50] (N=2)
	Less active	82.22 (N=2)	1.14 (N=2)	--	--	Shs. 1/- [$.14] (N=2)

a"More active" villages were the top 50 percent of those sampled in each region—ranked according to the number of participants in communal production divided by the number of families in each village. "Less active" villages were the bottom 50 percent. Several villages were excluded because of incomplete data.
N = Number of villages surveyed.

likely to increase the incentive effect of remuneration. The smaller the work group, the more difficult it is for an individual to work sluggishly, for social controls become more operative.

The system for measuring the amount of work accomplished also affects the incentive power of remuneration. The more closely the system is linked with work accomplished, the more likely it is to encourage the accomplishment of work. The basis of most remuneration systems is a day's work. In Swahili it is called a "heshima," which means honor or respect. An editorial in the party newspaper praised this use of the word:

> By deciding to call the member's contribution to the community his daily respect, the villagers have . . . established a yardstick for the individual's contribution to nation-building at his work and life centre.

> In this renewed practice of the peasants, urban workers have much to learn. The amount of production attributed to an individual in a day's work should also be a measure of his respect.[20]

The work of a day was measured in different ways, however, the two most common being time-rate and piece-rate systems. The former allocates one heshima for five or six hours of work, and the latter, one heshima for performing a given piece of work. Piece-rate systems more directly link actual work accomplished and remuneration. In general, one would expect to find a higher proportion of piece-rate than of time-rate systems of remuneration in those villages with higher levels of peasant participation in communal production than in those with lower levels of participation. The four-region survey of ujamaa villages supports such a conclusion, as shown in Table VI.8. Although identification of the principal system of remuneration is complicated by mixed systems and piece-work assigned to small groups, the conclusion—shared by many government officials— that the piece-work system is an improvement is confirmed by these data. In certain places the piece-rate system has been abandoned after initial trial because of the difficulty of equating and supervising tasks,[21] but generally the trend is toward its greater use because it enhances the incentive affect of remuneration.

When communal agricultural production was profitable, not all the income earned was used for incentive purposes. One model system for distribution of the product was outlined in TANU's ideological college journal, *Ujamaa*:

Table VI.8

RELATIONSHIP BETWEEN SYSTEMS OF REMUNERATION AND
DEGREE OF PARTICIPATION IN COMMUNAL PRODUCTIVE WORK
(FOUR-REGION SURVEY): TANZANIA, 1975

	Ratio of Villages w/Piece-Rate Systems to Villages w/Time-Rate Systems	
Region	Higher Rate of Participation	Lower Rate of Participation
Dodoma (N = 6)	4:2	2:4
Iringa (N = 6)	3:3	2:4
Kigoma (N = 4)	0.4	0.4
Kilimanjaro (N = 2)	1:1	1:1

N = Number of villages for which data were available.

1. A portion should go to development activities and investment in farm implements, starting small-scale industries and initiating village shops.

2. A portion should go for different village services such as taking care of children, school fees, dispensary expenditures, etc.

3. A portion should be distributed according to members' work or attendance.

4. A portion should be saved for such things as emergency famines, floods and other types of difficulties.

5. A portion should be for the disabled, old and crippled members.[22]

This pattern for use of the product of communal activity is found in many widely scattered villages from ones in (or proposed for) Kilimanjaro Region, such as Ruvu Mferejini, Kigonigoni, Kimunyu, and Ruvu Chamamba, to ones in Kigoma Region, such as Songambele Mzila and Kitagata. A second model for the use of the product of communal farming was more specific:

1. Only a part of the crop should be sold.

2. The rest should be reserved for food, seeds and emergencies.

3. That part distributed in the form of food should follow either of two principles to be decided upon at the village meeting: (a) the number of days each villager has participated in village work or (b) the number of people in each family.

4. That part in the form of money should be used as follows:
   a. Payment of all village debts, e. g., for fertilizer, insecticide and petroleum.
   b. Wages for skilled workers employed by the village, if any.
   c. Payments for licenses, taxes, duties, insurance, if any.
   d. Some should be set aside for office stationery and equipment.
   e. Some should be set aside for the maintenance of village properties, e. g., truck, flour mill, village buildings, store and other equipment.
   f. 25% of village net profit should be compulsory saving for emergency cases.
   g. 2% should be set aside, as agreed by the village meeting, for education and culture in the village.
   h. 73% should then be distributed among the villagers. Each villager should get money equivalent to his work contribution.

5. Distribution and payments should be made once per year after auditing has been done.[23]

This guideline for distribution was contained in general form in model cooperative society constitutions ranging from Dodoma to Iringa to Kigoma Regions. The models sought to overcome problems encountered in the distribution of the product. For example, in 1973 Iringa district officials argued that some portion had to be distributed rapidly as an incentive for continued participation:

If villages should be required to pay all their debts without leaving anything to distribute among themselves, this can result in the retardation of village progress. And, also, if the decision on how much the villages should be allowed to distribute takes a long time this can reduce the morale of the villagers and make them not want to participate in farming and other development activities in their areas this year.[24]

In Kibondo district, the same year, difficulties arose over the distribution of what was considered too large a proportion of the income and the failure to tie income to work contributed:

There have been many complaints from some of our Ujamaa villages with respect to the distribution of village-produced wealth. Often the complaints are over the distribution of income without regard to the amount of work done by each villager. Both those who worked and those who didn't work much for the village get an equal amount. Sometimes the village distributes money/product of the village without making considerations for saving part of it for future developmental projects, etc.[25]

That any portion of the product of communal agriculture should be distributed as individual incentives to work harder was disputed by some Tanzanian leaders. An editorial in the *Daily News* put the argument in the following way:

The attitude that at the end of the harvest season the people should divide their earnings clouds and distorts the concept of Ujamaa. The effect is that those villages which have no liquid cash to share will be discouraged. . . . Services given to the community at large by the village should determine its success. A village that makes a big payout to its members but fails to provide essential services hardly deserves the name of an Ujamaa village. It is a voluntary labour camp whose inmates are paid something but have no concern about the welfare of the whole.[26]

Such a position also assuaged the discontent produced by the absence of significant production in many ujamaa villages. In all cases, a proportion of the product, if there was any, went to finance village activities. In effect, participants in communal production were being taxed to pay for village needs, and the more one participated, the more he contributed to the welfare of others. Such behavior was in accord with ujamaa ideals, yet conflicted with prevalent values. Villagers were taxed for doing what was wanted of them—i. e., work on the communal farm—but not taxed for doing what was not wanted of them—i. e., work on private farms. The incentive effect of the system of distribution was, therefore, counterproductive.

Great variation existed, however, in systems of distributing the product. Although in some villages nothing was distributed, in others almost all produce was passed on to participants. The final decision on distribution usually was made by the village executive committee and approved by the village conference, but at times the finance subcommittee helped the village executive, at other times the ujamaa and cooperative officer made the decision, and at still other times the whole decision was left up to the village conference. Although as a rule the basis of distribution was specified as effort and attendance in work, other factors were sometimes introduced. For example, in the proposed constitution for Seri Chini in Moshi district a system similar to that found in the Chinese Tachai model is proposed. It suggests that the division of the product be made on the basis of (1) duration of work, (2) technical qualification, (3) know-how and experience, and (4) capability.[27] In most villages an effort was made to divide the product annually, but in a few cases this was done more frequently. Thus the problems with the use of inducement involved not only the limits on available resources, but also the manner in which such resources should be used.

APPLICATION OF COMPULSION

Throughout the period of major operations to get people to live in villages the President argued that the use of force was inappropriate in getting people to work together in ujamaa villages. When asked in mid-1974 whether it was true that Tanzanians were to be compulsorily "ujamaaized," he replied that it was impossible: "How can you compel people to go into Ujamaa, to share their labour and so on? We think it's a jolly good thing . . . but socialism is a matter of conviction. And you can't convince by law."[28] As mentioned earlier, this was a view that he repeated in many forums. Nevertheless, the milieu in which ujamaa villages were established was one in which compulsion had been commonly employed in both colonial and independent Tanzania. It had been used not only in getting people to move into villages but also to cause them to grow more food and to participate in self-help schemes. In fact, the President had encouraged the resort to force for similar purposes at various times. One might therefore expect that strictures against its use for ujamaa purposes would not have been entirely successful.

In an important directive on development issued in 1968,[29] the President had encouraged local governments to use sanctions under certain conditions. He maintained that traditional sanctions imposed on those who did not participate in collective activities, including the deprivation of the use of the result of community work, fines in the form of chickens, goats, or sheep, and the refusal of a share of the beer or food provided to participants, were no longer being employed. On the contrary, he observed, "We prosecuted people for imposing the traditional fines on those who did not take part in self-help schemes. It was almost as if we disapproved of the schemes and approved of laziness!" In order to counteract this tendency he called for the imposition of sanctions by village development committees, predecessors of the village councils, provided they had obtained the support of a majority of those affected. The qualification was necessary because, in his words, "There is no alternative to education and persuasion—in other words to leadership. For although the village development committee may be able to force everyone to come and gather at the work place, it cannot force everyone to work hard when they get there." The underlying reason for giving the village committees power to impose sanctions was said to be "to ensure that the mass of the people shall never have any reason to lose their enthusiasm through the feeling that they are being exploited by the few who do not want to work but do want to benefit." It will be recalled that an identical argument was put forth during the colonial period by officials seeking legal sanctions for turnouts, as described in Chapter II.

The President specifically urged the use of sanctions in 1974 when the drought and forced villagization brought a decline in agricultural production. In July he was reported to have directed

> that a system be devised to ensure that every family in Mara Region cultivate a minimum acreage and cooperate with others in nation building. . . . The order would first apply to Mara Region, later becoming effective in other regions.

> Every Tanzanian had to work diligently of their own free will, but Government would not hesitate to force lazy people to work, should this prove the only way.[30]

His request amounted to a call for the enforcement of the by-laws described in Chapter III. The response by other officials was widespread. Drinking local beer during weekdays was banned; the number of liquor licenses issued was limited; unemployed youths were rounded up and sent to farm; minimum acreages were established for parastatals, government departments, and private companies; fees were added to trading licenses to assist farming; leaders were threatened with the loss of work if they refused to farm; identity cards issued only to those who farmed were required for travel in some areas; sales of green corn that might reduce eventual harvests were banned; and many other regulations were introduced.[31] All contributed to a state of mind of people in rural areas which condoned compulsion.

In fact, sanctions, the most common forms of which were fines, have been employed by both local and national leaders to get peasants to participate in the communal work of ujamaa villages. In many of the poorer areas, failure to participate might result in the loss of a chicken or even a goat. Monetary fines were more common, especially in the more prosperous areas, as in Kimunyu village in Pare district, where a fine of Shs. 3/- was imposed for failure to participate.[32] In Chikereni ujamaa village, Moshi district, where most members lived several miles away on the slopes of Mt. Kilimanjaro, the constitution specified that

A villager who fails to turn up for communal work or to send a representative in his place will be fined Shs. 5/-. This applies to the employees of government or other institutions who do not get time to work on the village farm. They have to pay Shs. 5/- on each working day missed.[33]

The major difficulty in imposing sanctions of this sort was the lack of much wealth that might be extracted as a penalty.

A sanction used in a limited way during the early years of the effort was expulsion. Normally it was used as a final resort after other sanctions had failed. At Msambara ujamaa village in Kasulu district, the following procedures were in force:

If villagers do not attend work, they would be advised to pay a fine for the days missed; if they continued to refuse, delegates would be sent to them a maximum of three times. If refusal continued, they would be dismissed from the village unless they apologized and made amends.[34]

In Newala district in 1972, six people who refused to take part in communal activities in ujamaa villages were expelled.[35] With the movement of virtually the entire rural population into villages, such extreme sanctions became less frequent. Little use has been made of the sanction of banning private cultivation as the alternative to communal farming, although in mid-1976 action was taken to halt private fishing in Lake Tanganyika.[36]

Private fishing for *dagaa* (a small, minnow-like fish) had flourished on the lake for well over a century. In 1971, frustrated fisheries department assistants complained that fishermen "were lazy and sometimes ignored communal fishing in favour of fishing for others or individually." By 1974 only about three of the twenty-five villages along the lake had any communal fishing. Apparently disheartened by the situation, the first vice-president, Aboud Jumbe, issued a directive banning all private production. The action was supported by an editorial in the government newspaper the following day:

Socialism requires fishermen no less than peasants to work together on the basis of equality for the good of all. . . .

Ndugu Jumbe's order must be seen as another step in the gradual
but consistent elimination of exploitation in Tanzania. . . .

We hope fishermen elsewhere will not wait for Ndugu Jumbe to
come around. It is not the Kigoma fishermen alone who have been
exploited. Along the Tanzanian coast, from Tanga to Lindi are a
host of fishmongers exploiting poor fishermen. The Kigoma order
must be extended to cover the whole of Tanzania.[37]

What is particularly interesting about this case is that the sanctions
were determined by the national government, rather than by the
villagers or village leadership, in contradiction to many earlier policy
statements.

Finally, by mid-1975 the President, although still stating his
formal opposition to the use of compulsion in communal agricultural activities, suggested to delegates at the TANU biennial conference that nonagricultural activities might not be so restricted:

You can compel people to live in villages, but a decision to work
in cooperation with others must be made entirely voluntarily. . . .
Any attempt to force the pace will lead to setbacks for the whole
policy of rural socialism. This warning refers to things like agriculture and livestock-keeping which the people are accustomed to
doing individually. But there is no need to delay cooperative
development in relation to shops and village industries. From the
beginning these should be Ujamaa property.[38]

A separate examination of these two aspects of "working together"
is appropriate.

WORKING TOGETHER IN AGRICULTURE

The President's early emphasis on communal agriculture in
ujamaa villages led implementers to devote considerable attention
to its achievement. Experiences elsewhere suggest that success often
is related to various village and individual characteristics. These relationships and other characteristics of ujamaa villages were examined in the four-region survey.

VILLAGE CHARACTERISTICS

Village characteristics likely to be related to the degree of participation in communal agriculture include the age of the village, the size of its population, its linguistic homogeneity, the extent of leadership participation, and the number of nonagricultural communal activities undertaken. Those villages in the sample with the highest rate of participation were compared with those with the lowest rate. The findings were suggestive and not conclusive.

1. *Age.* Villages founded in the early years of the ujamaa village effort more often formed around the nucleus of a communal farm than did those founded in later years. The increasing use of incentives and force lured/forced peasants into the villages for reasons other than to benefit from communal work. Thus we might expect that participation would be greater in the older villages than in the newer ones, and this is confirmed by data in Table VI.9. In three of the four regions, the villages with more active participants were older than those with less active ones. In the fourth, the villages were of the same age. There is therefore some evidence that the age of villages is directly related to the degree of participation in communal work by their inhabitants, confirming what might be expected given the historical development of the effort.

Table VI.9

AGE OF VILLAGES AND LEVEL OF PARTICIPATION IN COMMUNAL
WORK (FOUR-REGION SURVEY): TANZANIA, 1975

| | Median Date of Village Formation | |
Region	High Level of Participation[a]	Low Level of Participation
Dodoma (N = 6)	August 1970	December 1970
Iringa (N = 6)	June 1970	August 1970
Kigoma (N = 4)	December 1969	September 1971
Kilimanjaro (N = 2)	June 1971	June 1971

[a]The level of participation for each village was calculated as the mean days participated by the random sample of participants observed in each village.
N = Number of villages for which data were available.

2. *Size*. The lack of agreement over what would be the best size for an ujamaa village was noted in Chapter IV. In the Villages and Ujamaa Villages Act a *minimum* of 250 families was established. The prime minister suggested a *maximum* of 600 families.[39] The former figure was probably specified in order to make efficient use of the investments required in schools and dispensaries. The latter reflected fears that large villages could not be managed. The problem of management suggests that the level of participation may be inversely related to the size of the village, but survey results, shown in Table VI.10, are inconclusive.

Table VI.10

SIZE OF VILLAGES AND LEVEL OF PARTICIPATION IN
COMMUNAL WORK (FOUR-REGION SURVEY): TANZANIA, 1975

| Region | Average Number of Families | |
	High Level of Participation	Low Level of Participation
Dodoma	573 (N=6)	397 (N=6)
Iringa	189 (N=6)	202 (N=6)
Kigoma	661 (N=4)	818 (N=1)
Kilimanjaro	140 (N=2)	70 (N=2)

N = Number of villages for which data were available.

The size of villages in 1974 varied greatly both within and among regions, but the averages for the samples do not appear to confirm the hypothesis. It appears possible to find within large villages a group of participants who work as hard as those who participated in smaller villages. That is, the size of the village does not seem to have an effect on the level of participation. Other factors, such as the presence of some subvillage organizational structures may offset management problems created by a large number of villages.

3. *Leadership Participation.* Several criticisms raised against the leadership have already been noted. One measure of the quality of the leadership according to criteria suggested by the President is the extent to which it participates in communal work. If he is right, the higher the level of peasant participation in communal production, the higher the level of leadership participation. Data are available for only three of the regions, but they support the hypothesis (as shown in Table VI.11): the more participant the leadership, the more successful it is.

Table VI.11

LEADERSHIP AND LEVEL OF PARTICIPATION IN COMMUNAL WORK
(FOUR-REGION SURVEY): TANZANIA, 1975

Region	Average Number of Days Worked per Year by the Chairman and Secretary	
	High Level of Participation	Low Level of Participation
Dodoma	79.0 (N=3)	15.4 (N=4)
Iringa	202.8 (N=4)	153.5 (N=2)
Kigoma	209.8 (N=4)	72.5 (N=2)
Kilimanjaro	--	--

N = Number of villages for which data were available.

4. *Linguistic Homogeneity.* At the state level, national integration often is seen as a condition that may facilitate development. Likewise, the lack of homogeneity is seen as a condition that may retard the achievement of objectives. In Chapter III it was noted that, ironically, the extreme ethnic diversity of Tanzania has led to a diminution of the importance of ethnicity in national politics. Because cooperation among many groups is a prerequisite for rule, appeals based on ethnicity may be counterproductive. Besides, the party has worked hard to eliminate appeals to tribal loyalty. Nevertheless, some argue that cooperation and communication are likely to be

easier among members of a single ethnic group than among members of different ethnic groups. If such a contention is true, lack of ethnic uniformity in a village may lead to lack of cooperation in communal production—that is, the greater the ethnic diversity, the lower the rates of participation. Slight support for such a proposition is provided by data in Table VI.12. For three of the four regions the hypothesized relationship holds, but the differences in percentages are very small in all cases. Consequently, although the available data do not contradict the notion that ethnic homogeneity facilitates a high rate of participation, they provide only minor support.

Table VI.12

LINGUISTIC HOMOGENEITY AND LEVEL OF PARTICIPATION
IN VILLAGES (FOUR-REGION SURVEY): TANZANIA, 1975

Region	Percent with Same First Language as 70 Percent or More of Other Peasants in Village	
	High Level of Participation	Low Level of Participation
Dodoma	72.0% (N=75)	77.0% (N=75)
Iringa	56.3 (N=94)	53.7 (N=95)
Kigoma	76.2 (N=42)	71.1 (N=38)
Kilimanjaro	44.4 (N=18)	37.5 (N=16)

N = Number of respondents.

5. *Nonagricultural Communal Activities.* Although an analytical distinction can be made between communal agriculture and non-agricultural activities, both are parts of a whole—i. e., "working together." One might reasonably expect that readiness to participate in communal agriculture would be associated with readiness to participate in nonagricultural communal activities. Table VI.13 suggests that the association is a valid one. In 69 percent of the cases (eleven out of sixteen) where there is any difference between those villages

Table VI.13

NONAGRICULTURAL COMMUNAL ACTIVITIES AND LEVEL OF PARTICIPATION IN VILLAGES
(FOUR-REGION SURVEY): TANZANIA, 1975[a]

Region	Percent of Villages Undertaking House Building		Percent of Villages Undertaking Road Work		Percent of Villages Undertaking Water Supply		Percent of Villages Undertaking Health Facility		Percent of Villages Undertaking Moving People		Percent of Villages Undertaking Shop Construction		Percent of Villages Undertaking Brickmaking	
	Participation High	Low	Participation High	Low	Participation High	Low	Participation High	Low	Participation High	Low	Participation High	Low	Participation High	Low
Dodoma (N = 6)	16.7%	16.7%	50.0%	83.3%	66.7%	50.0%	0	50.0%	83.3%	0	50.0%	16.7%	66.7%	66.7%
Iringa (N = 6)	16.7	0	66.7	16.7	0	0	50.0	16.7	0	0	16.7	0	0	33.3
Kigoma (N = 4)	25.0	0	25.0	25.0	0	0	50.0	25.0	0	0	75.0	100.0	50.0	25.0
Kilimanjaro (N = 2)	50.0	0	0	0	0	50.0	0	0	0	0	0	0	0	0

[a]During the lifespan of the village.
N = Number of villages for which data were available.

with more and less active participants, communal activity other than commodity production was more common in the former type of village than in the latter. The results therefore are not inconsistent with the hypothesis posed. An implication is that recent emphasis on nonagriculture communal activities may enhance, rather than detract from, communal agriculture.

INDIVIDUAL CHARACTERISTICS

Various characteristics of villagers may also affect the degree of participation in communal agriculture. Among such traits are his/her wealth, age, education, sex, party membership, satisfaction with life, level of aspirations, and motives for joining the village.

1. *Wealth*. The ujamaa village policy was initiated partly as a response to the growth of a group of farmers, normally called "kulaks" or "progressive farmers"—i. e., those who had greater wealth. The argument was advanced that their increasing wealth meant increasing inequality and their employment of labor meant exploitation. President Nyerere and other advocates of the ujamaa village policy considered communal agriculture a way of providng the poor with a chance equal to that of the rich to accumulate wealth. The poor might therefore reasonably be expected to respond more enthusiastically than the rich to the lure of communal production. The survey results, summarized in Table VI.14, tend to refute that supposition. In all three regions a higher percentage of the more active than of the less active were wealthy, and in two of the three regions a lower percentage of the more active than of the less active were poor. There thus appears to be a slight tendency for the wealthier to be more active participants than the less wealthy. The relationship suggests that the communal farm was not achieving one of its principal objectives—i. e., to serve as a means by which the poorer peasant might improve his condition relative to the richer peasant.

2. *Age*. As we have seen, efforts to establish communal farms and start ujamaa villages were made by the TANU Youth League in the years preceding the formal initiation of the policy in 1967. This early trend was enhanced by the President's stress on building socialism for the young and for future generations, and it contrasted with the hesitancy of older peasants to change established habits. It was therefore expected that the young would play a more active

Table VI.14

LEADERS ESTIMATE OF VILLAGERS' WEALTH AND LEVEL
OF PARTICIPATION (FOUR-REGION SURVEY): TANZANIA, 1975

Region	High Level of Participation			Low Level of Participation		
	Percent Wealthy	Percent Average	Percent Poor	Percent Wealthy	Percent Average	Percent Poor
Dodoma	4.0%	17.3% (N=75)	78.7%	3.8%	20.5% (N=78)	75.6%
Iringa	7.3	74.4 (N=82)	18.3	2.4	61.0 (N=82)	36.6
Kigoma	23.8	42.9 (N=42)	33.3	10.8	51.4 (N=37)	37.8
Kilimanjaro	--			--		

N = Number of respondents.

role in communal production than the older members of the population. The survey data, however, contradict that expectation, as
shown in Table VI.15. A more accurate conclusion would be that
the higher the level of peasant participation in communal production, the older the participants. For three of the four regions, the
more active participants were, on the average, older than the less
active participants. The fact that the young no longer appear to
be taking the lead in communal commodity production may have
adverse long-term consequences.

3. *Education.* After independence, Tanzania sought to change the
thrust of its educational system. Nyerere has criticized the colonial
system of education in his paper "Education for Self-Reliance" in
the following terms: "It was based on the assumptions of a colonial-
ist and capitalist society. It emphasized and encouraged the individualistic instincts of mankind, instead of his cooperative instincts. It
led to the possession of individual material wealth being the major
criterion of social merit and worth."[40]
Reorganization brought socialism and self-reliance in both
theory and practice into the schools. Encouragement of "coopera-

Table VI.15

AGE OF PARTICIPANTS IN COMMUNAL ACTIVITY AND LEVEL OF PARTICIPATION (FOUR-REGION SURVEY): TANZANIA, 1975

| | Average Age | |
| | High Level of Participation | Low Level of Participation |
Region		
Dodoma	36.4 (N=75)	32.6 (N=78)
Iringa	39.9 (N=89)	34.1 (N=91)
Kigoma	41.7 (N=42)	48.1 (N=38)
Kilimanjaro	48.9 (N=16)	38.5 (N=18)

N = Number of respondents.

tive instincts" replaced encouragement of "individualistic instincts." Nevertheless, Table VI.15 indicates that most of those who are participating in communal production would have received their primary education, if any, under the British colonial system. Since that system supported values opposed to communal farming, one might expect that the more active participants were those who had received less of such indoctrination. Table VI.16 indicates that on two measures of "level of education"—the number of years of schooling and the percent who attended government or mission schools—the relationship does not hold. Instead, in all regions except Kilimanjaro, the higher the level of peasant participation in communal production, the higher the level of education received. Two possible reasons for this may be a greater susceptibility of the more educated to socialization through recent adult education or a greater tendency on their part to engage in productive labor, regardless of the type. The situation in Kilimanjaro may have been due to the special conditions in its villages in 1973/74. Most of them were established in the lowlands, and many were nonresidential. Peasants lived on the mountain and came down to work on village fields. Those attracted to the lowland villages were the poorer and generally

Table VI.16

TYPE/AMOUNT OF EDUCATION AND LEVEL OF PARTICIPATION
(FOUR-REGION SURVEY): TANZANIA, 1975

Region	Percent Attending Regular Government or Mission Schools		Average Years of Schooling of All Types	
	Participation		Participation	
	High	Low	High	Low
Dodoma	38.7% (N=75)	33.3% (N=78)	3.4 (N=75)	2.8 (N=78)
Iringa	50.0 (N=95)	38.9 (N=95)	2.5 (N=87)	2.3 (N=89)
Kigoma	35.7 (N=42)	28.9 (N=38)	2.4 (N=42)	2.2 (N=38)
Kilimanjaro	44.4 (N=18)	56.3 (N=16)	2.5 (N=13)	3.4 (N=13)

N = Number of respondents.

less educated ones who did not have sufficient land on the mountain to survive. Such a situation is very unusual in Tanzania. Elsewhere, the appeal of communal production does not appear to be greater to the poorly educated than to the slightly better educated.

4. *Sex.* President Nyerere has criticized "traditional" Tanzanian society for its treatment of women. In "Socialism and Rural Development" he stated: "It is impossible to deny that the women did, and still do more than their fair share of the work in the fields and in the homes."[41] This inequality is considered wrong in itself and wrong because it reduces the overall labor going into production. The communal farms were to be places where men and women were to contribute equally to production, but the survey results, shown in Table VI.17, indicate that such equality was not attained. In three of the four regions more men than women worked, and in all four regions the average male worked longer than the average female. This situation may be the result of two factors: (1) fear by the women that communal production might not meet the food requirements of

Table VI.17

COMPARISON OF MALE AND FEMALE PARTICIPATION IN
COMMUNAL PRODUCTION DURING 1974
(FOUR-REGION SURVEY): TANZANIA, 1975

Region	Average Number of Participants Village			Ratio of Male to Female Partici- pants	Average Duration of Participation per Participant (Days)			Ratio of Male to Female Partici- tion
	Total	Male	Female		Total	Male	Female	
Dodoma (N = 9)	353	189	165	1.1:1	15.6	16.1	14.8	1.1:1
Iringa (N = 19)	170	75	95	.8:1	54.4	63.8	47.5	1.3:1
Kigoma (N = 8)	316	250	67	3.7:1	59.9	61.8	54.4	1.1:1
Kilimanjaro (N = 5)	77	48	29	1.7:1	107.5	110.6	100.1	1.1:1

N = Number of villages for which data were available.

the family, for which they were generally responsible, and (2) the customary male role of protecting the family from outside interference which might result from nonparticipation.

5. *Party Membership.* Because of the close relationship between the party and the ujamaa village policy, one might reasonably expect that membership in TANU would be closely associated with participation in communal production. That is, one might expect that a low level of participation is associated with the failure of TANU members to participate. In Chapter III it was noted that the determination of whether a peasant is a member of the party is not as simple a matter as it appears. Official records of membership are either lacking or greatly in error; membership is frequently claimed by an individual if he once obtained a card, whether or not he continues to pay dues; and membership is often claimed by those closely associated with someone calling himself a member, such as a wife or son.[42] Nevertheless, information supplied by village leaders regarding individual membership indicates that the suggested rela-

tionship is false, as shown in Table VI.18. TANU membership is positively related to participation in all regions; in other words, the higher the degree of participation in communal production, the higher the proportion of TANU members participating.

Table VI.18

TANU PARTY MEMBERSHIP AND LEVEL OF PARTICIPATION
IN COMMUNAL PRODUCTION (FOUR-REGION SURVEY):
TANZANIA, 1975

| Region | TANU Members | | Nonmembers | |
| | Participation | | Participation | |
	High	Low	High	Low
Dodoma	73.3% (N=75)	44.9% (N=75)	26.7%	55.1%
Iringa	90.5 (N=84)	65.9 (N=82)	9.5	34.1
Kigoma	85.7 (N=42)	83.8 (N=37)	14.3	16.2
Kilimanjaro	100 (N=18)	93.8 (N=16)	0	6.3

N = Number of respondents.

6. *Satisfaction with Life*. The motivation of an individual to participate in something like communal farming may reasonably be linked with the degree of his satisfaction with the trend of improvement in his life. If he feels that the trend of changes introduced by the party and government is satisfactory, one might suppose that he would respond more positively to the advice of the party and government. Participation in communal production has been urged by both organs. The expected relationship might be more formally stated as follows: the higher the level of peasant participation in communal production, the greater the degree of satisfaction with the trend of improvement in their lives. Table VI.19, which compares the relative

satisfaction with life expressed by peasants for 1970 and 1975 and predicted for 1980 tends to support the hypothesis.* In three

Table VI.19

PEASANT EVALUATION OF THE TREND IN LIVING
CONDITIONS AND LEVEL OF PARTICIPATION
(FOUR-REGION SURVEY): TANZANIA, 1975

Region	Percent Who Felt 1975 Was Better than 1970		Percent Who Felt 1980 Would Be Better than 1975		Percent Who Felt 1980 Would Be Better than 1970	
	Participation		Participation		Participation	
	High	Low	High	Low	High	Low
Dodoma	63.5% (N=74)	47.4% (N=78)	93.2% (N=74)	93.6% (N=78)	83.6% (N=73)	80.8% (N=78)
Iringa	66.7 (N=93)	64.1 (N=92)	81.5 (N=81)	81.7 (N=82)	85.0 (N=80)	80.5 (N=82)
Kigoma	90.5 (N=42)	89.5 (N=38)	92.9	86.8	92.9	86.8
Kilimanjaro	52.9 (N=18)	81.3 (N=16)	100	100	94.1	93.8

N = Number of respondents.

of the four regions a higher percentage of the more active participants than of the less active participants saw 1975 as better than 1970; the relative optimism concerning the possible improvement of life between 1975 and 1980 is virtually identical between more and less active participants, except in Kigoma, where the more active are likelier to be optimistic than are the less active; and in all four regions a higher percentage of the more active participants than of the less active expect life to be better in 1980 than it was in 1970. In other words, the dissatisfied and discouraged are less likely to be active participants than the satisfied and encouraged.

*The high level of satisfaction with the probable future as compared with the present and with the present as compared with the past may be partly due to the peasants' desire not to express discontent with the ujamaa village lest party or government officials condemn them for doing so.

7. *Levels of Aspiration.* Satisfaction with a *trend* of improvement in life differs from satisfaction with an existing condition of life. The latter may breed inaction; the former need not. One of the arguments for the British policy of concentrations, described in Chapter II, was that village life stimulated individual desires and aspirations which, in turn, stimulated work and production. The relationship between aspirations and participation in communal work might be hypothesized as follows: the higher the level of peasant participation in communal production, the greater the aspirations of the peasants. Table VI.20, which shows the relative percentage of the more and less active participants expressing a desire for various aspects of what they considered the good life, supports the hypothesis. In only five of thirty-six comparisons made was the percentage of less active participants desiring an aspect of what was considered the good life higher than that of the more active participants. This relationship held whether the item desired was one of the more "modern," such as motorized transport, or one of the more "traditional," such as livestock.

8. *Reasons for Living Together.* There has been considerable debate in Tanzania over whether there is a relationship between the motives for joining ujamaa villages and the motives for participating in communal production. As previously noted, the President has referred to the old proverb (rephrased for Tanzania), "You can drive a donkey to water, but you cannot make it drink." In essence, "driving the donkey to water" was undertaken through the various operations, but there was considerable fear that the use of force in moving people to the villages would make it doubly difficult to "get them to drink." The validity of claims in the debate may be assessed by an examination of the relationship between the extremes of self-identified motives for joining the village—the expectation of material gain and the fear or experience of force—and the degree of participation in communal production, as shown in Table VI.21. Those who joined the villages because of the promise of material gain tended to be among the more active participants in communal work more often than among the less active—i. e., the higher the level of peasant participation in communal production, the more likely that peasants joined because of the expectation of material benefit. One might expect that failure to receive significant material benefit from communal work would lead to a diminution of this trend, but this was not the case in the 1973/74 crop year. The more active participants joined because their expectations of receiving

Table VI.20

PEASANT ASPIRATIONS AND LEVEL OF PARTICIPATION
(FOUR-REGION SURVEY): TANZANIA, 1975

Region	Percent Desiring Corrugated-Iron Roof		Percent Desiring Plenty of Food or Crops		Percent Desiring Plenty of Money		Percent Desiring Livestock	
	Participation High	Low	Participation High	Low	Participation High	Low	Participation High	Low
Dodoma	58.7% (N=75)	49.4% (N=77)	66.7%	72.7%	52.0%	55.8%	50.7%	49.4%
Iringa	85.5 (N=87)	80.9 (N=94)	47.1	41.5	44.8	43.6	34.5	26.6
Kigoma	78.6 (N=42)	66.7 (N=36)	38.1	36.1	21.4	13.9	4.8	8.3
Kilimanjaro	82.4 (N=17)	81.3 (N=16)	58.8	50.0	47.1	37.5	11.8	0

Region	Percent Desiring Clothing		Percent Desiring Good Farm		Percent Desiring Motorized Transport		Percent Desiring Tractor		Percent Desiring Other Agricultural/ Fishing Equipment	
	Participation High	Low	Participation High	Low	Participation High	Low	Participation High	Low	Participation High	Low
Dodoma	32.0%	20.8%	16.0%	26.0%	6.7%	5.2%	5.3%	2.6%	1.3%	0
Iringa	17.2	25.5	24.1	21.3	24.1	20.2	13.8	8.5	3.4	3.2
Kigoma	23.8	19.4	4.8	2.8	11.9	11.1	4.8	2.8	9.5	2.8
Kilimanjaro	35.3	6.3	0	0	17.6	6.3	0	0	0	0

N = Number of respondents.

Table VI.21

RELATIONSHIP BETWEEN MOTIVES FOR JOINING UJAMAA
VILLAGES AND LEVEL OF PARTICIPATION IN COMMUNAL
PRODUCTION (FOUR-REGION SURVEY): TANZANIA, 1975

Region	Percent of Participants Who Joined Because of Expectation of Material Gain[a]		Percent of Participants Who Joined Because of Force	
	Participation		Participation	
	High	Low	High	Low
Dodoma	4.3% (N=69)	0 (N=75)	10.1%	8.0%
Iringa	15.7 (N=83)	14.6 (N=82)	7.2	8.5
Kigoma	20.7 (N=29)	10.7 (N=28)	6.9	10.7
Kilimanjaro	47.1 (N=17)	25.0 (N=16)	0	0

[a]The most common response by peasants to the question of why they moved into villages was that they thought it would be generally beneficial, without specific reference to material benefits. The percentages above refer only to those who specified material gain as the principal incentive.

N = Number of respondents.

money were relatively higher than those of the less active participants. Undoubtedly, insecurity and fear prevented many villagers from identifying force as the motive which brought them to join ujamaa villages. In two of the three regions where villagers indicated force was used, those who joined the villages because they were forced tended to be among the less active participants in communal work more often than among the more active participants. Yet the proportion of villagers forced to join who participated actively in communal farming is too high to substantiate the notion that the use of force is necessarily detrimental to the active participation of peasants in communal farming.

The individual characteristics of the more active participants, then, differ from those that might be predicted from the underlying ideology. Although it might be expected that such a participant would be poorer, less educated, more likely female, and more likely to be seeking benefits from mutually working together with others than the less active participants, he turns out to be less poor, slightly better educated, older, more likely male, and more likely one who seeks money by joining the village. Ironically, these characteristics are close to those of the "kulak" or "progressive farmer," who was to be eliminated by the introduction of communal farming. In no case is the difference extreme. The differences may well be those between an "upper" and a "lower" middle peasant in Chinese terminology. They suggest, though, that communal production is not serving well the interests of the poorer peasants.

LEGITIMACY OF COMPLIANCE TECHNIQUES

The attitudes of villagers and village leaders toward the use of persuasion, inducement, and compulsion can be assessed indirectly through a review of methods they suggest as appropriate for increasing participation. In the late 1960s, Clyde Ingle found in both Tanga and Handeni districts that "the legitimacy of compulsion as a developmental technique may have been more accepted by the peoples . . . than by their leaders."[43] In the four-region survey the reverse was true.

Villagers were very reluctant to suggest methods for increasing participation in communal work, this being perhaps indicative of the value they place on the enterprise. Nevertheless, of those who did respond, four principal responses were offered, as shown in Table VI.22.

Although no clear differences between the more- and the less-active participants are evident, in every region the former appear, more than do the latter, to feel that greater government assistance would encourage them, and in every region except Iringa the latter appear, more than do the former, to feel that greater material reward for work on the communal farm would encourage them. In fact, the lack of adequate material return appears to be the most important factor in the villagers' decision not to work more in communal production. The third response—"changed work situation"— groups together suggestions for better leadership, cultivation of a different crop, and a better or fairer system of distributing the product. The fourth response—"get others to work"—is somewhat circular, but suggests that so long as some opt out of the work others will want to opt out.

When village leaders were asked how participation might be

Table VI.22

VILLAGER SUGGESTIONS FOR IMPROVING PARTICIPATION AND
LEVEL OF PARTICIPATION IN COMMUNAL PRODUCTION
(FOUR-REGION SURVEY): TANZANIA, 1975

Region	Improve Material Profit		More Government Assistance		Changed Work Situation		Get Others to Work	
	Participation High	Low	Participation High	Low	Participation High	Low	Participation High	Low
Dodoma	68.5% (N=54)	75.0% (N=52)	25.9%	15.4%	9.3%	7.7%	3.7%	9.6%
Iringa	77.6 (N=76)	77.1 (N=83)	30.2	25.3	14.5	21.7	10.5	4.8
Kigoma	39.4 (N=33)	59.3 (N=27)	27.3	22.2	27.2	29.6	18.2	11.1
Kilimanjaro	29.4 (N=17)	38.5 (N=13)	58.5	53.8	41.2	15.4	0	100

N = Number of respondents.

improved, the responses were considerably different. They did not focus on the inducements of "improved material profit" or "more government assistance," as did the villagers, but rather on "changed work situation"—i. e., technical improvements in running the operation—and on the use of sanctions. Table VI.23 summarizes their suggestions. Because regional variation did not appear to be a significant variable determining the attitude of leaders toward what would increase peasant participation in communal production, Table VI.23 compares quartiles of villages arranged on the basis of the degree of peasant participation, regardless of region. The most frequent suggestion was the imposition of fines, something which not unexpectedly was not mentioned by the villagers. There is a very clear inverse relationship between the degree of participation by villagers and the suggestion by leaders that fines be imposed—i. e., the lower the rate of participation, the higher the desire for the imposition of fines. The lowest quartile was characterized by relatively strong desires for a more rapid division of the crop after harvest and the need for persons of authority to come and explain the utility of

Table VI.23

VILLAGE-LEADER SUGGESTIONS FOR IMPROVING PARTICIPATION IN COMMUNAL PRODUCTION
(FOUR-REGION SURVEY): TANZANIA, 1975

Quartiles of Villages by Level of Participation	Suggestions							
	General Sanctions	Fines	Send Offender Before Authority	More Rapid Crop Division	Work Groups	Piece-Work	Status Person to Explain Benefits	Meetings or Seminars
Highest (N = 7)	28.6%	14.3%	14.3%	14.3%	0	28.6%	14.3%	28.6%
Medium High (N = 7)	0	28.6	28.6	14.3	14.3	0	28.6	0
Medium Low (N = 7)	28.6	42.9	14.3	14.3	14.3	14.3	0	14.3
Lowest (N = 7)	14.3	57.1	14.3	42.9	14.3	14.3	42.9	14.3

N = Number of villages in each quartile.

participating in communal farming. Both suggestions appear to indicate frustration with the absence of sufficient outside support for their efforts, for delay in crop division is often a consequence of delayed approval at the district level.

District and regional officials in several areas have begun to undertake reforms that seek both short- and long-term solutions to the problem posed by low peasant participation in communal production. First, as we have noted, there is a noticeable trend toward the adoption of piece-rate systems and smaller work-team organization. These ideas have filtered down to village leaders, as shown in Table VI.23. In other countries, both have improved productivity and have been incentives to participate more fully. Second, there is a shift of emphasis in several areas from communal farming to block farming. The latter involves the assignment of individuals to plots of land adjacent to each other. The idea is that the movement from scattered private plots to communal farming is too abrupt to be successful. The block farm is seen as an intermediary form that will eventually transform itself into a communal farm. Kigoma Region is one area where the policy is explicit. Planning for the transition from block to communal farming has not advanced greatly;[44] hence some feel that it is merely a mechanism for retreating to the private farm, rather than one for advancing over a new path toward the communal farm. Nevertheless, after the massive influx of people into villages during the 1974/75 operations, this became an important alternative to immediate movement toward communal farming. Theoretically, it would permit the gradual socialization of the peasant to accept work on the communal farm as valuable and eventually lead to increased participation.

WORKING TOGETHER IN NONAGRICULTURAL ACTIVITIES

Although the core of an ujamaa village initially was conceived to be communal agriculture, collective work was not to be confined to it. With the increase in block farming came increased attention to manufacturing, construction, and commercial activities undertaken on a communal basis.

MANUFACTURING

Although small-scale industries have been established in several villages, participation in them has involved a relatively small portion of the village population. Their early importance has been more symbolic than material. An Indian team visited Tanzania in January 1974 and proposed a plan to establish 1,000 small-scale industries during the period of the forthcoming five-year development plan, employing about 5,000 people at a cost of some Shs. 5,000 per worker. This plan contemplated that 10 percent of the investment would be raised by the local group and the rest would be provided by credit institutions.[45] Although initiation of the third five-year plan was delayed until 1978, efforts to promote such industries proceeded. Most common were those in carpentry and blacksmithing, but there were also sawmills, shoe-making plants, soap factories, a coffee-processing plant, and others.[46] One of the most widespread was the milling of corn and millet. The establishment of small-scale industries was encouraged primarily by inducement, as facilities, equipment, and training were provided by the government. In some areas, however, as in Mpwapwa district, the forcible exclusion of private mills was a key mechanism in getting village maize mills under way.

CONSTRUCTION

Much of the assistance given to ujamaa villages that functioned as collective incentives to induce people to join, including equipment for small-scale industries, required cooperative work on the part of villagers to realize its benefits. Materials for schools, dispensaries, water projects, and housing might be provided, but most of the construction had to be done jointly by the villagers. The aid initiated a chain of activities necessitating cooperative enterprise if the desired end was to be reached.

1. *Schools.* The government normally contributed corrugated iron for a roof, cement, beams, and nails for construction of schools. It supplied a few skilled workers for difficult portions of work, such as installing doors and windows and putting up the roof, and promised to provide a teacher after the school was completed. Labor for making bricks and for constructing the school and the teacher's house was supplied primarily by the villagers. Often the demand for government help outran available resources, so assistance was not always provided as quickly as villagers wished. Even when it came promptly, villagers did not automatically turn out to work, despite the general desire for schools. For example, the author worked on the construction of a school in Mpamantwa ujamaa village in Dodoma district during 1973, where turnouts sometimes fell to four

or five people out of a village of several hundred families. Village leaders became disappointed and threatened the ten-cell leaders with fines in the form of chickens or goats should they not get families for which they were responsible to participate. The school building was eventually finished. The attitude of the villagers appeared to be based on the belief that they would be able to benefit from the school without contributing to its construction.

2. *Dispensaries.* Although villages with dispensaries numbered only about half of those with schools, the form of government assistance to promote collective work for construction was identical. Materials that were not available locally were provided, as was training for the person to run the dispensary after it was built. The provision of such aid was dependent on the availability of funds from the ministry of health and other organizations. In the same way that such assistance reduced the cost/benefit assessment of participation in building schools, it was likely to facilitate working together to build dispensaries.

3. *Water Projects.* Water was an even greater need, and the desire for it facilitated government efforts to get people to work together to obtain it. Some water projects, such as deep wells or water tanks, involved little joint work by villagers, but others, such as some in Kondoa and Nachingwea, did require it. The Tomoko water scheme in Kondoa brought water over a distance of 124 kilometers from a mountain range above the Kondoa Irangi plains to a series of ujamaa villages. To accomplish the work, 2,800 villagers were reported to have taken part in digging the trench for the pipe.[47] The Sambwa project, also in Kondoa, involved the digging of a ditch for an eighteen-mile pipeline by nearby villagers.[48] In Nachingwea district, 5,000 villagers were reported to have worked together in digging a thirty-kilometer trench from Ruponda to various ujamaa villages.[49] Tschannerl has studied the provision of rural water supply and found that in general "the nature of communal water supplies is such that no privileged group can enjoy a considerably larger share of the benefits than the rest."[50] This, though, did not mean that everyone benefitted in the same proportion to his participation in the joint work involved.

4. *Housing.* The building of permanent housing was important not only because it could be used as a method for getting people to work

together, but also because it meant more than a passing commitment to living together. To promote the construction of houses, the government established the Tanzania Housing Bank at the end of 1972.[51] In some regions, major efforts were exerted shortly after the completion of operations to move people into villages. For example, Operation Ngodano in Kigoma Region was initiated following a suggestion by Nyerere in December 1973 and by the regional TANU secretary in March 1974.[52] Its objective was to replace all temporary housing in ujamaa villages in the region. First, lists of the old houses were compiled; then the people were told what to do; finally, if they refused to obey, the old houses were burned. Early in 1976 the prime minister announced that Operation Nyumba (Operation Houses) would be undertaken. The government paper noted that he "was optimistic that by the end of this year 'Operation Vijiji' will have been fulfilled to give way to Operation Nyumba which is the second important stage in the villagisation programme."[53] He complained about the fact that many villages looked like refugee camps rather than permanent villages. Just as the other construction efforts—the schools, dispensaries, and water projects—required collective work for their completion, so did the operations to build permanent housing, and government assistance together with forms of compulsion brought people to work together in its construction.

COMMERCE

As mentioned earlier, Indian traders had dominated buying and selling of goods in rural areas since the early years of British colonial rule. Chapter II commented upon the rise of the cooperative movement, which by the late 1950s had wrested control over purchasing most crops from the traders. Peasant control of the cooperative movement in parts of the country such as Kilimanjaro antedates the initiation of the ujamaa village policy by forty years. Inasmuch as both undertakings involved a form of cooperative work among peasants, it is not surprising that there was an eventual merger of the two efforts. The development of peasant control over retail trade has progressed much more slowly. Nevertheless, the ujamaa village provided an ideal setting for the elimination of both Indian and African private traders.

1. *Cooperatives.* Until the Villages and Ujamaa Villages Act of 1975, the highest stage of development of the ujamaa village was

registration as a multipurpose cooperative society. According to the *Economic Survey and Annual Plan for 1970/71*, "The ultimate aim of the Ujamaa village programme is that the village should become a fully collectivized unit, i. e., a production and marketing cooperative. Most Ujamaa villages are still a long way from this level."[54] Nevertheless, the proportion of villages so registered increased considerably during the early 1970s, as shown in Table VI.24. Despite the impli-

Table VI.24

NUMBER AND PERCENT OF UJAMAA VILLAGES REGISTERED AS
COOPERATIVE SOCIETIES: 1969-1974

Year	Number of Ujamaa Villages	Number Registered as Cooperatives	Percent Registered as Cooperatives
1969	809	7	0.9%
1970	1,956	9	0.5
1971	4,464	79	1.8
1972	5,556	323	5.8
1973	5,628	342	6.1
1974	5,008	393	7.8

Source: Calculated from Jedwali, 1.1 and 3.0 in Sehemu ya Mipango no Utafiti Kikundi cha Takwimu, Ofisi ya Waziri Mkuu na Makamu wa Pili wa Rais, *Maendeleo ya Vijiji yva Ujamaa* (Dar es Salaam: National Printing Co. June 1974), pp. 1 and 8, respectively.

cation that cooperative registration meant that significant collective work had been undertaken, this often was not the case. The 1975 act sought to rectify the situation. It called for the registration of all villages as cooperative societies and the designation of those cooperatives with extensive communal work as ujamaa villages.[55] The former cooperative movement virtually disappeared with the disbanding of cooperative unions and the merger of primary societies into the villages in 1976.[56] What really happened in the mid-1970s was the transmutation of the old cooperative movement into the new ujamaa movement.

The rapid expansion of the cooperative movement in the early 1960s led to problems that threatened cooperative ideals. Peasants in several parts of the country were bitterly disappointed by mismanagement and losses.[57] Some party leaders were angry because marketing cooperatives seemed to benefit wealthy peasants more than poor ones. As a consequence, the government intruded more and more into the operation of cooperatives in order to improve their efficiency and to mould them into instruments for socialist construction. Yet the problems persisted.

Perhaps partly because of the frustration of efforts to solve problems in the cooperative movement, the party/government began to use what strength was left in the movement to further the ujamaa village policy. In a sense, the cooperative movement was used to pave the way for its successor. The highest cooperative organization in the country, the Cooperative Union of Tanganyika (CUT), recognizing that "the activities of the Ujamaa village will usually be more communal than the present cooperative societies," called on them to help keep village records, to train villagers to keep accounts, to distribute seeds and fertilizer to the villages, to demonstrate the use of good seeds and good animal husbandry, and in all other ways possible to facilitate the success of ujamaa villages.[58] The purpose of registration of villages as multipurpose cooperatives was to give them access to government services, such as loans, which had been established for the cooperative movement. Even before registration, the government suggested that cooperatives might facilitate ujamaa village efforts to market crops:

> It is not, however, necessary for an Ujamaa village to be a registered multipurpose cooperative society before it starts to play a part in, and benefit from the cooperative movement. As a first step, the Ujamaa village *as a whole* may join an existing primary society to market its produce, and in this way will benefit from scale economies—e. g., in transport—that would not be available to individual members. Ujamaa villages will normally go through this stage before registering as cooperatives.[59]

The organizational link between the ujamaa village and the cooperative movement might take one of two primary forms. The villages themselves might become multipurpose cooperatives or they might join with other villages as individual members of a larger cooperative. The latter form was especially appropriate where villages were small and skills were few. Even where several villages became members of a single cooperative there were gradations in the degree of independence each exercised, as illustrated by the case of Iringa Region:

> The first type is where villages are united but each village continues to carry out its economic activities. It is only the major

tasks (e. g., the ordering of fertilizers and the application for loans, etc.) which will be performed by the joint cooperative society. The second type is where the villages unite and all economic activities and other functions are handled by the joint cooperative.[60]

While efforts to assist the creation of new ujamaa villages and facilitate their evolution into cooperative societies were continuing, President Nyerere embarked on a second approach. Existing cooperatives were to be transformed into ujamaa villages. In a visit to Mwanza in 1972 the President called for the well-developed cooperative societies which dealt with cotton marketing to become ujamaa villages.[61] A full year passed, however, before a plan was drawn up to accomplish the task. The importance of Nyerere's action was to indicate clearly to the cooperative movement that the ujamaa village and not the old cooperative society was to be the future form of cooperative activity.

The old cooperative movement, while providing assistance to ujamaa villages, continued to decline. Thefts and corruption appeared to grow worse. In 1974 alone, millions of shillings disappeared from just two unions—Mtwara Regional Cooperative Union and the Nyanza Cooperative Union.[62] The government newspaper commented in late 1974 that

> Thefts and inefficiency within this country's cooperative movement seem to have become so rampant that hardly a day goes by without news of such sad events breaking out. . . . There appears to be some indication that our cooperative movement has fallen victim of bureaucratisation—so much so that those who work in the movement have become a power unto themselves, leaving the owners of the movement . . .—the peasants, isolated and hardly with any possibility to know, let alone to check what goes on in the daily running of their cooperatives. . . . The inspectorate division which is supposed to act as a complementary watch-dog, particularly where accounting is concerned, has lost its teeth.[63]

The Cooperative Union of Tanganyika replied a few days later that the fault was not that of the movement but of the police and courts for failing to stop corruption.[64] Nevertheless, the demise of the cooperative movement and its partial replacement by the ujamaa village was already widely expected, and, as has been noted, this occurred two years later.

2. *Retail Trade.* Efforts by the government during the 1960s to transfer control of most retail trade from private traders to state or cooperative bodies had not been marked by success. With the advent of ujamaa villages, some districts decided to speed the establishment of village shops by banning competition from private shops. In 1974, Dodoma district banned them outside urban areas; Mpwapwa district followed in 1975. In August of the latter year the President, while visiting Kilimanjaro Region, called on ujamaa and cooperative officers to take the lead in mobilizing peasants to start cooperative shops in ujamaa villages. He was reported to have said that "It would be absurd to allow an individual to own a shop in an Ujamaa village because such an act would be tantamount to allowing the peasants who have accepted the ideology of socialism to be exploited freely."[65] Shortly afterwards the district party executive in Liwali district reacted by banning all private businesses.[66] Tukuyu district followed with a more modest move which banned private shops only where village and cooperative shops had been established.[67] This piecemeal approach gave way to a national one early in 1976.

At a rally at Kimamba in Kilosa district on 16 February 1976 the prime minister was reported to have ordered the closure of all private shops in villages by the end of the month as part of Operation Maduka (Operation Shops).[68] The move was not unprecedented, for, as already noted, several districts had acted both before and after Nyerere's statement the previous August. However, the order was another of the major policy decisions which, like Nyerere's call for a 1976 deadline for villagization, appear to have been made almost on the spur of the moment. Kawawa continued to order the closure of private shops in villages in the days that followed his initial announcement.[69] The Lindi regional party executive complied with a resolution banning all privately owned shops in the region,[70] and it sent the regional TANU chairman to Dodoma to learn from the experiences of that district.[71] The Mwanza regional party executive committee also issued an order that all private shops be closed.[72]

The move by the prime minister and the quick response by party leaders prompted a quick "clarification" a couple of days later: the order was intended to be limited to private shops competing with cooperative ones at Kilombero Sugar Company and those in nationally owned farms, estates, plantations, industries, parastatals, and national institutions.[73] Elsewhere the phasing out of privately owned shops would be done step by step. An editorial in the government newspaper cautiously stated that eventually all private shops would have to give way to people's shops, but this could not be done overnight.[74] In addition to these clarifications, an emergency meeting was called by the prime minister to plan implementation of the new directive.[75] The minister of finance was told to establish a committee, coopting officials of the National Bank of Commerce, the Board of Internal Trade, the Tanzania Housing Bank, and the prime minister's office, to submit a plan for implementation in ten days.

The guidelines for implementation of Operation Maduka were issued a few days after the committee reported to the prime minister. Kawawa insisted that the roots of the policy were in decisions made at the national party conference the previous year, which declared:

> To accelerate the pace of socialist revolution in the villages and build a society which will ensure basic ujamaa requirements in land use—public ownership of all the means of production, distribution and exchange—the Party's 17th Biennial Conference resolved that Ujamaa shops must be established in villages and ensure that services such as village produce mills are owned by the villages throughout the country.

> Therefore, the recent Government directive of "OPERATION MADUKA" is a significant step in implementing Party resolutions aimed at advancing the country towards ujamaa.[76]

The caution implicit in the prime minister's clarifications the previous month was explicitly stated in the guidelines:

> In the villages and Ujamaa villages to ensure efficiency and avoid measures that could lead to shortages of goods, the implementation of "Operation Maduka" will be as follows:

> In villages and Ujamaa villages where there are Ujamaa and individual shops, if necessary, Ujamaa shops should be expanded and individual shops should be closed.

> In villages where at present there are no such shops, immediate steps should be taken to establish Ujamaa shops.

> In villages and Ujamaa villages where, at the moment Ujamaa shops have not been established, but where there are privately owned shops, these individual shops should be allowed to continue rendering services while plans are being worked out to establish Ujamaa shops.[77]

A training program of seminars for district ujamaa and cooperative officers and regional commercial officers and assistants was to begin almost immediately in Dar es Salaam. This was to be followed by "a one-month crash training programme" for those who would work in the shops. Many national institutions were ordered to become involved in giving loans for construction, improving roads, getting supplies, transportation, and politicization. Obviously, it was to be a huge undertaking, and this was probably a factor prompting reconsideration of the intention to close all private shops immediately.

The prime minister's office responded to critics of the policy by arguing that previous unhappy experiences with cooperative shops were unlikely to be repeated, for several reasons: first, there would be training for both officers and managers; second, there would be a cooperative shop subcommittee of the finance and planning committee of each village which would meet weekly to discuss the progress of the shops, and two committee members would be assigned to verify records daily; third, a monthly report on the cooperative shop would be presented to the village assembly; fourth, merchandise would be "distributed by Regional Trading Companies to the village cooperative shops and therefore it is hoped that there will be an effective regular supply of goods and suitable price margins will be fixed."[78]

Despite the more temperate policy pronouncements following the initial statements by the prime minister, attacks on private shops and shopkeepers were often virulent. For example, the Shinyanga regional party secretary was reported to have said that "the government will take severe action against individuals who utter slanderous remarks intended to frustrate Operation Maduka."[79] The Mara regional commissioner closed private shops "as their owners were sabotaging the country's economy."[80] Toward the end of May, serious concern had arisen among some government officials about the conduct of the operation. A government newspaper editorial noted:

> To close a private shop does not in any way constitute a step toward socialism. In fact it may constitute a denial of service to the people. . . . Operation Maduka cannot afford to fail. If the People's shops being started through Operation Maduka fail, that will be a terrible demoralizing blow to the people. It will be a setback for socialist development.
>
> Operation Maduka is not a trial and error game. Therefore the People's shops should not be started as if they were a joke, a make-shift or temporary affair. These shops are going to be a permanent feature of our life. Hence the imperative need to start them properly.[81]

This was followed by another editorial directed at party and government leaders:

> Ever since the operation was announced, actions being taken by certain leaders at regional and district levels have given the impression that to them this operation is about the closure of private shops. . . . We are asking the authorities to temper their over-enthusiasm and approach this "Operation Maduka" with the calmness and resolve that it requires. This operation is not a competition to close shops. It is one for the establishment of people's shops.[82]

The President went even further the same day and declared that the closing of shops, without replacing them with village shops, "by leaders, causing suffering to the masses simply because they want publicity on the radio and in newspapers, is aimed at frustrating our socialist policy and not building it."[83] The result was a slowing of the implementation process. By September 1976 it was announced that 2,170 new cooperative and ujamaa shops had been established under Operation Maduka—i. e., about one in every third village. The total number of cooperative and ujamaa shops was 3,110, or about 11 percent of the total number of private shops.[84] Although many problems remain, the commercial activities of most ujamaa villages have been growing.

CONCLUSIONS

Implementation of the "working together" aspect of the ujamaa village policy has not met with the same success as has implementation of the "living together" aspect. Permeating the implementation effort has been some conceptual confusion over the meaning of "working together." On the one hand was the initial view that it meant communal production and the division of whatever was produced; on the other was the view of the villagers that it entailed a wide range of other types of activities. Lack of agreement among implementers and villagers, however, permitted what is generally called a tactical shift of objective from working together at communal farming to working together at other communal activities. This could be done without admitting failure because of the range of activities that still might be pursued within the broad conception given to "working together." In other words, the conceptual fuzziness gave the party and government ways of covering major setbacks in implementation.

Much as the two aspects of the policy were split to permit the use of compulsion for villagization without contradicting the ideological commitment to persuasion, the split in the conception of "working together" appears to permit the use of compulsion. At the seventeenth biennial conference of TANU in 1975 the party's opposition to compulsion for communal farming was restated, but its support for the use of force in other communal activities was implied. With the shift in emphasis to those other activities as the major arena for the achievement of the goal of "working together," the use of compulsion may increase.

All these shifts and redefinitions appear to have been the consequence of the clash between the ideology behind ujamaa villages and the practical problems faced in implementation. The mechanisms and goals appear to shift, thereby modifying the policy, as difficulties in implementation arose. As we have seen, communal farming and fishing failed to expand to make it a significant part of the rural economy. The reaction of party officials and administrators was to seek reform or abandonment of the exercise. In some villages smaller work groups have been introduced and piece-rates have been tried. In others the communal farms have been abandoned for private plots in block farms. The latter trend is widespread. Joseph Angwazi and Benno Ndulu in their study of Rufiji noted that "the way to ujamaa by directly communalizing agricultural production has failed. The level of political consciousness is not high enough to cater for that. I would therefore suggest . . . the indirect way to ujamaa through the 'bega kwa bega' [block farm]."[85] An observer in Kigoma Region noted that in ujamaa villages, "Government's initial objective was that all ujamaa productive activity should be communal; early difficulties with communal agriculture have caused the block farm approach, in which each family is responsible for a particular plot, to be the most likely form of production for the foreseeable future."[86] How long the "foreseeable future" is likely to be depends on many factors, including how successfully the problems are worked out, who wins internal struggles for power, and even the weather. The shift of attention to nonfarming communal activities meant a shift to work that was not as essential to survival. Operation Maduka and Operation Nyumba were undertaken to get people to participate in forming shops and building houses. Rival private shops were closed and poor housing was destroyed. As in the case of villagization, short-term use of force was successful, yet the type of activity it stimulated was not the form of collective work originally stressed in "Socialism and Rural Development." It is evident that the effort to induce people to "work together" is unfinished. Whether the current impasse continues or whether it is overcome will be of considerable interest to much of the rest of Africa and to countries elsewhere in the world.

Chapter VII

AN ASSESSMENT:
IMPLEMENTATION OF THE UJAMAA VILLAGE POLICY

The purpose of this concluding chapter is threefold. First, the material considered in preceding chapters will be summarized. Second, an evaluation of the ujamaa village policy and its implementation will be undertaken. Third, the implications of this policy and its implementation for the general study of policy implementation will be assessed.

SUMMARY

The summary will be organized around the four major divisions of the study. First, the two foci of investigation, their significance and their relationship to other studies, considered in Chapter I, will be reviewed. Second, the environmental factors that conditioned both the policy and its implementation, examined in Chapters II and III, will be summarized. Third, the goals and plans for implementation of the policy, dealt with in Chapter IV, will be recapitulated. Fourth, the actual implementation of the policy, examined in Chapters V and VI, will be briefly summarized.

OBJECTIVES

The primary focus of the preceding chapters—the specific process by which the ujamaa village policy has been implemented in rural Tanzania—is important both in its own right and because of its inductive relation to the general process of policy implementation. Its relevance to peoples of other African countries lies in the fact that they face problems similar to Tanzania's and their needs for models of change are similar. It is valuable to social scientists because of the increasing significance attached to implementation in building general knowledge of the policy process.

The distinction made by several scholars between policy and implementation is useful. The former refers to government's *decision to act* to attain specific ends, whereas the latter refers to government's *action* to achieve those ends. Implementation has much the same meaning as one of the principal conceptions of development: both refer to the process of moving toward goals set by political leaders. The crux of implementation is behavioral change. Among the many concepts used in the vast literature on behavioral change, persuasion, inducement, and compulsion are the most useful in an analysis of how compliance necessary for policy implementation is gained. The utility of each of these three mechanisms ultimately depends on a general assessment by individuals of the costs and benefits that they expect will result from compliance or noncompliance.

SITUATION

The specific context in which the ujamaa village policy arose and was implemented was considered in two parts—one dealing with local history and the other with local conditions. Historical experiences with policies whose objectives were similar to those of the ujamaa village policy, principally to cause people to live and work together, were reviewed in Chapter II. Most important of these were the concentration policy of the colonial period and the village settlement policy of the early years of independence. Both of these policies were successful in causing people to move into villages. Mass recruitment into concentrations required compulsion; selective recruitment into village settlements was accomplished by inducement. Part of the reason for the use of compulsion in the villagization aspect of the ujamaa village policy may have been its success with concentrations, and part of the formal aversion to the use of inducement may have been the demoralization and inaction of those recruited by such means in village settlements. The ujamaa village policy was aimed specifically at overcoming problems that were thought to be associated with the failure of previous efforts to bring about sustained change, such as the lack of democratic control of the village, the lack of politicization to new values, and the continued existence of the private plot as the basis of production. The concentration and village settlement schemes foreshadowed the possibility of successful villagization and the probability of major difficulties in bringing about post-settlement change. Collective work, which was the central objective of the ujamaa village policy after villagization, was the principal objective of various other policies.

205

Although the colonial government condoned the resort to force to move people into concentrations, it formally condemned its use to get people to work together. Nevertheless, while it maintained formal opposition to forced labor, it found various ways to permit it in the form of tax labor, conscript labor, or broadly interpreted "minor communal service." The decision to use force appeared to be pragmatic—i.e., it followed the failure of other mechanisms to cause people to work on tasks the colonial government deemed broadly beneficial. To minimize financial and authority costs, administrative decentralization of responsibility for the use of force to regional, district, and most important, native-authority levels was undertaken. Peasant hesitancy to work together and administrative hesitancy to employ force in ujamaa villages may have been conditioned by the unhappy historical associations.

Not only historical experience but also immediate conditions affected the formulation and implementation of the ujamaa village policy. For example, the fact that most Tanzanians were peasants meant that if the country were to become socialist, the rural population had to be politicized to accept a concept of ujamaa that included more than immediate family members. The fact that migration was traditional meant that if investments for change were to be made efficiently, more permanent settlement was required. Because unoccupied land was available for cultivation, resettlement, if it were desired, might be possible without seizing land already cultivated. The existence of a great variety of ethnic groups in the country meant that if ethnic mixing were sought, villagization might be a means to bring diverse people together. The decline of the non-African population indicated that if opposition from that quarter were to be expected, it probably would be lessening. The stagnation of the agricultural sector demonstrated that if people were to be fed, something had to be done to increase food production. The government's policy of widening control over the economy meant that if full control were to be attained, organizational forms encompassing the peasantry were needed. And the fact that the Tanzanian economy was closely tied to the West meant that if self-reliance were to be achieved, rural production must be restructured. These elements that conditioned the formation of the ujamaa village policy also conditioned its implementation. For example, because of the large proportion of peasants in the total population, the task of gaining their compliance was a major one. The tradition of migration may have facilitated the movement of people into villages, but it also made it more difficult to keep them settled. Conflict in Tanzania's villages was a possibility because of the country's ethnic diversity. Despite the decline of the non-African population, its importance to the economy remained substantial. The stagnation of agriculture increased the danger that even minor disruptions would bring famine. The growing control of the economy by the government added to peasant suspicion of the real intentions behind the creation of ujamaa villages. And attempts to reduce the dependence inherent in the economic links with Western nations might be met by resistance from capitalist countries and their proteges in Tanzania.

Finally, in addition to historical experiences and the socio-economic situation, characteristics of the agents most actively involved—government and party leaders—affected the formulation and implementation of the ujamaa village policy. Adoption of a policy by the party did not inevitably lead to compliance by the peasantry. Most Tanzanians were not members of TANU, and even most of TANU's members were separated from decision-making by the many structural layers and the control maintained by higher party organs over who might hold decision-making positions. This situation did not mean that there was no opposition to the party, but rather that such opposition was controlled. In both theory and fact the role of the party was more significant in the formulation than in the implementation of the ujamaa village policy. Government agents were assigned the main burden of implementation, yet previous experiences did not bode well for success. Popular participation in the decision-making involved in implementation had been limited; representative councils had failed; continuous modification of administrative structures had contributed to a low public awareness of how decisions were made; politico-administrative officers who were supposed to link party and government tended to adopt the style of the latter; functional officers had great difficulty in promoting rural development; and time and again observers attributed problems of implementation to bureaucratization. These factors affected both policy formation and policy implementation.

POLICY

The policy that arose out of these circumstances was primarily the product of President Nyerere. In order to contend with the great variety of conditions found in Tanzania, his vision of goals and the means to attain those goals permitted a wide range of interpretations. The indefiniteness of the *goals* provided administrators with a flexibility that helped in getting people to move into villages, but it caused considerable confusion over what was to be done once the peasants came to live in villages. For a time, the designation "ujamaa village" became virtually meaningless. A degree of uniformity was finally introduced with the enactment of the Villages and Ujamaa Villages Act in mid-1975, but much of the confusion about what an ujamaa village is and what it implies remains. The President's argument in "Socialism and Rural Development" concerning the appropriate *means* to establish ujamaa villages appeared much more definite. Persuasion was to be the only legitimate method of implementation. However, the slow movement of people into ujamaa villages brought new interpretations. First, inducement was made appropriate if it took the form of "aid" to villages already started. Second, "village" was separated from "ujamaa," and compulsion was made appropriate for the former. Thus both the more flexibly stated policy goals and the more rigidly stated policy means were modified for the same purpose—that of facilitating implementation of the policy.

IMPLEMENTATION

Although successful implementation required peasants to live *and* work together, the two facets are analytically distinguishable. The former, examined in Chapter V, involved the phased introduction of persuasion, inducement, and compulsion. The latter, described in Chapter VI, does not appear to have moved past an inducement phase, but because of the many more types of "working together" than of "living together," simplification into phases would be virtually impossible. The reasons it has not moved into a compulsion phase include the following: first, the central government has not been as involved as it was in the effort to get people to live together, and local leaders are not as free of local pressures against the use of force as are central government officials; second, because living together was seen as a prerequisite for working together (but not vice versa), greater costs might be borne to get peasants to live together; third, movement of people into villages required only short-term use of force, whereas getting people to work together required its long-term use. The costs to the government in terms of reduced authority and legitimacy of the former were likely to be much less than those of the latter.

Additional specific factors appear to have prompted the shift to compulsion in nation-wide operations after 1973. Flood in Rufiji, famine in Dodoma, and severe poverty in Kigoma had stimulated local operations well before the President established a deadline for moving. These experiences provided a basis for believing that the addition of force was likely to bring success. Decentralization of administration in 1972 resulted in a stronger central government presence in rural areas that might undertake the application of force and movement of people. Finally, movement into villages had stagnated. When the costs of failing to implement a policy on which the government had staked so much both domestically and internationally were weighed against the possible costs of adding the use of force, compulsion was introduced on a broad scale. It was masked, as described in Chapter IV, by splitting "ujamaa" and "village" so that formally it was applied only to the latter.

Implementation of the working-together aspect was hampered by confusion over the meaning of "ujamaa." By the mid-1970s, few villagers identified it with working together and sharing the proceeds, yet communal production of this sort was envisaged in most policy pronouncements as the principal factor distinguishing a village from an ujamaa village. A detailed analysis of communal agricultural production in four regions for the crop year 1974 indicated that part of the reason for the discrepancies between the policy and the peasant conception of "ujamaa" may be the combination of unpleasant experiences with communal farming and the desire not to oppose what public officials support. The exclusion of communal production from what was considered "ujamaa" was a rational reaction to the two factors. Participation in communal farming is low; it makes a very small contribution to per capita income; it attracts most the peasants it least wanted to attract, and it attracts least those it most wanted to attract; and it is not viewed as a reliable base of food supply, as indicated by limited female participation. With a few exceptions, central government officials are not taking the lead in seeking to get more peasants to participate in communal production. A major reason appears to be fear that it may upset the production of foodstuffs, which during the operations had been insufficient to feed the country's population.

Control of incentives and sanctions that might be used to foster communal production is primarily in the hands of village leaders. For the most part, neither inducement nor compulsion has been used in the past as widely or as effectively as it might have been. Although there is a general trend from communal to block farming, some improved forms of organization and remuneration are being introduced to facilitate increased participation in communal production. Working together at other tasks such as building schools, dispensaries, water supply facilities, and so on has been undertaken in almost every village. In these activities, also, control over most incentives and sanctions is mainly in the hands of village leaders, who appear to wield them more effectively than in the case of communal production. The central government, however, has not remained entirely aloof. Its most important intervention has been to ban private shops and to assist in initiation of communal ones. The use of force to promote the implementation of this aspect of "ujamaa" appears to be the result of the expectation that it would "work." And the principal criterion determining the use of a given mechanism of implementation always appears to be based on pragmatic rather than ideological grounds.

EVALUATION

Tanzania's ujamaa village policy has caused considerable local and international controversy. The Western press has tended to be pessimistic or critical, or both. One observer, Robin Wright, wrote in early 1975 that "Tanzania's socialist experiment, once hailed as the most hopeful in Africa, is in trouble. . . . [The country] now faces failure in its efforts to collectivize a massive but scattered rural population."[1] A similar view was expressed a few months later by Richard Cardinale, who said that the ujamaa village policy had been "a potential model for the developing world" but that "now it is foundering."[2] And Roger Mann reported from Sumbawanga in early 1977 that "Tanzania's widely publicized system of collective *ujamaa* villages is not popular among farmers in this remote and backward southwestern corner of the country."[3] In reaction to such reports, a bitter editorial appeared in the government newspaper, the *Sunday News*:

> The policy of Ujamaa Vijijini has . . . been singled out for vicious attack. Imaginary hardships and sufferings are being conjured up and said to have been caused by the country's rural transformation policy. . . . The aim of all this dirty campaign is to confuse us and plant doubts in the minds of our friends and fellow socialists in Africa and elsewhere so that they begin to have second thoughts about their support for our cause.[4]

Many Western journalists have overstressed the problems faced and underemphasized the successes achieved, thereby depreciating Tanzania's efforts to build a socialist society. Nevertheless, Chapter VI indicated that reports of only very limited progress in the communal production aspect of the policy have a factual basis.

On the tenth anniversary of the formal initiation of the move toward socialism, the President presented a critical analysis of what had transpired in a document entitled "The Arusha Declaration: Ten Years After."[5] He summarized his assessment of experiences in the following terms:

> In 1956 I was asked how long it would take Tanganyika to become independent. I thought 10 to 12 years. We became independent 6 years later! In 1967 a group of the Youth who were marching in support of the Arusha Declaration asked me how long it would take Tanzania to become socialist. I thought 30 years. I was wrong again: I am now sure that it will take us much longer!

Nevertheless, he asserted that the foundation on which to build a socialist society, rather than a capitalist one, had been laid. He suggested the temporary difficulties that were being experienced might be understood through an analogy that likened constructing such a foundation to getting a vaccination:

> We are like a man who does not get smallpox because he has got himself vaccinated. His arm is sore and he feels sick for a while; if he has never seen what smallpox does to people he may feel very unhappy during that period, and wish that he had never agreed to the vaccination.

He declared that the effort to get peasants to live together was a "tremendous achievement . . . of TANU and Government leaders in cooperation with the people of Tanzania." Village life was "proving itself to be beneficial and popular." Yet Tanzanians, he said, did not appreciate the extent of their success:

> We have become defensive about the villagisation exercise because there were widely publicized cases of maladministration, and even of mistreatment of people. Some few leaders did act without thinking, and without any consultation with the people who had to move. Therefore we did have cases of people being required to move from an area of permanent water to an area which is permanently dry. We had other cases where the new villages were made too large for the amount of land available. And there were cases where people were rounded up without notice, and dumped on the village site, without time to prepare shelter for themselves.

In reality, Nyerere contended, such experiences were not typical of the operations. He felt that villagization had laid "the foundation for a permanent improvement in people's lives." Nyerere offered virtually no evaluation of the other aspect of the ujamaa village policy—that of getting people to work together. Such avoidance of the subject suggests possible embarrassment in regard to its progress and probable desire to deemphasize its significance. This interpretation is supported by his emphasis on providing compensation for those whose property had been taken in villagization, rather than on the encouragement of further strides toward communal farming. It is supported also by reports of statements of Prime Minister Sokoine, who told a Kivukoni College audience in mid-1977 that "each village will be left to develop at its own pace on the path to socialism."[6] Obviously, the lull is not complete, for some activities such as Operation Maduka, described in Chapter VI, continued to be pursued. Nevertheless, the fervor of implementation activity reached in villagization has clearly dissipated.

Neither the assessment of Western correspondents nor that of President Nyerere claimed that the policy had been either completely successful or unsuccessful. Within a decade of its launching, over 13,500,000 peasants had moved into, or come to identify themselves with, more than 7,300 villages.[7] In other words, about 90 percent of the rural population had complied with at least one of the two major objectives of the policy. Although considerably less than a third of the villages have any communal farming or fishing and well under 2.5 percent of the GDP from agriculture is derived from such production, joint work has produced many new schools, dispensaries, and water supply facilities. Even where successes were achieved, however, they were not gained without difficulty. Explanations for the fact that peasants did not invariably comply with the demands of the ujamaa village policy have been the subject of considerable thought and review. They may be grouped into three categories. The first includes those that attribute the difficulties to weaknesses of, or flaws in, the groups involved. The second consists of those that trace the problems to the approaches used by implementers. And the third embraces those that ascribe slow progress to various virtually uncontrollable factors.

GROUPS INVOLVED

Each of the major groups involved in implementation has been attacked for thwarting the rapid achievement of the goals of ujamaa. The bases of the criticisms can be summarized as follows:

*1. Government officials: The charge that bureaucratic domina-
tion of implementation hindered implementation.* Many observers
have contended that reliance on the party/state bureaucracy to the
extent that occurred distorted initial objectives and undermined
long-run success. Their arguments take two principal forms. On the
one hand, the interests of the bureaucracy are said to be threatened
by the establishment of ujamaa villages; as a result, bureaucrats
subvert or do not seriously attempt to implement the policy. On
the other, bureaucratic style, methods, or modus operandi are said
to be detrimental to the successful implementation of the policy;
as a result, bureaucrats inadvertently block rapid implementation.
The two viewpoints are often merged in attacks on government
officials, although they rest on quite different assumptions.

An important critic, Issa Shivji, has stated that a central problem was "bureaucratic (as opposed to democratic) and technocratic
(as opposed to political) methods in implementing the programme."[8]
A.C. Coulson, after a review of the many failures of bureaucratic
transformation of rural areas, suggests that alternatives are necessary.[9] P.L. Raikes has written of the "bureaucratic distortion of
ujamaa into villagization." He amplified this by asserting that "The
ujamaa policy was changed to conform more closely with the pre-
conceptions and interests of the bureaucratic bourgeoisie who
controlled its implementation. . . . Large numbers of democratically
controlled ujamaa villages would pose a real threat to their status."[10] Ralph Ibbott commented bitterly on the bureaucratic take-
over of the Ruvumu Development Association in 1969 by remarking,
similarly, that such interests were basically opposed to those of the
settlers because of the competition for dominance that might develop as a result of self-reliant village democracies. He contended also
that the modus operandi of the bureaucracy was detrimental to
the sound long-term development of ujamaa villages:

> Time and again we have come up against this idea that the bigger
> the number of settlements and the more the number of people
> in them the greater the development. As a result of this Area and
> Regional Commissioners generally believe that their performance
> in their positions will be judged by the number of "villages" they
> found. This fact is responsible for so much force being used by
> these officials in order to drive people into settlements.[11]

In each case, bureaucratic interests or style, or both, are said to have hindered implementation. To what extent are such arguments valid?

Two claims are being made: (1) that government officials dominate implementation and (2) that they have hindered implementation because of their interests or style of operation, or both. There is little disagreement over the first claim. The growth of de facto government power in the state and the tendency for joint party/ government positions to become less political and more governmental were described in Chapter III. In fact, the party has assigned to the government formal responsibility for implementation of policies and for the application of force to that end. The implicit claim by critics that this role has been usurped by the government from the party to the detriment of implementation efforts is, therefore, misleading. There is more disagreement over the second claim. Because government officials were given the dominant role in implementation, they were automatically assigned responsibility for successes and failures. In a technical sense, then, they may be blamed for implementation problems. However, the data are ambiguous. For example, if their modus operandi was detrimental to implementation, one might expect that the more significant their role, the more significant the difficulties. Yet such a proposition is not borne out in the case of ujamaa villages. Government officials were more involved in villagization than in communal agriculture, and success was greater in the former than in the latter. Likewise, if their interests were not likely to be served by implementation, one might expect resistance. Many observers, such as Raikes, did not see bureaucratic interests served by villagization, although they saw that party/government officials worked hard to get peasants into villages. Certainly problems did arise with what is called bureaucratic domination of the implementation process. Nevertheless, the implication by critics that alternative agents would have led to greater success assumes abilities of such agents that do not correspond to Tanzanian realities. The decision to rely more heavily on the bureaucracy was, in Nyerere's view, a necessity because other agents were unable to accomplish the task.

2. *Party leaders: The charge that the absence of political socialization hindered implementation.* One of the major tasks assigned to the party in the ujamaa village effort was that of getting peasants to accept the values implied by the policy. In many areas this was not accomplished. Several observers argued that the need to add inducement and compulsion to persuasion arose because politiciza-

tion had not been sufficient to gain compliance. J. Angwazi and B. Ndulu, commenting on Rufiji, stated that the "greatest problem of Ujamaa is the absence of political consciousness all the way from village leaders to the villagers."[12] J. Rald, referring to Bukoba, observed that "the most important problem today is to make the people in the Ujamaa villages understand that all land, individual plots as well as Ujamaa plots, belong to the people in the village."[13] Cliffe suggested that implementation "will . . . depend on developing some socialist consciousness among the rural population."[14] Lack of politicization has been cited as the reason for compliance problems with regard to both aspects of the policy.

The change of values involved in politicization is most commonly thought to derive from persuasion, but it may also follow behavior initiated by compulsion and inducement. Whether the latter two mechanisms will be employed appears related to the certainty of decision-makers that the action so induced/compelled will politicize those complying so that they accept such behavior as valuable. President Nyerere appears to have been much more certain that life in villages would be valued by peasants once they were brought together than he was that communal cultivation would be valued. Consequently, he did not try to induce or force behavioral change in the latter, but he did in the former. Ideally, however, politicization was expected to follow from persuasion. Why was its success so limited?

John Nellis suggests that persuasion using "rhetoric and symbolism" has not worked in Tanzania because of the absence of four necessary characteristics:

> (1) a considerable amount of cultural unity; (2) an aura of national solidarity stemming from a recent history of violence or war; (3) a powerful and penetrative organizational-administrative mechanism or mechanisms arising from the same source; and (4) a dedicated political leadership, sufficiently capable and sufficiently ruthless to use the organizational-administrative mechanism to force on society at large their vision of a desirable future state.[15]

The villagization operations indicated that organizational mechanisms and political leadership were more in evidence in the early 1970s than they had been in the late 1960s. Perhaps that accounts for what has already been suggested is an increase in the effectiveness of persuasion during the operations. Political socialization requires credibility. TANU leaders who claimed they would seize power from the British gained great credibility with independence in 1961. When an improvement of life did not follow during the 1960s as rapidly as was expected by the peasantry, the credibility of political leaders declined. A parallel situation arose in the villages. Communal agriculture did not lead to the good life. The credibility of those political leaders who encouraged it declined, and a high value was not attached to participation in communal agriculture. Disillusionment was probably greater for the more marginal because their very survival was threatened. Political socialization is not independent of experience. Had communal agriculture "worked," it probably would have been valued.

3. *Village leaders: The charge that lack of leadership skills hindered implementation.* Delays in furthering collective work often have been attributed to village leadership by both the bureaucracy and the peasants. The situation is much like that of Chinese cadres who were caught at various times between the pressures from above and below. The view from above is illustrated by a regional ujamaa and cooperative officer in Mwanza who ascribed problems with ujamaa villages to "poor leadership which often stagnates development" and observed that "it was difficult to correct elected leaders."[16] The view from below is illustrated by several cases in Dodoma Region.[17] At Mlali ujamaa village in 1975, villagers complained that the chairman used village funds for various projects without informing them, thereby creating suspicions that theft was occurring. At Sagara ujamaa village, members believed that their shop had gone bankrupt because the chairman had stolen from it and that the communal farm had not prospered partly because the chairman had failed to participate. Such complaints were common in all regions studied by the author. Many criticisms seemed exaggerated, however, and many concerned actions or inaction over which village leaders have little control.

The pressures from above and below on village leadership are enhanced by a tendency in Tanzania, encouraged by President Nyerere, to demand considerable sacrifice on the part of leaders. Individuals can be lured into leadership positions by various incentives. Leaders get to travel to meetings, attend seminars, and control much of the outside assistance that enters the village, but almost none receives any direct compensation for his leadership work. Moreover, the benefits have not been sufficient to attract peasants to leadership positions in many of the new villages. As a result, several villages have not yet established governing structures.[18] The village leader has been given the extremely difficult task of convincing peasants that participation in communal agriculture will be beneficial. He has little in the way of outside incentives to apply, compulsion is frowned upon by villagers and the central government, and previous experiences generally have not convinced peasants that life would be improved by such work. Even the most skillful village leader would have difficulty in achieving the policy objectives.

4. Peasants: The charge that peasant ignorance has hindered implementation. Many administrators involved with implementation of the ujamaa village policy account for the problems by reference to peasant "faults." Peasants are said to be lazy, ignorant, superstitious, devious, and conservative. Such characteristics, it is contended, hinder efforts to gain their compliance with policy directives. Often the criticisms are means of avoiding charges of administrative responsibility for implementation delays or difficulties. As Coulson observed: "When peasants will not do what the staff think they ought to do the staff react by calling the peasants lazy."[19] Many, including the President, have attacked those who blame the peasants for implementation problems. Despite the fact that party ideology holds the peasant in high esteem, the criticism continues. Certain customs and values, however, have interfered with ready peasant compliance. For example, Jonathan Barker notes that communal production undermines the family head's direct control of family labor and can be a base for some women's economic independence.[20] It would be rational, therefore, for the family head to resist full compliance. Even more important is the peasants' need for an adequate food supply. Experiences with communal agriculture generally were bad. It was not rational for the peasants to devote much time to such work if the possible result was hunger. Often what may seem an irrational peasant response is, in fact, a rational one.

APPROACHES USED

A number of critics have suggested that the problems with establishing ujamaa villages stemmed not so much from the characteristics of the groups assigned a role in implementation as from the particular approaches they adopted. Among such criticisms are the absence of class struggle, poor use of incentives, faulty policy formation, and poor implementation planning.

1. Absence of class struggle. Several observers have suggested that limited differentiation or lack of awareness of significant differentiation, or both, hindered the development of peasant-controlled ujamaa villages. Shivji attributes many problems of implementation to the "complete lack of any analysis of the differentiation among the peasantry in the area concerned and which sections can be potentially mobilized to effect the programme and which sections are likely to oppose it."[21] Consequently, he asserts, "ujamaa does not come to the exploited as a process of political struggle in which they themselves are involved but as something imposed from above."[22] Lack of awareness of differentiation after villages are established poses, according to Cliffe, "the danger of better-off peasants acquiring a dominating political position in these supposedly self-governing communities and distorting the ujamaa aim by, for instance, stopping short at villagisation without cooperative production, or arranging the sharing of the proceeds to their own benefit."[23]

The view that class struggle is a requisite of implementation is derived principally from the experiences of the USSR and, to a lesser extent, China, yet those two countries differ significantly from Tanzania. Differentiation, for instance, is much less in Tanzania, where a landlord class is virtually nonexistent. In fact, the President has maintained from the time the policy was initiated that the objective of ujamaa villages was not to overthrow an established rich peasant or landlord class, but to stop one from forming. On most issues affecting rural areas, the interests of the richer peasants parallel those of the poorer ones. Although an effort was made to characterize Mwamwindi's killing of Klerruu—recounted in Chapter VI—as indicative of kulak resistance to ujamaa, it was largely ineffectual because of the facts of the case and the absence of similar conditions in many other parts of the country. Finally, as noted in Chapter VI, an attack on the more wealthy peasants would have been an attack on the more active participants in communal agriculture—an action more likely to hinder implementation than to help it. Conditions in Tanzania, therefore, were such that it was virtually impossible to make class struggle an effective tool of implementation.

2. *Use of ineffective systems of organization and remuneration.* Critics attacking the failure to employ class struggle in implementation were addressing themselves primarily to villagization; those attacking the poor use of systems of internal organization and distribution of income were addressing themselves, of course, to the

effort to get people to work together. In fact, a significant obstacle to full participation in communal work has been the disincentives associated with the system of organization and remuneration. Hyden has observed that "the system of regulating and assessing work has usually been rudimentary with emphasis only on attendance."[24] Payment for attendance is an incentive to attend, but productive labor does not necessarily follow. Sometimes hundreds of people turned out to work at an assigned task. Such organization makes it very easy to "slack off" and perform little work. As noted in Chapter VI, much of the product of communal work is not distributed to those who work to produce it, but is kept for the use of village leaders or for village projects. In effect, a tax is being levied against those who participate in communal activity, but not against those who do not participate. The net result of the most generally used systems of remuneration, organization, and distribution has been to discourage participation. Even those who valued the communal farm for the contribution it made to collective goods for the village must have been discouraged by the small yield realized through their efforts. Although changes that tie the return more closely to work have been instituted in many villages, the systems employed in most villages in the mid-1970s were not conducive to hard work.

3. *Flawed policy.* Many observers contend that the problems of implementation were a consequence of faults in the policy. Such criticisms come from both the "right" and the "left." On the one hand are those, especially Western-influenced scholars, who insist that communal production is inefficient and therefore unlikely to prosper. Barker uses the term "production liberals" to refer to those "skeptical of the effectiveness of communal or collective production in agriculture."[25] Because it would not prosper, they argue, rational peasants would reject it and a rational government would not persist in seeking to institute it. On the other hand are those, especially non-Western-influenced scholars, who insist that failure to deal with the relations between ujamaa villages and national and international conditions seriously jeopardizes the possibility of full implementation. Both Shivji and Mapolu have contended that unless neocolonial ties are broken, all the ujamaa villages would do would be to link the peasants more closely with the exploitative international system.[26] They hold, moreover, that without a concomitant industrial strategy, little significant advance could be made in the agricultural sector.[27] Both the "right" and the "left" criticism of the ujamaa village policy targeted not so much on

the goal of villagization as on that of post-settlement efforts. The critics questioned the possibility that the policy objectives would be achieved.

The "left" criticism denies the possibility of the success of communal production so long as Tanzania remains linked with the world capitalist economy. It amounts to a call to opt out of the system. Tanzania's policy toward trade and aid has always been based on two pragmatic considerations: (1) sources should be diversified, and (2) the best terms possible should be obtained. The imbalance of both trade and aid connections in favor of the non-Communist, rather than the Communist, world is chiefly a result of the application of these principles. It is questionable whether the abandonment of such principles would benefit either Tanzania or the peasantry. A necessary contradiction between communal production and participation in the world economy is not apparent. Furthermore, the general isolation of the peasantry from that economy has not in the past brought significant prosperity to Tanzanian peasants. The "right" criticism denies the possibility of communal production whether or not Tanzania remains linked with the world capitalist economy. The fact that there have been cases in China, in the Soviet Union, in Mexico, and elsewhere of successful communal agriculture suggests that the enterprise is not intrinsically faulty. That the basic assertions of the two criticisms of the policy seem unreasonable does not deny the validity of associated arguments. Continued contact with the West may sustain individualistic values and retard the movement toward self-reliance, both of which may slow the acceptance of ujamaa. Communal agriculture in many countries is on the decline, suggesting that it is a difficult enterprise to undertake. The policy, however, does not by itself forbid its implementation.

4. *Poor planning for implementation.* Rather than place the blame on the plans of policymakers, some critics place it on the plans of policy implementers. Such criticism has been raised persistently. It charges failure to locate villages near water supplies, to limit or expand the size of villages to a reasonable level, to provide sufficient land for cultivation nearby, to complete the movement of peasants in time for planting, to provide cattle-grazing areas, to order and distribute fertilizer and insecticide at the proper time, to purchase crops at designated places, and so on. Had planning for implementation been better, those critics argue, disenchantment would have been less and compliance would have been greater. Yet,

as has been noted, despite errors in planning, villagization was accomplished. It appears possible, by the addition of sanctions or incentives, to offset costs imposed on the peasants as a result of poor planning for implementation. The same may eventually occur in communal agriculture. As villagization indicates, implementation may become more costly, but it need not be blocked.

UNCONTROLLABLE FACTORS

One of the factors most frequently mentioned in explaining the shift away from communal agriculture is related neither to the groups involved nor to the approaches adopted: it is drought. Yet its relationship to the ujamaa village effort is controversial. Party/ government officials have said that the huge imports of food in 1974 and 1975 were prompted by low rainfall. Critics lay the blame on the ujamaa village policy. Although a thorough empirical analysis of the issue has not been undertaken, available evidence suggests that both drought and policy contributed to the problem.

On the one hand, villagization sometimes meant that people were moved after the start of the planting season, that cleared land was abandoned, that some crops were left untended as a result of the operations, and that, as a consequence of the move, many new tasks were demanded of the villagers that took time away from agriculture. In addition, no neighboring country unaffected by villagization had an agricultural problem of the magnitude of Tanzania's, suggesting that villagization was a contributory factor.

On the other hand, rainfall in parts of the country was low; hence crop yields were meager. The combination of villagization and the drought had considerably reduced food supplies. Communal farming, however, probably contributed only marginally to the problem, for in few villages did it ever occupy the major portion of many villagers' time. It was nevertheless affected by the food shortages. Because avoiding a recurrence of the problem became of central importance to the party/government, it tended to shift emphasis to the most secure form of production—the individual plot. Thus a deemphasis on communal agriculture was partly a response to the food crisis of 1974/75.

There were other effects as well. For example, the country became more dependent on support from abroad, including that from countries which did not consider communal production worthy of major investment. Although charges that donors directly hindered implementation of the policy are probably false, indirect influence may have contributed to the lull described earlier in this chapter.[28] Several other factors not easily controlled by the government affected the time and wealth that might be devoted to implementation, including the oil price rise, continued friction with Uganda, commercial problems with Kenya, and moves for the liberation of southern Africa. Obviously, Tanzania was not free of external constraints that hindered implementation.

None of the explanations considered in the foregoing pages is without merit. The ujamaa village policy and its implementation are like the elephant described by the blind men. The image of the man who touched only the tail was quite different from that of the man who touched only the leg. The whole creature, or the whole implementation process, is the sum of diverse parts. The view of the implementation of the ujamaa village policy provided by this study, however, suggests that these explanations are not of equal utility in accounting for success and failure.

The goals of the ujamaa village policy were not and are not impossible to attain. "Living together" has been achieved; "working together" has been realized in part. The policy is a flexible one that may require a step back now and then, but its complete abandonment is unlikely. The real power of the party has been overstressed in much of the literature. The assumption that it could politically socialize such a diverse population in such a short time without clear material proof that the ujamaa village policy would significantly better peasant life was unrealistic. Likewise, the assumption that the interests of government officials and the peasants were diametrically opposed in the ujamaa village policy is unrealistic. Class lines and class interests in Tanzania are not as sharp or as distinct on such issues as many contend. Using class struggle as a means of implementing the policy was unnecessary for villagization and appears inapplicable for communal production in most areas. A material base of significant differentiation and significant exploitation is not present in Tanzania to the degree necessary for it to be effective. Drought has been used as an excuse both for exonerating ujamaa villages from responsibility for the sudden fall in agricultural production and for shifting emphasis in ujamaa villages toward private production. In neither case was it as unimportant or as important a factor as claimed. It was used both to facilitate and to retard implementation. Peasant "ignorance" has not been a crucial element. In most cases, peasant resistance to moving into villages was either a bargaining technique to extract more assistance from the government in return for compliance or an indication that real problems would probably result from compliance, such as inadequate water supplies at the village site.

One of the major difficulties in implementing the policy was the frequent failure of party/government officials to analyze sufficiently the nature of peasant assessment of costs and benefits to be derived from compliance. The efficient use of any compliance technique is intimately related to peasant evaluation of costs and benefits. Such a failure is reflected most conspicuously in the remunerative systems for participation in communal agriculture, which discourage rather than encourage work. The net result is a peasantry unconvinced about the benefits of further compliance.

IMPLICATIONS

Several features of the ujamaa village effort may have more general relevance to the field of policy implementation, and several experiences of other countries may have specific relevance to the future of the ujamaa village policy. The former include the following:

1. LEADERSHIP

The more limited popular participation is in policymaking and implementing decisions which require widespread compliance, the more extensive the impact of a few top leaders on the course of the policy's implementation. Not only did President Nyerere formulate the ujamaa village policy in "Socialism and Rural Development," but he also profoundly affected its implementation. His decision while on tour in November 1973 to set 1976 as the deadline for getting people to move into villages had a greater impact on implementation than any action before or since. Prime Minister Kawawa's decision in February 1976, also while on tour, to push for the implementation of Operation Maduka led to immediate activity. Despite the obvious importance of such decisions, the President has criticized the manner in which they appear to have been made: " 'Platform policy-making' is not the answer to our problems. The people must be fully involved in drawing up policies. They must always be made to understand the need and the purpose of a particular public decision; and they must be involved in its implementation."[29] In essence he asserts that an inverse relationship exists between the extent of "platform policy-making" and participation, and he implies that participation is a requisite of implementation.

Experience with the ujamaa village policy indicates that numerous problems arise when the President's warning is ignored.

2. RESPONSIBILITY

The higher the peasant cost/benefit ratio for compliance with policy demands, the greater the effort of implementers to dissociate themselves from the means used or objectives sought. Responsibility for implementing policies during the colonial period which involved the use of force, as noted in Chapter II, was decentralized first to the provinces and districts and then to the native authorities, partly to avoid peasant animosity toward the British administration. The situation was more complex in the case of the ujamaa village policy. When the President set the deadline for movement in late 1973, he did not say that force should be used, but left the matter to regional and district officials. In several parts of the country, however, these officials dissociated themselves from the policy and told the peasants that it was the President's idea or the party's idea. The fact that the President received twice as many "No" votes in the 1975 election as he had in the 1970 election (he still received over 90 percent "Yes") has been interpreted as indicative of animosity aroused by the operations. Studies of the 1975 elections made in various districts indicated that some incumbent MPs had sought to stay away from their districts during the operations because they feared voter retribution. The need for force indicated a high peasant cost/benefit ratio for compliance. Consequent efforts by some administrators to dissociate themselves from the policy indicated a sensitivity to at least some elements of the peasantry.

3. POLICY ALTERATIONS

Changes in the means by which a policy is implemented are more likely to be a consequence of modifications in policy interpretation than of changes in policy substance. There appears to be a belief, at least in Tanzania, that the legitimacy of a government is related to the consistency of its policies. At the same time there seems to be a belief that the legitimacy of a government is related to its ability to implement its policies. When the two principles clash, new policy interpretations conducive to effective implementation are usually the result. For example, the President's decision at the 1972 NEC meeting to separate "ujamaa" from "village," retaining the notion of persuasion for the former but permitting compulsion for the latter, has been referred to earlier. The President's distinction at the biennial conference in 1975 between agricultural and nonagricultural activities in ujamaa villages has also been pointed out. Force, he suggested, was still inappropriate for the former, but not necessarily for the latter. The forcible closure of private shops suggests that the distinction is being acted upon. When pragmatism clashes with ideology, the former wins if the latter can be retained through some form of rationalization or reinterpretation.

4. IMPLEMENTATION

A. Compliance mechanisms are introduced by stages until the policy end is attained or discarded, starting with persuasion, moving to inducement, and culminating with compulsion. The addition by stages of new techniques to get people to move into villages was described in Chapter V. Although geographical variations existed, persuasion was important from 1967, inducement from 1969, and compulsion from 1973. The immediate reason for the addition of a new technique was the slackening of recruitment into ujamaa villages, and in fact a rise in membership did follow the application of the new method. The decision concerning whether or when to "up the ante" appears to have depended on whether the costs or benefits (or both) of lost momentum in implementation were greater or less than those likely to be involved in adding the new mechanism. There was certainly no need to move through all three to get compliance from some peasants, but with others it was necessary. Obviously, if compliance could be elicited through persuasion, the government would not want to bear the additional costs to authority or to the treasury of using inducement or compulsion. The order of introduction indicates the government's perception of the relative costs implied. In the case of communal agriculture, the central government made a decision to hold implementation temporarily at the compliance level of persuasion. Some villages, however, are attempting to proceed with inducement and compulsion.

B. The smaller the resources available for implementation, the farther down the "chain of action" leading to the goal sought will incentives be applied. The term "chain of action" is used to refer to a set of activities that are interconnected so that performance of one leads to performance of another, and so on. When large resources are available, governments simply pay people to do what they want done. When such resources are severely limited, however, instead of applying the incentive directly to gain the desired end, they must apply a smaller one to an action that might lead to an action that could be expected to bring about the result desired. For example, instead of providing food, they might supply seeds or fruit trees. Most resources to facilitate implementation of the ujamaa village policy were "stretched" in this way. The indirect application of incentives requires an awareness of the connections among actions and peasant assessments of costs and benefits to be derived from them. Considerable skill therefore is involved in effectively applying incentives to induce compliance.

5. RESISTANCE

As compliance mechanisms move from persuasion to compulsion, resistance forms move from frontal to adaptive. In some areas, the direct or frontal resistance of peasants to living in ujamaa villages was broken by the addition of compulsion, but this did not mean the end of resistance to the goals of ujamaa villages. Clashes occurred in many places between villagers who had entered because they believed in seeking such goals and those who had joined because they were forced to do so. The former felt that the latter were diluting and destroying the ideals of ujamaa. In other areas, as Raikes pointed out, "far-sighted rich farmers have learned that they can turn ujamaa to their own advantage."[30] This adaptive resistance has made progress of the villages toward the general goals of ujamaa more difficult than did frontal resistance because it operates within, rather than outside, the village. That is, opposition to the general principles of ujamaa was not necessarily eliminated by membership in the villages but may have been merely transformed.

The Tanzanian experience with the ujamaa village differed in some important respects from the Soviet experience with the kolkhozy and the Chinese experience with the commune.[31] The prominent role played by the "dekulakization" campaign in the Soviet effort had no equivalent in Tanzania. The level of compulsion involved in Soviet collectivization was much higher than that in Tanzania. The famine associated with collectivization in the Soviet Union led to starvation, whereas in Tanzania it resulted in massive food imports. The strong rural cadres in China had no parallel in Tanzania, and the great Chinese irrigation systems that necessitated some cooperative work had no equivalents in Tanzania. Neither China nor the Soviet Union was as dependent on Western countries as was Tanzania. Tanzania's rural population, moreover, was only a tiny fraction of that of the Soviet Union or China.

Although the situations are by no means identical, greater resemblance exists between Tanzanian experiences with the ujamaa village and Mexican experiences with the *ejido*. When President Echeverria of Mexico visited Tanzania in 1975 he pointed out the similarity between the two.[32] The Mexican experience, however, preceded that in Tanzania by about thirty years. When Cardenas came to power in 1934, the area granted to ejido communities greatly expanded, and many ejido grants previously worked individually began to be worked cooperatively.[33] With the end of the Cardenas administration in 1940, government encouragement of the efforts lapsed. Then, during the early 1940s, the land in most collective ejidos was divided into individual parcels for private cultivation.[34] Discontent with collective production involved complaints similar to those heard in Tanzania. According to Raymond Wilkie, "The principal factor favoring decollectivization was the absence, under the collective system, of an adequate system of rewards for ability and effort. Many ejidatarios felt that they were not being paid enough for their efforts, and that others were being paid too much in comparison."[35] Since the early 1940s, government attention and assistance has turned to private, rather than collective, farming. Nevertheless, formal opposition to collective ejidos is not voiced. Wilkie observed that "politicians and government officials who oppose the collective ejidos seldom do so openly or directly. Rather, they count on the slow decline of the ejidos through a combination of inefficiency, graft, and governmental indifference."[36]

Whether the move toward communal production will suffer the same fate in Tanzania as it did in Mexico will probably be determined by the interests of those who hold political power. Although there has been a shift from concern with communal production in Tanzania which has parallels with a similar shift that occurred in Mexico in the early 1940s, it is not certain that the result will be similar. The influence of the private sector is much less, counterweights to the dominance of capitalist countries are present, and the ujamaa ideology may have penetrated more deeply than was the case in Mexico. Consequently, Tanzania's political leadership may not be so ready to abandon the effort.

Appendix 1

SELECTION AND MEMBERSHIP OF TANU ORGANS
(POST-1973)

Cell:
    All TANU members in ten-house unit
    By   all members: Cell leader

Sub-branch conference:
    All members of sub-branch

Sub-branch executive committee:
    By   sub-branch conference: Ten delegates, chairman, secretary
    By   sub-branch chairman: Up to four delegates

Branch conference:
    By   branch conference: Branch chairman, district conference delegates in branch
    By   electorate: Councillors
    By   cell: All rural cell leaders
    By   virtue of membership: All TANU members if branch is urban, industry-based, or an ujamaa village
    By   sections of party: One representative from women's section, elders' section, and TANU Youth League (TYL)
    By   Central Committee: Branch secretary
    All branch and sub-branch executive committee members not included above

Branch executive committee:
    By   branch conference: Branch chairman, six delegates, annual district conference delegates
    By   sections of party: One representative from women's section, elders' section, and TYL
    By   Central Committee: Branch secretary

District conference:
    By   district conference: District chairman, three regional executive committee members, five delegates to regional conference
    By   branch conference: Three delegates from each rural branch, branch chairman
    By   cells: All urban ten-cell leaders
    By   electorate: Councillors and MPs resident in district
    By   National Assembly: E. A. legislative assembly members in district
    By   President: Area commissioner
    By   District Chairman: Up to four delegates to the district working committee

By Central Committee: Branch secretary
By sections of party: One representative from women's section, elders' section, and TYL
By affiliated organizations: One representative from each
All district executive committee members and non-elected MPs resident in district not included above

District executive committee:
By district conference: District chairman and ten delegates
By electorate: MPs resident in district
By National Assembly: E. A. legislative assembly members in district
By branch conference: Branch chairman
By Central Committee: Branch secretary
By President: Area commissioner
By district chairman: Up to four delegates to district working committee
By sections of party: One representative from women's section, elders' section, and TYL
By affiliated organizations: One representative from each
All regional executive committee members and non-elected MPs resident in district

District working committee:
By district conference: District chairman and ten delegates to the district executive committee
By regional conference: Three regional executive committee delegates
By President: Area commissioner
By district chairman: Up to four delegates

Regional conference:
By regional conference: Regional chairman
By district conference: Five delegates from each district, district chairmen
By National Conference: Any NEC member resident in region
By branch conference: Branch chairmen and eight delegates from each branch
By President: Regional and area commissioners
By regional chairman: Up to four delegates chosen for the regional working committee
By Central Committee: Branch secretaries
By sections of party: One representative from women's section, elders' section, and TYL
By affiliated organizations: One representative from each

Regional executive committee:
By regional conference: Three delegates from each district, regional chairmen
By President: Regional and area commissioners
By National Conference: Any NEC member resident in region
By electorate: MPs resident in district
By district conference: District chairmen
By regional chairman: Up to four delegates chosen for the regional working committee
By sections of party: One representative from women's section, elders' section, and TYL

By   affiliated organizations: One representative from each
By   National Assembly: E. A. legislative assembly members in district

Regional working committee:
By   regional conference: Five delegates from each district elected to the regional executive committee, regional chairman
By   National Conference: Central Committee delegate
By   President: Regional commissioner
By   regional chairman: Up to four delegates

National Conference:
By   National Conference: President, vice-president, and NEC members
By   President: Area commissioners, not more than five persons chosen for the Central Committee
By   regional conference: Regional chairmen
By   district conference: District chairmen, ten delegates
By   TANU Youth League: Eighteen delegates
By   electorate: MPs
By   affiliated organizations: One representative from each
All NEC members and MPs not included above

National Executive Committee:
By   National Conference: One person from each region chosen for the Central Committee, President, and vice-president
By   President: Not more than five persons chosen for the Central Committee, regional commissioners
By   regional conference: Regional chairmen
By   TYL: Two delegates
By   virtue of office: Secretary-generals of NUTA, CUT, TAPA and UWT, attorney general, principal secretary to the President
By   affiliated organizations: One representative from each

Central Committee:
By   National Conference: President, vice-president, and one person from each region
By   President: Not more than five persons

Sources: Derived from TANU, *Katiba ya TANU,* 1973, with some revisions; *Daily News* (Dar es Salaam), 30 September 1975, p. 1.

Appendix 2

VILLAGE LEADER QUESTIONNAIRE

Village: Date:

Name and Position of Leader:

Name of Interviewer:

1. Kijiji hiki kilianzishwa lini? (*When was this village established?*)

2. Familia ngapi zinaishi hapa mwaka huu? (*How many families live here this year?*)

   Familia ngapi ziliishi hapa mwaka jana? (*How many families lived here last year?*)

3. Wanakijiji wameshiriki katika kazi za aina gani? (*What communal activities have villagers engaged in?*)

Kazi za Kijiji (*Village work*)	Mwaka (*Year*)	Kazi za Kijiji	Mwaka	Kazi za Kijiji	Mwaka
_____	_____	_____	_____	_____	_____
_____	_____	_____	_____	_____	_____

4. Mmekua na shamba la bega kwa bega? (*Have you had a block farm?*)

   Mwaka Jana? (*Last year?*)

   Mwaka Huu? (*This year?*)

   Kama ndiyo, eneo gani limelimwa na wanakijiji katika mashamba ya bega kwa bega? (*If yes, how much area has been farmed by the villagers in block farms?*)

Zao (*Crop*)	Mwaka Jana (*Last year*) Ekari (*Acres*)	Hekta (*Hectares*)	Mwaka Huu (*This year*) Ekari	Hekta
_____	_____	_____	_____	_____
_____	_____	_____	_____	_____

5. Mmekua na shamba la kijamaa? (*Have you had a communal farm?*)

Mwaka Jana? (*Last year?*)

Mwaka Huu? (*This year?*)

Kama ndiyo, eneo gani limelimwa na wanakijiji katika shamba la kijamaa? (*If yes, how much area has been farmed by the villagers in communal farms?*)

Zao (*Crop*)	Mwaka Jana (*Last year*)		Mwaka Huu (*This year*)	
	Ekari (*Acres*)	Hekta (*Hectares*)	Ekari	Hekta
――――	――――	――――	――――	――――
――――	――――	――――	――――	――――

6. Eneo gani limelimwa na wanakijiji *licha* ya mashamba ya kijamaa *na* bega kwa bega? (*How much area has been farmed by the villagers outside the communal and block farms?*)

Zao (*Crop*)	Mwaka Jana (*Last year*)		Mwaka Huu (*This year*)	
	Ekari (*Acres*)	Hekta (*Hectares*)	Ekari	Hekta
――――	――――	――――	――――	――――
――――	――――	――――	――――	――――

7. Tofauti kati ya mashamba ya kijamaa na mashamba ya bega kwa bega ni zipi? (*What are the differences between communal farms and block farms?*)

8. Kuna kazi yo yote katika mashamba ya bega kwa bega inavyofanywa kijamaa? (*Is any of the work in block farms done on a communal basis?*)

Kama ndiyo, ipi? (*If yes, what work?*)

9. Mazao gani yamelimwa kwenye mashamba ya kijamaa?[*] (*What has been produced on the communal farm?*)

Zao (*Crop*)	Mwaka Jana (*Last year*)		Mwaka Huu (*This year*)	
	Thamani (*Value*)	Kiasi (*Amount*)	Thamani	Kiasi
――――	――――	――――	――――	――――
――――	――――	――――	――――	――――

[*]Tunatumia maneno "shamba la kijamaa" kumaanisha aina ya shamba ambako wanakijiji ushiriki kwa pamoja katika kazi za shamba hilo na ugawanya kwa pamoja mazao au fedha zipatikanazo kutokana na shamba hilo. (*We are using the expression "communal farm" to refer to the farm where villagers work together and then distribute whatever is produced among themselves.*)

10. Umeridhika kiasi gani kutokana na kushiriki kwa wanakijiji katika shamba la kijamaa? (*How satisfied have you been with the degree of participation by the villagers in the communal farm?*)

	Mwaka Jana (*Last year*)	Mwaka Huu (*This year*)
(a) Sana (*Very satisfied*)	————	————
(b) Kiasi (*Satisfied*)	————	————
(c) Sikuridhika (*Not satisfied*)	————	————

11. Njia gani ulizoona zinafaa zaidi kwa kuwafanya watu washiriki katika shamba la ujamaa? (*What methods have you found for getting people to participate in the communal farm?*)

12. Unaweka kumbukumbu ya kazi inayofanywa na kila mwanakijiji katika shamba la kijamaa? (*Do you keep a record of the work done by individual villagers on the communal farm?*)

Kama ndiyo, (*If so,*)

(a) Nani anayeweka kumbukumbu hiyo? (*Who normally keeps the record?*)

(b) Yule anayeweka kumbukumbu huandika jina la yule aliyefana kazi au jina mkubwa wa familia? (*Does the recorder usually write the name of the person who actually works, or the name of the head of the household from which the person comes?*)

(c) Yule anayeweka kumbukumbu huandika shambani au badaye? (*When does the recorder record participation?*)

(d) Kumbukumbu hiyo inakuwa na vipimo vifuatavyo? (*Does this record contain measures for the following?*)

   (i) Saa zilizofanywa kazi? (*The hours worked?*)

   (ii) Siku zilizofanywa kazi? (*The days worked?*) Kama ndiyo, kazi ya siku moja ni kazi ya saa ngapi? (*If yes, how many hours are included in a day's work?*)

   (iii) Bidii kiasi gani? (*The effort put into the work?*)

   (iv) Aina ya kazi inayofanywa? (*The kind of work done?*)

13. Kuna msaada wowote kutoka nje uliotolewa kwa kijiji? (*Has any outside help been provided to the village?*)

Kama ndiyo, msaada ya aina gani? (*If so, what kind of help?*)

Aina Gani (*Type of help*)	Kutoka Wapi (*Source*)	Thamani (*Value of help*)	Mwaka (*Year provided*)
————	————	————	————
————	————	————	————

14. Namna gani maazimio yanafanywa kuhusu ugawanyaji wa mazao yana-yotokana na kazi za ujamaa? (*How are decisions made on the way the product of collective production will be distributed?*)

15. Mgawanyo wa mapato ya kijiji kwa wanakijiji unafuata misingi ipi? (*On what basis was the amount to be received by each villager determined?*)

16. Kila mwanakijiji alipata kiasi gani? (*What was returned to each villager?*)

	Mwaka Jana (*Last year*)	Mwaka Juzi (*Year before last*)
Zao (*Crop*)	————	————
Fedha (*Money*)	————	————

17. Wanakijiji walipata kiasi chao lini? (*When did the villagers get their share?*)

18. Kile kiasi ambacho hakikungawanywa kilitumikaje? (*What was done with that proportion which was not returned to participants?*)

VILLAGER QUESTIONNAIRE

Village: Date:

Name of Participant:

Relation to Head of Household:

Name of Interviewer:

1. Una umri gani? (*How old are you?*)

2. Umepata kwenda shule? (*Have you ever attended school?*)

   Kama ndiyo, (*If yes,*)

   (a) Shule ya aina gani? (*What kind of school?*)

   (b) Ulisoma kwa muda wa miaka mingapi? (*For how many years did you attend?*)

3. Una watoto? (*Do you have some children?*)

   Kama ndiyo, (*If yes,*)

   (a) Una watoto wangapi? (*How many children do you have?*)

   (b) Una watoto wanaokwenda shule? (*Are any in school?*)

   Kama ndiyo, kila mmoja amefika darasa gani? (*If yes, up to what level has each studied?*)

4. Lugha yako ya kwanza ni ipi? (*What is your first language?*)

5. Ni mazao gani mawili makubwa unayolima? (*What are the two most important crops you raise?*)

6. Unayo kazi nyingine zaidi ya ile ya shambani wako? (*Do you have any other work besides that on your shamba?*)

   Kama ndiyo, ni kazi gani? (*If yes, what is it?*)

7. Kuna tofauti kati ya mashamba ya kijamaa na mashamba ya bega kwa bega? (*Is there a difference between communal farms and block farms?*)

   Kama kuwa, tofauti ni zipi? (*If yes, what is the difference?*)

8. Unapenda kufanya kazi katika shamba la kijamaa?* (*Do you like to work on the communal farms?*)

   Kwa nini? (*Why?*)

9. Umepata nini kutokana na kazi yako katika shamba la kijamaa? (*What did you get in return for your work on the communal farm?*)

10. Unaelewa nini kutokana neno "Ujamaa"? (*What do you understand the word "Ujamaa" to mean?*)

11. Kwa nini ulijiunga na kijiji hiki? (*Why did you join this village?*)

12. Unafikiri ni nini kinachoweza kukufanya ushiriki zaidi katika kazi ya shamba la kijamaa? (*What would make you want to participate more in communal work?*)

13. Kama ungaliishi maisha mazuri sana, unayofikiria yangekuwa maisha namna gani? (*If you were to live a very good life, what do you think that life would be like?*)

14. Hapa kuna picha ya ngazi. Tuseme juu ya ngazi hiyo ni maisha yako mazuri sana, na chini ya ngazi ni maisha mabaya sana. (*Here is a picture of a ladder. Let me say that the top of the ladder is your very good life, while the bottom of the ladder is your very poor life.*)

    (a) Uko mahali gani katika ngazi hiyo wakati huu? (*Where are you on the ladder now?*)

    (b) Katika miaka mitano iliyopita ulikuwa mahali gani katika ngazi hiyo? (*Five years ago, where were you on the ladder?*)

    (c) Unafikiri utakuwa wapi kwenye ngazi hiyo katika miaka mitano ijayo? (*In five years, where do you expect to be on the ladder?*)

*Tunatumia maneno "shamba la kijamaa" kumaanisha aina ya shamba ambako wanakijiji ushiriki kwa pamoja katika kazi za shamba hilo na ugawanya kwa pamoja mazao au fadha zipatikanazo kutokana na shamba hilo. (*We are using the expression "communal farm" to refer to the farm where villagers work together and then distribute whatever is produced among themselves.*)

15. Ni nini hasa ambacho TANU na Serikali ingefanya ili kuwasaidia wanavijiji wa sehemu hii? (*What could TANU and the Government do which would most help the villagers in this area?*)

Asante sana! (*Thank you very much!*)

SURVEY AND SURVEY ANALYSIS

Sample

A random sample of villages with communal farming/fishing was selected for each of the four regions. A comparison of regional samples is given below.

COMPARISON OF REGIONAL SAMPLES

	Total Number of Villages Identified by District Leaders	Number of Villages with Com- munal Farming in 1974 Identified by District Leaders	Number of Villages Said to Have Com- munal Farming in 1974 Studied	Percent of Villages Said to Have Com- munal Farming in 1974 Studied	Percent of Villages Said to Have Com- munal Farming in 1974 Which Actually Did	Corrected Number of Villages with Com- munal Farming in 1974
Dodoma	391	152	20	13%	95%	144
Iringa[a]	263	160	23	14	86	138
Kigoma	196	18	10	56	78	14
Kilimanjaro	18	12	9	75	83	10

[a]In Iringa only Mufindi and Iringa districts were studied: Njombe was not, because of government restrictions on noncitizens (even those with research clearance) entering the district.

Participation lists were sought in each village from which a random sample of approximately twenty villagers was selected. In many villages, participation lists for the 1973/74 crop year were lacking or incomplete. Complete records were available in only about half the villages. Where possible, partial lists, leader estimates, or 1972/73 crop year village lists were used. The latter were used for three villages in Dodoma Region and six villages in Iringa Region.

The interviews were carried out by the following persons who were students at the University of Dar es Salaam in 1975 when the study was made: J. Sakumba (Kigoma), J. H. Haule, L. Gambi, and B. J. C. Sanyagi (Iringa), H. J. Kivina and A. M. Mughwira (Dodoma), and E. D. A. Mrindoko (Pare district of Kilimanjaro). Nd. Maganya (Kigoma) and E. Marandu (Kilimanjaro) also worked on the project.

Analysis

1. *Villager participation rates.* The quartile division of participants on the basis of the number of days worked on communal production was made separately for each village. The lowest quartiles in all the villages were combined to produce the sample of less active participants, and the highest quartiles in all the villages were combined to produce the sample of more active participants. The rule followed for exclusion/inclusion was as follows:

> If the top of the lowest quartile or the bottom of the highest quartile fell among villagers with the same level of participation, then all such participants were included if such inclusion did not boost the percent within the quartile by an amount above 25 percent greater than its exclusion would have reduced the percent within the quartile below 25 percent.

A division based on Z scores was produced, but because of the skewed distribution of Z scores it produced significantly greater differences in the number of participants included in the top and the bottom quartile. Therefore it was not used.

2. *Village participation rates.* Village participation rates are based on a rank ordering of villages according to the average number of days participated by the sample of villagers. The villages in the top half are considered the more active participant villages; the bottom half are considered the less active participant villages.

NOTES

Chapter I

1. A comparison of such policies is contained in the author's "The Ujamaa Village in Tanzania: A Comparison with Chinese, Soviet and Mexican Experiences in Collectivization," *Comparative Studies in Society and History* 18, 3 (July 1976): 347-70.

2. Press Release (PR) A/323/73, 7 February 1973; *Daily News* (Dar es Salaam), 20 May 1975, p. 5; *ibid.*, 3 November 1972, p. 5; *Nationalist* (Dar es Salaam), 2 April 1971, p. 1; PR C/3134/73, 24 November 1973; *Daily News* (Dar es Salaam), 10 July 1972, p. 1; PR A/1643/73, 5 July 1973; *ibid.*, A/1036/73, 8 May 1973; *ibid.*, A/1074/73, 11 May 1973; *ibid.*, A/1654/73, 6 July 1973; *ibid.*, C/3309/73, 14 December 1973; *ibid.*, C/2483/73, 21 September 1973; *idem*; *Daily News* (Dar es Salaam), 3 July 1972, p. 5; *ibid.*, 24 June 1972, p. 1 respectively.

3. *Daily News* (Dar es Salaam), 10 July 1972, p. 1.

4. *Ibid.*, 9 February 1973, p. 5.

5. *Ibid.*, 2 July 1974, p. 1.

6. *Ibid.*, 24 June 1972, p. 1.

7. *Ibid.*, 16 August 1973, p. 1.

8. Jeffrey L. Pressman and Aaron Wildavsky, *Implementation* (Berkeley: University of California Press, 1973), p. 166.

9. Donald Van Meter and Carl Van Horn, "The Policy Implementation Process," *Administration and Society* 6, 4 (February 1975): 449.

10. Thomas Smith, "The Policy Implementation Process," *Policy Sciences* 4 (1973): 197.

11. Erwin C. Hargrove, *The Missing Link: The Study of the Implementation of Social Policy* (Washington, D. C.: The Urban Institute, 1975), p. 117.

12. Walter Williams, "Implementation Analysis and Assessment," *Policy Analysis* 1 (1975): 531.

13. Smith, "Policy Implementation Process," p. 197, and Van Meter and Van Horn, "Policy Implementation Process," p. 450.

14. Tanzania, *Quarterly Statistical Bulletin* 26, 1 (June 1975): sec. 1.

15. Nikos Georgulas, "Settlement Patterns and Rural Development in Tanganyika," *Occasional Paper No. 29*, Program of Eastern African Studies, Syracuse University, May 1967, p. 28.

16. Soren Jensen and Jumanne Mkama (compilers), *District Data* (Dar es Salaam: Ministry of Economic Affairs and Development Planning, 1968), p. 77.

17. Calculated from data in Tanzania, *Statistical Abstract*, 1966 and 1970 (Dar es Salaam: Government Printer, 1968 and 1972), pp. 144-45 and 165 respectively.

18. Calculated from *ibid.*, pp. 24 and 143 (1966) and pp. 44 and 165 (1970).

19. *Ibid.*

20. Jensen and Mkama (compilers), *District Data*: Kilimanjaro, p. 28; Shinyanga, p. 59; Arusha, p. 4; Kasulu, p. 24; Kibondo, p. 24; Sumbawanga, p. 37.

21. For example, Julius Nyerere, "Socialism and Rural Development," in Julius Nyerere, *Freedom and Socialism* (Dar es Salaam: Oxford University Press, 1968), p. 342.

22. Tanzania, *Statistical Abstract*, 1970, p. 195.

23. Calculated from Bertil Egero and Roushidi Henin, "Distribution by Sex and Age," in *The Population of Tanzania*, eds. Egero and Henin (Dar es Salaam: Bureau of Resource and Land Use Planning and Bureau of Statistics, 1973), p. 206, and Tanzania, *Statistical Abstract*, 1970, p. 200.

24. Calculated from Tanzania, *Statistical Abstract*, 1970, p. 144.

25. Cranford Pratt, *The Critical Phase in Tanzania, 1945-1968* (Cambridge: Cambridge University Press, 1976), p. 257; James Finucane, *Rural Development and Bureaucracy in Tanzania* (Uppsala: Scandinavian Institute of African Studies, 1974), p. 173; Julius Nyerere, "Decentralization," in Julius Nyerere, *Freedom and Development* (Dar es Salaam: Oxford University Press, 1973), p. 344.

26. Nyerere, *Freedom and Socialism*, pp. 231-50.

27. In Lucian Pye's *Aspects of Political Development* (Boston: Little, Brown and Co., 1966), pp. 31-48, he reviews at least fifteen meanings given to the concept of political development.

28. Lucian Pye, "Introduction: Political Culture and Political Development," in *Political Culture and Political Development*, eds. Lucian Pye and Sidney Verba (Princeton: Princeton University Press, 1965), p. 19; other non-choice-oriented definitions include Daniel Lerner, "Modernization," in *International Encyclopedia of the Social Sciences*, vol. 10, ed. David L. Sills (New York: Macmillan and Free Press, 1969), pp. 386-87, and Samuel Huntington, "The Change to Change," *Comparative Politics* 3, 3 (April 1971): 288.

29. Inayatullah, "Toward a Non-Western Model of Development," in *Communication and Change in the Developing Countries*, eds. Daniel Lerner and Wilbur Schramm (Honolulu: East-West Center Press, 1967), pp. 100-101.

30. J. J. Nettl, "Strategies in the Study of Political Development," in *Politics and Change in Developing Countries*, ed. Colin Leys (London: Cambridge University Press, 1969), p. 17; other choice-oriented definitions include Inayatullah, "Non-Western Model of Development," pp. 98-102.

31. This is implicit, for example, in Tanzania, *Second Five-Year Plan for Economic and Social Development*, 1st July, 1969—30th June, 1974, Vol. 1 (Dar es Salaam: Government Printer, 1969), p. x.

32. Yehezkel Dror, *Public Policymaking Reexamined* (San Francisco: Chandler Publishing Company, 1968), p. 12.

33. Theodore Lowi, "Decision Making vs. Policy Making: Toward an Antidote for Technocracy," *Public Administration Review* 30, 3 (May/June 1970): p. 317; Charles E. Lindblom, *The Policy-Making Process* (Englewood Cliffs: Prentice-Hall, 1968).

34. Lowe, p. 315.

35. Vernon Van Dyke, "Process and Policy as Focal Concepts in Political Research," in *Political Science and Public Policy*, ed. Austin Ranney (Chicago: Markham Publishing Co., 1968), p. 27.

36. Ira Sharkansky, "The Political Scientist and Policy Analysis," in *Policy Analysis in Political Science*, ed. Sharkansky (Chicago: Markham Publishing Co., 1970), p. 1.

37. Lewis A. Froman, Jr., "Public Policy," in *International Encyclopedia of the Social Sciences*, Vol. 13, p. 204.

38. The utility of cost/benefit analysis is argued by Harold S. Luft in "Benefit-Cost Analysis and Public Policy Implementation: From Normative to Positive Analysis," *Public Policy* 24, 4 (Fall 1976): 437-62.

39. Van Meter and Van Horn, "Policy Implementation Process," p. 459, support this proposition, citing Neal Gross et al., *Implementing Organizational Innovations* (New York: Basic Books, 1971), pp. 24-29, in confirmation.

Chapter II

1. H. Fairbairn, "The Agricultural Problem Posed by Sleeping Sickness Settlements," *East African Agricultural Journal* 9 (1943-44): 17.

2. *Ibid.*, and George Maclean, "The Relationship Between Economic Development and Rhodesian Sleeping Sickness in Tanganyika Territory," *Annals of Tropical Medicine and Parasitology* 23 (1929): 41.

3. F.I.C. Apted, "Sleeping Sickness in Tanganyika, Past, Present and Future," *Transactions of the Royal Society of Tropical Medicine and Hygiene* 56 (1962): 16.

4. *Ibid.*

5. C.F.M. Swynnerton to Chief Secretary, 17 March 1924; TNA: 2702, Vol. 2.

6. A journalist's account of the scheme may be found in Alan Wood, *The Groundnut Affair* (London: The Bodley Head, 1950).

7. Tanganyika Agricultural Corporation, *Report and Accounts for 1957-58* (Dar es Salaam: Government Printer, 1957), p. xii.

8. International Bank for Reconstruction and Development (IBRD), *The Economic Development of Tanganyika* (Baltimore: Johns Hopkins Press, 1961), p. 131.

9. Benjamin Kaplan, *New Settlement and Agricultural Developments in Tanganyika* (Jerusalem: State of Israel, Ministry of Foreign Affairs, Department for International Cooperation, August 1961).

10. Julius K. Nyerere, "President's Inaugural Address," in Nyerere, *Freedom and Unity* (Dar es Salaam: Oxford University Press, 1966), p. 184.

11. E. Yalan, *Report on the Creation of an Organizational Framework for the Villagisation of Tanganyika* (Jerusalem: State of Israel, Ministry of Foreign Affairs, Department for International Cooperation, April 1963), p. 11.

12. Tanganyika, *Rural Settlement Planning* (Dar es Salaam: Rural Settlement Commission, Vice President's Office, n.d. [1964?]), p. 1.

13. Sleeping Sickness Officer (Fairbairn) to DVS, 28 December 1942; TNA: 31351.

14. H. Fairbairn, "Resettlement of the Population as a Medical and Social Measure in the Development of Tanganyika Territory," Memorandum No. 5, June 1943; TNA: 31731.

15. H. Fairbairn, "Resettlement of Population as a Preventive Measure Against Sleeping Sickness: The Development and Reorientation of This Policy," forwarded to Governor via letter 17 September 1943; TNA: 31731.

16. Minute to J.E.S. Lamb, 6 November 1943; TNA: 31731.

17. To Director of Medical Services from Acting Chief Secretary, 3 January 1944; TNA: 31731.

18. To Chief Secretary from PC, Southern Province, Lindi (J. Rooke Johnson), 3 May 1945, "Closer Settlement" (mimeo); TNA: 31351.

19. Minute copied from TNA: 34273, DAS from FAM, 25 January 1946; TNA: 31351.

20. Minutes, August-September 1947; TNA: 31351.

21. Minute to SAA and CS from FAM, 7 July 1948; TNA: 31351.

22. Minute to SAA and CS, 20 August 1948; TNA: 31351.

23. IBRD, *Economic Development*, p. 131; Kaplan, *New Settlement*, p. 15.

24. Tanzania, Ministry of Lands, Settlement, and Water Development, *The Rural Settlement Commission, A Report on the Village Settlement Programme from the Inception of the Rural Settlement Commission to 31st December, 1965* (Dar es Salaam, 1966), pp. 6-7.

25. United Republic of Tanganyika and Zanzibar, *Tanganyika Five-Year Plan for Economic and Social Development, 1st July, 1964-30th June, 1969, Vol. 1, General Analysis* (Dar es Salaam: Government Printer, 1964), p. 33.

26. Fairbairn, "The Agricultural Problems," pp. 18-19.

27. Tanzania, Ministry of Lands, Settlement, and Water Development, *The Rural Settlement Commission*, p. 49.

28. Nikolaus Newiger, "Village Settlement Schemes, The Problem of Cooperative Farming," in *Smallholder Farming and Smallholder Development in Tanzania*, ed. Hans Ruthenberg (Munich: Weltforum Verlag, 1968), pp. 258-59.

29. Tanzania, Ministry of Lands, Settlement, and Water Development, *The Rural Settlement Commission*, p. 40.

30. P.M. Landell-Mills, "Village Settlement in Tanzania, An Economic Commentary," University of Dar es Salaam, Economics Seminar 1965/66, Paper No. 2 (9 November 1965) [mimeo], p. 5.

31. John R. Nellis, "Transformation and Village Settlement: From Abstraction to Reality," Syracuse University, Village Settlement Project, Paper 23 (August 1965), pp. 6-7.

32. Chief Secretary from Director of Game Preservation (Swynnerton), 5 July 1927; TNA: 2702, Vol. 2.

33. To Chief Secretary from PC, Central Province, 2 February 1928; TNA: 11771.

34. To Chief Secretary from PC, Tabora, 21 February 1928; TNA: 11771.

35. To Acting Director of Game Preservation from Chief Secretary, 17 May 1928; TNA: 11771.

36. Circular No. 40, 1934; TNA: 22494.

37. *Ibid.*

38. To Sleeping Sickness Officer, Tabora, from Surveyor (Macquarie), Uyowa, 20 July 1937; TNA: 63/934.

39. A.O. Ellman, "Agricultural Improvements through Cooperative Farming in Tanzania: A Brief Outline," University of Dar es Salaam, Economic Research Bureau Paper 69.23, p. 3.

40. Newiger, "Village Settlement Schemes," p. 261.

41. Ellman, "Agricultural Improvements," p. 3; John R. Nellis, *A Theory of Ideology: The Tanzanian Example* (Nairobi: Oxford University Press, 1972), pp. 125-26, makes the same point.

42. *Ibid.*, p. 128.

43. Fairbairn, "The Agricultural Problems," p. 24.

44. Ellman, "Agricultural Improvements," p. 2.

45. Garry Thomas, "Division of Crop Proceeds, Upper Kitete Village Settlement 1965/66," Syracuse University, Village Settlement Project, Report 37 (28 February 1966), pp. 1-2.

46. Landell-Mills, "Village Settlement," p. 4.

47. Tanzania, Ministry of Lands, Settlement, and Water Development, *The Rural Settlement Commission*, p. 43.

48. *Ibid.*, p. 6.

49. *Ibid.*, p. 44.

50. Calculated from chart included in letter to Director of Medical Services from Sleeping Sickness Officer (Fairbairn), 14 November 1945 (TNA: 11771, Vol. 2), by multiplying by 3.3 the number of taxpayers given; and Tanzania, Ministry of Lands, Settlement, and Water Development, *The Rural Settlement Commission*, p. 10, respectively.

51. Samuel S. Mushi, "Modernization by Traditionalization: Ujamaa Principles Revisited," *Taamuli* 1, 2 (March 1971): 22.

52. Margaret Digby, *Agricultural Cooperation in the Commonwealth* (Oxford: Blackwell, 1951), p. 148.

53. F.G. Sayers, Acting Chief Secretary, to Secretary of Federated Chambers of Commerce Section, Indian Association, 24 June 1935; TNA: 22181.

54. Minutes on a report by W.K.H. Campbell entitled "Report on a Visit to Tanganyika" by the Registrar of Cooperative Societies, 31 August 1944; TNA: 33017.

55. J. Gus Liebenow, *Colonial Rule and Political Development in Tanzania: The Case of the Makonde* (Nairobi: East African Publishing House, 1971), p. 157.

56. Goran Hyden, "The Politics of Cooperatives in Tanzania," in *Cooperatives in Tanzania: Problems of Organisation*, ed. Hyden (Dar es Salaam: Tanzania Publishing House, 1976), p. 11.

57. B.T.G. Chidzero, *Tanganyika and International Trusteeship* (London: Oxford University Press, 1961), Appendix A, pp. 257-62, contains the mandate document.

58. To Chief Secretary from PC, Dodoma, 16 October 1936; TNA: 21181, Vol. 2.

59. To Chief Secretary from PC, Southern Highlands Province, 4 October 1938; TNA: 21181, Vol. 2.

60. Minute to PAS (LG) from ACs (SS), 11 November 1950; TNA: 10953.

61. To Chief Secretary from Ag. PC, Northern Province (Mitchell), 26 July 1927; TNA: 10953.

62. Typed copy of government reply to H.R. Ruggles-Brise, MC, question in Legislative Council, 9 January 1931; TNA: 13235.

63. Minute by Governor Cameron, 29 May 1930; TNA: 13235.

64. To J.E.S. Lamb, Secretariat, Dar es Salaam, from W.S. Marchant, Secretariat, Nairobi, 19 October 1945; TNA: 34003.

65. To W.S. Marchant, Secretariat, Nairobi, from J.E.S. Lamb, Secretariat, Dar es Salaam, 10 November 1945; TNA: 34003.

66. Note on round-table discussion held at Secretariat, 20 August 1942, with Chief Secretary, Administrative Secretary, Director of Agriculture, Labour Commissioner, Director of Manpower, PCs Central and Northern Provinces, and Assistant Director of Public Works; TNA: 256/1/63.

67. Churchill to Byatt, 27 August 1921; TNA: 3299.

68. Cable, Secretary of State to Governor, 5 May 1922; TNA: 3299.

69. Cameron to Secretary of State, 5 April 1929; TNA: 13235.

70. "Memorandum on Tax Labour," probably prepared in February 1932 [typescript]; TNA: 13804. (Emphasis added.)

71. Memorandum No. 54 for Executive Council, 11 April 1951; TNA: 26377, Vol. 2.

72. To Chief Secretary from Director of Game Preservation (Swynnerton), Kilosa, 4 February 1928; TNA: 10953.

73. Colonial Office, *Labour Conditions in East Africa* (London: His Majesty's Stationery Office, 1946), p. 42.

74. Chief Secretary to PC, Northern Province, 6 May 1932; TNA: 19461.

75. Orde Brown to Chief Secretary, 18 January 1929; TNA: 10672.

76. To Chief Secretary from Director of Game Preservation (Swynnerton), Kilosa, 4 February 1928; TNA: 10953.

77. Minute to Chief Secretary, 8 March 1928; TNA: 10953.

78. To Chief Secretary from Ag. PC, Lindi Province, 18 December 1935; TNA: 13435, Vol. 2.

79. *Ibid.*

80. Typed notes on choosing thirty-day tribal labour, 1956; TNA: 256/A2/33.

81. To all Jumbes, 21 March 1956, from DC, Kondoa; TNA: 256/A2/33.

82. Extract from Napier-Bax's personal letter to Swynnerton, 20 November 1932; TNA: 11883.

83. Minute by Cameron, 11 September 1926; TNA: 2702, Vol. 3.

84. Minute to D.C.S. from G.F.S., 23 April 1927; TNA: 2702, Vol. 4.

85. To PCs, Tabora, Mwanza, Central Provinces, from Acting Chief Secretary (Sayers), 18 April 1929; TNA: 13435.

86. Tanganyika, Government Circular No. 16 of 1938.

87. Tanganyika, Circular No. 25 of 1925; TNA: 7777.

88. Liebenow, *Colonial Rule*, figure 5 between pp. 146 and 147.

89. Fairbairn, "Resettlement of the Population as a Medical and Social Measure."

90. Appended to Director of Medical Services to Chief Secretary, 12 June 1946; TNA: 11771, Vol. 2.

91. Translation of report dated 15 July 1970 by Freiherr von Rechenberg, Governor of German East Africa, to Colonial Office, Berlin, on Explanatory Memorandum (Denkschrifft) relating to the Rebellion of 1906; TNA: 11601.

92. Tanganyika, *Report on Administration of Tanganyika Territory for 1927* (London: His Majesty's Stationery Office, 1931), pp. 78-79.

93. Minute by SNA, 3 February 1928; TNA: 10953.

94. Minute to H.C.S., 23 July 1930; TNA: 19094.

95. To DC, Kondoa, from Acting PC, Central Province, 23 September 1955; TNA: 256/A2/30.

96. Cameron, Confidential letter on "Native Administration," 16 July 1925; TNA: 7777.

97. *Ibid.*

98. Acting PC, Central Province, to Secretary of Labour Board, n.d.; TNA: 10953.

99. Tanganyika Territory, *Native Administration Memorandum, No. 1, Principles of Native Administration and Their Application* (Dar es Salaam: Government Printer, 1930), pp. 38-39.

100. Tanganyika, *Local Government Memoranda, No. 1*, Part 1 (Dar es Salaam: Government Printer, 1954), pp. 43-50.

101. To Chief Secretary from PC, Mwanza, 15 June 1928; TNA: 11883.

102. Typed proposals for call-up of thirty-day tribal turnout labour in Kondoa, 1956, signed by DO, Kondoa, 2 October 1955; TNA: 256/A2/33.

103. To officer in charge of police, Moshi, from DC, Kondoa, 11 April 1956; TNA: 265/A2/33.

104. To member for local government from PC, Lindi Province, 13 October 1952; TNA: 10953.

105. Hans Ruthenberg, *Agricultural Development in Tanganyika* (Berlin: Springer-Verlag, 1964), p. 61.

Chapter III

1. Chinmoy Koley, "Agricultural Data," in *The Population of Tanzania*, Census Vol. 6, eds. Bertil Egero and Roushdi Henin (Dar es Salaam: BRALUP and Bureau of Statistics, 1973), p. 151.

2. *Ibid.*, p. 155.

3. *Idem.*

4. John Sender, "Some Preliminary Notes on the Political Economy of Rural Development in Tanzania Based on a Case-Study in the Western Usambaras" (Economic Research Bureau paper 74.5, University of Dar es Salaam, May 1974), p. 6.

5. Manuel Gottlieb, "The Extent and Character of Differentiation in Tanzania Agriculture and Rural Society, 1967-1969" (University of East Africa Social Science Conference, Nairobi, 18-23 December 1972).

6. Issa G. Shivji, *Class Struggles in Tanzania* (Dar es Salaam: Tanzania Publishing House, 1975), p. 51.

7. Henry Mapolu, "The Social and Economic Organization of Ujamaa Villages" (Department of Sociology, University of Dar es Salaam, September 1973; mimeo), p. 35.

8. Tanganyika, *Report on the Native Census, 1921* (Dar es Salaam: Government Printer, 1921), table III, pp. 11 and 12; Tanganyika, *Census of the Native Population, 1931* (Dar es Salaam: Government Printer, 1932), pp. 23 and 25; Stephen Lucus and Gerard Philippson, "Ethnic Characteristics," in *The Population of Tanzania*, eds. Egero and Henin, pp. 160-61.

9. The annual rate of growth in the population of Dar es Salaam between 1967 and 1977 was estimated to have been 7.8 percent (*Weekly Review* [Nairobi], 13 March 1978, p. 6).

10. *Daily News* (Dar es Salaam), 8 February 1973, p. 4, and *Weekly Review*, 27 February 1976, p. 5, respectively.

11. *The Standard* (Dar es Salaam), 16 December 1970, p. 1.

12. *Sunday News* (Dar es Salaam), 10 August 1975, p. 1.

13. *Ibid.*, 25 January 1976, p. 6.

14. Tanganyika, *African Census Report, 1957* (Dar es Salaam: Government Printer, 1963), p. 1, and Tanzania, *Statistical Abstract, 1970* (Dar es Salaam: Government Printer, 1972), p. 44.

15. *Ibid.*

16. Calculated from Tanganyika, *Report on the Census of the Non-Native Population Taken on the Night of 25th February, 1948* (Dar es Salaam: Government Printer, 1953), table X, p. 11; Tanganyika, *African Census Report, 1957*, p. 1; and Tanzania, *Statistical Abstract, 1970*, p. 44.

17. John Moore, "Population Distribution and Density," in *The Population of Tanzania*, eds. Egero and Henin, p. 55.

18. *The Population of Tanzania*, eds. Egero and Henin, appendix 3.1, p. 255.

19. Moore, "Population Density," p. 41.

20. Tanzania, *Statistical Abstract, 1970*, table A3, p. 3.

21. R. W. James and G. M. Fimbo, *Customary Land Law of Tanzania* (Nairobi: East African Literature Bureau, 1973), pp. 27 and 28.

22. *Ibid.*, p. 35.

23. R. C. Northcote, *A Memorandum on Native Land Tenure* (Dar es Salaam: Government Printer, 1945), pp. 3 and 5.

24. James and Fimbo, *Customary Land Law*, p. 69.

25. *Ibid.*, pp. 365-66.

26. Tanzania, *National Accounts of Tanzania, 1964-1972* (Dar es Salaam: Bureau of Statistics, February 1974), table 21, p. 30.

27. Among the works on East Africa dealing with this question are Colin Leys, *Underdevelopment in Kenya* (London: Heinemann, 1975); Issa Shivji, *Class Struggles in Tanzania* (New York: Monthly Review Press, 1976), esp. pp. 158-78; and for the colonial period, E. A. Brett, *Colonialism and Underdevelopment in East Africa* (London: Heinemann, 1973).

28. *Daily News* (Dar es Salaam), 8 October 1975, p. 4.

29. TANU, *Taarifa ya Ofisi Kuu Kuhusu Hali na Kazi za Chama*, April 1969.

30. P. Msekwa, "Towards Party Supremacy: The Changing Pattern of Relationships between the National Assembly and the National Executive Committee of TANU Before and After 1965," (M. A. program, 1973/74, Department of Political Science, University of Dar es Salaam; typescript), p. 61.

31. James R. Finucane, *Rural Development and Bureaucracy in Tanzania: The Case of Mwanza Region* (Uppsala: The Scandinavian Institute of African Studies, 1974), p. 63.

32. *Daily News* (Dar es Salaam), 31 January 1975, p. 1.

33. *Sunday News* (Dar es Salaam), 2 February 1975, p. 1.

34. *Weekly Review* (Nairobi), 26 September 1977, pp. 76 and 77.

35. This is the theme of Msekwa in "Towards Party Supremacy."

36. Henry Bienen, *Tanzania, Party Transformation and Economic Development* (Princeton: Princeton University Press, 1967), p. 176.

37. *Daily News* (Dar es Salaam), 4 October 1975, p. 1.

38. *Ibid.*, 20 August 1975, p. 1.

39. *Ibid.*, 8 October 1975, p. 4.

40. Helge Kjekshus, "The Elected Elite: A Socio-economic Profile of Candidates in Tanzania's Parliamentary Election, 1970," Research Report No. 29 (Uppsala: The Scandinavian Institute of African Studies, 1975), p. 25.

41. *Ibid.*, p. 26.

42. University of Dar es Salaam Election Study materials: 81 of a sample of 168 were living in ujamaa villages; 40 were defeated and 41 won.

43. *Daily News* (Dar es Salaam), 19 November 1975, p. 4.

44. See H. U. E. Thoden Van Velzen and J. J. Sterkenburg, "The Party Supreme," in *Socialism in Tanzania*, Vol. 1, *Politics*, eds. Lionel Cliffe and John Saul (Nairobi: East African Publishing House, 1972), pp. 257-64.

45. *Daily News* (Dar es Salaam), 29 November 1973, p. 1.

46. *Ibid.*, 14 December 1973, p. 1.

47. *Ibid.*, 26 April 1975, p. 1.

48. The complete treason-trial judgment was published in six parts from February 1 to February 6, 1971, in the *Nationalist* (Dar es Salaam).

49. From TANU *Directories*, December 1967, November 1968, April 1969, January 1970, and October 1970.

50. TANU, *Taarifa ya Ofisi Kuu Kuhusu Hali na Kazi za Chama*, November 1967, April 1969, and 1971, and *Daily News* (Dar es Salaam), June 9, 1975, p. 1; respectively.

51. *Nationalist* (Dar es Salaam), 18 February 1972, p. 8.

52. *Daily News* (Dar es Salaam), 10 March 1976, p. 5.

53. *Nationalist* (Dar es Salaam), 1 June 1971, p. 1.

54. *Ibid.*, 18 June 1971, p. 1.

55. *Ibid.*, 16 September 1971, p. 4.

56. *Sunday News* (Dar es Salaam), 16 March 1975, p. 6.

57. *Daily News* (Dar es Salaam), 16 April 1975, p. 1.

58. *Ibid.*, 16 June 1975, p. 1.

59. Stanley Dryden, *Local Administration in Tanzania* (Nairobi: East African Publishing House, 1968), p. 106.

60. *Ibid.*, p. 108, and William Tordoff, *Government and Politics in Tanzania* (Nairobi: East African Publishing House, 1967), p. 113.

61. Finucane, *Rural Development*, p. 56.

62. At the highest level in the regions there were regional development committees. According to Bienen: "It is at the level of the RDC that the development committees really enter into formulation of the central plan" (Bienen, *Tanzania, Party Transformation*, p. 327); Tordoff made the point, however, that "the regional development committee is essentially an advisory rather than an executive body in respect of any major project and requires central government assistance" (Tordoff, *Government and Politics*, p. 108). Another observer pointed out that "the Regional Development Committees are . . . mainly employed for the purpose of looking after the implementation of central decisions" (Rolf E. Vente, *Planning Processes: The East African Case* [Munchen: Weltform Verlag, 1970], p. 151).

63. Dryden, *Local Administration*, p. 112.

64. *Ibid.*, and R. G. Penner, *Financing Local Government in Tanzania* (Dar es Salaam: East African Publishing House, 1970), p. 10.

65. Tordoff, *Government and Politics*, p. 119.

66. Julius K. Nyerere, *Decentralization* (Dar es Salaam: Government Printer, 1972), p. 3.

67. Vente, *Planning Processes.*

68. Dryden, *Local Administration*, p. 111.

69. Bienen, *Tanzania, Party Transformation*, p. 352.

70. Dryden, *Local Administration*, p. 49.

71. *Ibid.*, and Finucane, *Rural Development*, p. 87.

72. Bienen, *Tanzania, Party Transformation*, p. 323.

73. Finucane, *Rural Development*, p. 86.

74. Vente, *Planning Processes*, p. 151.

75. Finucane, *Rural Development*, p. 100.

76. A. T. Kundi, "Popular Participation in Tanzania, A Case Study of Initiation and Implementation of Water Projects in Kirua Vunjo West Ward in Moshi District" (Dissertation [P. S. 307], Department of Political Science, University of Dar es Salaam, 1976), p. 39.

77. R. M. Mayaya, "Decentralization and Popular Participation in Shinyanga District" (Dissertation [P. S. 307], Department of Political Science, University of Dar es Salaam, 1976), p. 54.

78. W. N. Lobulu, "Popular Participation Since Decentralization in Tanzania, A Case Study of Health Projects in Kinondoni District" (Dissertation [P. S. 307], Department of Political Science, University of Dar es Salaam, 1976), p. 46.

79. A. P. Mosha, "Decentralization: Popular Participation in Planning and Implementation of Health Projects in Moshi District" (Dissertation [P. S. 307], Department of Political Science, University of Dar es Salaam, 1976), p. 64.

80. By Ward Development Committee Act (No. 6 of 1969).

81. Dryden, *Local Administration*, p. 23 and Finucane, *Rural Development*, p. 108.

82. Finucane, *Rural Development*, p. 124.

83. *Ibid.*, p. 126.

84. Nyerere, *Decentralization*, p. 4.

85. Seminar by M. von Freyhold, January 31, 1975, at the University of Dar es Salaam.

86. *Ibid.*

87. Dryden, *Local Administration*, p. 35, and Finucane, *Rural Development*, pp. 120 and 123.

88. Nyerere, *Decentralization*, p. 4.

89. *Ibid.* The positions of regional and district financial and personnel officers were abolished in 1976; *Daily News* (Dar es Salaam), 6 July 1976, p. 5.

90. Tordoff, *Government and Politics*, p. 116.

91. *Ibid.*, and Dryden, *Local Administration*, p. 117.

92. Nyerere, *Decentralization*, p. 4.

93. Goran Hyden, "The Politics of Cooperatives in Tanzania," in *Cooperatives in Tanzania*, ed. Goran Hyden (Dar es Salaam: Tanzania Publishing House, 1976), p. 15.

94. Herbert C. Kriesel et al., *Agricultural Marketing in Tanzania, Background Research and Policy Proposals* (East Lansing: Michigan State University, June 1970), figure 11, p. 30.

95. Cooperative Union of Tanganyika, "Structure of Agricultural Marketing in Tanzania," January 1975, mimeographed, pp. 4 and 9.

96. *East African Standard* (Nairobi), 17 May 1976, p. 5.

97. N. V. Rounce, *The Agriculture of the Cultivation Steppe of the Lake, Western and Central Provinces* (Capetown: Department of Agriculture, Tanganyika Territory by Longmans, 1949), pp. 92-93.

98. Government Notice No. 1, 1976.

99. R. Hulls, "An Assessment of Agricultural Extension in Sukumaland, Western Tanzania" (Economic Research Bureau, University of Dar es Salaam, 1971); cited by A. C. Coulson in "The Evolution of Rural Policies in Tanzania or Can a Government Bureaucracy Bring About Development," presented at Economic Research Bureau seminar, January 21, 1975, University of Dar es Salaam.

100. *Daily News* (Dar es Salaam), October 21 and 22, 1975, pp. 1 and 2 respectively. An interesting response by an agricultural officer may be found in *Daily News* (Dar es Salaam), December 31, 1975, p. 1.

101. Shivji, *Class Struggles*, p. 88.

102. Phil Raikes, "Ujamaa and Rural Socialism," *Review of African Political Economy*, No. 3, pp. 51 and 52.

103. Finucane, *Rural Development*, p. 10.

104. *Ibid.*, p. 174.

105. Gerhard Tschannerl, "Rural Water Supply in Tanzania: Is 'Politics' or 'Technique' in Command?" (paper presented at East African Universities Social Science Conference, Dar es Salaam, 18-20 December 1973), p. 17.

106. H. U. E. Thoden Van Velzen, "Staff, Kulaks, and Peasants," in *Socialism in Tanzania*, Vol. 1, eds. Cliffe and Saul, pp. 153-79.

107. Michaela von Freyhold, "The Government Staff and Ujamaa Villages" (paper presented at East African Universities Social Science Conference, Dar es Salaam, 18-20 December 1973), p. 1.

108. Discussions with M. von Freyhold, December 1975, and seminar, January 31, 1975, at the University of Dar es Salaam.

Chapter IV

1. See *Daily News* (Dar es Salaam), 24 January 1975, p. 4.

2. Julius K. Nyerere, "Socialism and Rural Development," in Nyerere, *Freedom and Socialism* (Dar es Salaam: Oxford University Press, 1968), pp. 337-66.

3. Jeffrey L. Pressman and Aaron Wildavsky, *Implementation* (Berkeley: University of California Press, 1973), p. xiv.

4. Nyerere, *Freedom and Socialism*, pp. 347-48. Emphasis added.

5. *Ibid.*, pp. 346-47.

6. *Ibid.*, p. 348; Julius K. Nyerere, "A Survey of Socialist Progress," in Nyerere, *Freedom and Development* (Dar es Salaam: Oxford University Press, 1973), p. 155.

7. Nyerere, *Freedom and Socialism*, p. 362.

8. *Ibid.*, p. 351.

9. *Ibid.*, p. 353.

10. *Daily News* (Dar es Salaam), 9 August 1973, p. 3; *ibid.*, 15 November 1973, p. 1; and Villages and Ujamaa Villages Act (No. 21 of 1975), sec. 4 (1) respectively.

11. Nyerere, *Freedom and Socialism*, p. 352.

12. *Ibid.*, p. 351.

13. Cooperative Union of Tanganyika, Ltd., "Shughuli za Vyama vya Ushirika Katika Vijiji vya Ujamaa" (C.U.T. Press, nd.), p. 2.

14. "Katiba ya Kijiji cha Ujamaa," Sharti la 3 (mimeo); District Cooperative Office: Mufindi and Iringa.

15. "Taarifa No. 1/1975 ya Mapato Kutoka na Uvuvi wa Kijamaa ya Kutoka Mwezi Februari 1975-Aprili 1975 na Mengineyo," from Kibirizi ujamaa village, Kigoma district. An "mjamaa" is a socialist or a member of an ujamaa village; "wajamaa" is the plural form.

16. Villages and Ujamaa Villages Act, section 16 (1).

17. *Ujamaa*, Toleo la 26 (1972), p. 10.

18. Letter from Kamishina wa Maendeleo Vijijini, Dar es Salaam, to Wakurugenzi wa Maendeleo wa Mkoa, Tanzania bara, 14 April 1973; DCO: Kibondo.

19. Letter from N. B. Magessa, Ujamaa and Cooperative Officer, Kigoma, to ujamaa and cooperative officers, Kigoma, Kasulu, Kibondo, 8 April 1974; DCO: Kibondo.

20. Muhtasari Mkutano wa Kamati ya Wilaya ya Vijiji vya Ujamaa vilioketi Makao Makuu ya Wilaya tarehe 24 April 1975; DCO: RD 63/A/iv, Same.

21. Summarized from "Katiba ya Kujiji cha Ujamaa," (mimeo); DCO: Mufindi and Iringa.

22. Letter from regional ujamaa and cooperative officer, Iringa, to district ujamaa and cooperative officers, Iringa, Mufindi, and Njombe, 8 May 1975; DCO: D/COOP/32, Iringa.

23. Nyerere, *Freedom and Socialism*, pp. 348-51.

24. R. W. James, *Land Tenure and Policy in Tanzania* (Nairobi: East African Literature Bureau, 1971), p. 244.

25. Julius K. Nyerere, "President's Report to the TANU Conference, September 1973" (Dar es Salaam: Government Printer, 1973), p. 8.

26. Abstracted from the Villages and Ujamaa Villages (Registration, Designation and Administration) Act, 1975, and the regulations issued under that act contained in Government Notice No. 162, published 22 August 1975.

27. Villages and Ujamaa Villages Act, section 16 (1).

28. Nyerere, *Freedom and Socialism*, p. 340.

29. Julius K. Nyerere, "The Arusha Declaration: Socialism and Self-Reliance," in Nyerere, *Freedom and Socialism*, pp. 231-32. The creed was simplified in the CCM constitution to include only three points. "(1)" and "(2)" of the TANU creed were retained and a summary third point was added: "The Party believes . . . that socialism and self-reliance is the only way of building a society of free and equal citizens" (CCM constitution, article I, section [4]).

30. *Ibid.*, pp. 233 and 234.

31. Summary of chapter 6 of P. K. Kimiti, *Siasa ya Tanu Katika Kilimo* (Dar es Salaam: National Printing Co., n.d.), pp. 27-32.

32. "Katiba ya Kijiji cha Ujamaa" (mimeo); DCO: Mufindi and Iringa.

33. Government Notice No. 168, 1975, sec. 8.

34. Nyerere, *Freedom and Socialism*, p. 356.

35. "Presidential Circular No. 1 of 1969," in *Rural Cooperation in Tanzania*, eds. Lionel Cliffe et al. (Dar es Salaam: Tanzania Publishing House, 1975), p. 27.

36. Julius K. Nyerere, "Freedom and Development," in Nyerere, *Freedom and Development*, p. 67.

37. *Daily News* (Dar es Salaam), 22 August 1972, p. 4.

38. *Ibid.*, 27 February 1973, p. 5.

39. *Ibid.*, 9 August 1973, p. 3.

40. Nyerere, *Freedom and Socialism*, p. 356.

41. Nyerere, "Freedom and Development," p. 61.

42. *Ibid.*

43. P. Msekwa, "Towards Party Supremacy: The Changing Pattern of Relationships between the National Assembly and the National Executive Committee of TANU Before and After 1965" (M. A. program 1973/74, Department of Political Science, University of Dar es Salaam; typescript), p. 60.

44. Julius K. Nyerere, "Hotuba ya Rais wa Chama Kwenye Mkutano Mkuu wa TANU wa 16," in TANU, *Maendeleo ni Kazi* (Dar es Salaam, 1973), p. 19.

45. *Ibid.*, p. 23.

46. *Ibid.*, p. 24.

47. Press Release A/2944/73, 6 November 1973.

48. Nyerere, "Hotuba ya Rais," pp. 21 and 22.

49. *Uhuru* (Dar es Salaam) 8 November 1973, p. 6.

50. *Daily News* (Dar es Salaam), 8 November 1973, p. 1.

51. *African Development* 8, 7 (July 1974): T9.

52. Interview with Nyerere by Hilary Ng'weno, reprinted from *Weekly Review*; *Daily News* (Dar es Salaam), 2 March 1976, p. 4.

53. *African Development* 8, 7 (July 1974): T9.

54. *Daily News* (Dar es Salaam), 24 September 1975, p. 4.

55. Nyerere, "Freedom and Development," p. 67.

56. Julius K. Nyerere, "To Plan Is to Choose," in Nyerere, *Freedom and Development*, p. 95.

57. *Ibid.*

58. "Presidential Circular No. 1 of 1969," p. 31.

59. Among the most recent is Jonathan Barker, "Socialism and the Rural Sector in Tanzania" (paper presented at the American Political Science Association meeting, Chicago, 2-5 September 1976), pp. 3-6.

60. Nyerere, *Freedom and Socialism*, p. 357.

61. Antony Ellman, "Development of Ujamaa Policy in Tanzania," in *Rural Cooperation in Tanzania*, eds. L. Cliffe et al., pp. 322 and 323.

62. *Daily News* (Dar es Salaam), 21 January 1973, p. 7.

63. "Maendeleo ya Vijiji vya Ujamaa," DCO: RD/KD/VVU/G, Kondoa.

64. "Hatua za Kuendeleza Vijiji vya Ujamaa Mkoa wa Iringa" (typescript, n.d.); DCO: Iringa.

65. *Daily News* (Dar es Salaam), 10 July 1972, p. 1.

66. Nyerere, *Freedom and Socialism*, pp. 357 and 358.

67. "Presidential Circular No. 1 of 1969," p. 20.

68. Nyerere, "Hotuba ya Rais," pp. 23 and 24.

69. Nyerere, *Freedom and Socialism*, p. 357.

70. "Presidential Circular No. 1 of 1969," p. 29.

71. Julius K. Nyerere, "Ten Years After Independence," in Nyerere, *Freedom and Development*, p. 307.

72. Julius K. Nyerere, "Implementation of Rural Socialism," in Nyerere, *Freedom and Development*, p. 11.

73. *Nationalist* (Dar es Salaam), 26 September 1969, p. 4.

Chapter V

1. Nikos Georgulas, "Settlement Patterns and Rural Development in Tanganyika," *Occasional Paper No. 29*, Program of Eastern African Studies, Syracuse University, May 1967, p. 28.

2. A.O. Ellman, "Progress and Prospects in Ujamaa Development in Tanzania" (paper delivered at the East African Agricultural Economic Society Conference, Dar es Salaam, 1970), pp. 6-7.

3. Phil Raikes, "Ujamaa Vijijini and Rural Socialist Development" (paper presented at East African Universities Social Science Conference, Dar es Salaam, 1973), pp. 15-20.

4. Hans Ruthenberg, *Agricultural Development in Tanganyika* (Berlin: Springer-Verlag, 1964), p. 60.

5. "Presidential Circular No. 1 of 1969," in *Rural Cooperation in Tanzania*, eds. Lionel Cliffe et al. (Dar es Salaam: Tanzania Publishing House, 1975), p. 30.

6. Henry Mapolu, "The Social and Economic Organisation of Ujamaa Villages" (University of Dar es Salaam, 1973; mimeo), p. 36.

7. Press Release A/370/74, 30 January 1974.

8. Press Release A/3081/73, 18 November 1973 (paraphrased).

9. *Daily News* (Dar es Salaam), 10 December 1974, p. 1 (paraphrased).

10. Press Release A/1977/72, 4 August 1972.

11. Press Release A/2971/73, 8 November 1973 (paraphrased).

12. *Daily News* (Dar es Salaam), 21 September 1973, p. 3.

13. *Nationalist* (Dar es Salaam), 25 March, 1971, p. 1.

14. Press Release A/2701/73, 13 October 1973.

15. Press Release A/1510/73, 23 June 1973 (paraphrased).

16. Press Release A/2212/72, 27 August 1972 (paraphrased).

17. Press Release A/1556/74, 14 April 1974 (paraphrased).

18. Press Release A/2929/72, 1 November 1972 (paraphrased).

19. *Nationalist* (Dar es Salaam), 14 June 1971, p. 1.

20. *Daily News* (Dar es Salaam), 16 October 1975, p. 1.

21. *Nationalist* (Dar es Salaam), 9 December 1969, p. 1.

22. *Ibid.*, 29 December 1969, p. 1.

23. *Daily News* (Dar es Salaam), 10 October 1972, p. 5.

24. Press Release A/1594/73, 1 July 1973.

25. Press Release A/2898/72, 30 October 1972.

26. Press Release C/2118/71, 24 September 1971.

27. Press Release A/479/73, 25 February 1973.

28. Press Release A/2927/72, 23 October 1973.

29. *Daily News* (Dar es Salaam), 26 March 1973, p. 5.

30. *Daily News* (Dar es Salaam), 12 February 1974, p. 4.

31. Press Releases: A/3081/73, 18 November 1973; A/2971/73, 8 November 1973; A/2701/73, 13 October 1973; *Daily News* (Dar es Salaam), 21 September 1973, p. 3; Press Release A/1556/74, 14 April 1974, respectively.

32. J. Rald, "Ujamaa, Problems of Implementation (Experiences from West Lake)," BRALUP Research Department, No. 10, May 1970, p. 25.

33. For example, Mancur Olson, Jr., *The Logic of Collective Action: Public Goods and the Theory of Groups* (Cambridge, Mass.: Harvard University Press, 1965); Leo Huberman and Paul Sweezy, *Socialism in Cuba* (New York: Monthly Review Press, 1969), pp. 141-53; E.L. Wheelwright and Bruce McFarlane, *The Chinese Road to Socialism: Economics of the Cultural Revolution* (New York: Monthly Review Press, 1970), pp. 143-61; Robert M. Bernardo, *The Theory of Moral Incentives in Cuba* (University, Alabama: University of Alabama Press, 1971); and Mikhail Laptin, *Material and Moral Incentives Under Socialism* (Moscow: Novosti Press, n.d.).

34. Olson, *Collective Action*, p. 14.

35. Leo Huberman and Paul Sweezy, "Editorial," *Monthly Review*, November 1967, p. 14.

36. Press Release A/1654/73, 6 July 1973.

37. Anaclet R. Rwegayura, "Operation Dodoma Enters the Second Phase," Maezelo Feature Service, C/59/72, 18 August 1972.

38. For example, Press Release A/1670/73, 7 July 1973.

39. Press Release A/995/72, 28 April 1972.

40. Press Release A/2914/72, 31 October 1972.

41. Press Release A/2752/72, 17 October 1972.

42. Press Release A/207/73, 26 January 1973.

43. Press Release A/3322/72, 13 December 1972.

44. Press Release A/903/73, 16 April 1973.

45. Press Release A/512/73, 1 March 1973.

46. Press Release A/737/73, 23 March 1973.

47. TANU, *Maendeleo ni Kazi* (Dar es Salaam: National Printing Co., 1973), p. 23.

48. *Daily News* (Dar es Salaam), 10 July 1972, p. 1.

49. *Ibid.*, 12 July 1972.

50. See Rwegayura, "Operation Dodoma"; Press Release A/151/73, 21 January 1973; Press Release A/675/73, 17 March 1973; *Daily News* (Dar es Salaam), 23 September 1972, p. 5; Press Release A/1937/73, 3 August 1973; Press Release A/2051/73, 13 August 1973; and *Daily News* (Dar es Salaam), 5 February 1973, p. 5.

51. *Daily News* (Dar es Salaam), 25 August 1972, p. 3.

52. *Ibid.*, 26 September 1972, p. 5.

53. *Ibid.*, 22 January 1973, p. 5.

54. *Ibid.*

55. Press Release A/666/72, 17 March 1972.

56. Press Release A/2535/73, 26 September 1973.

57. *Daily News* (Dar es Salaam), 21 January 1974, p. 3.

58. Anaclet R. Rwegayura, "Ujamaa Villages Turned into Cooperatives," Maelezo Feature Service, C/60/72, 18 August 1972.

59. John F. Chant, "Problems and Prospects of Credit to Small Holder Agriculture: The Experience of the National Development Agency in Tanzania" (Economic Research Bureau, n.d. [c. 1969]), p. 117.

60. *Tanzania Rural Development Bank: Annual Report and Accounts for 1972/73 and 1971/72*, pp. 9 and 12 respectively.

61. *Nationalist* (Dar es Salaam), 24 March 1971, p. 1, and *Daily News* (Dar es Salaam), 27 June 1973, p. 3.

62. *Daily News* (Dar es Salaam), 5 January 1973, p. 9.

63. *Ibid.*, 2 October 1972, p. 5.

64. *Ibid.*, 15 June 1972, p. 3.

65. *Ibid.*, 10 October 1972, p. 5.

66. *Ibid.*, 1 September 1972, p. 5.

67. Ujamaa villages appear to be virtually the only points of distribution of such relief.

68. *Nationalist* (Dar es Salaam), 8 May 1971, p. 4.

69. Ellman, "Progress and Prospects," pp. 19-20.

70. *Daily News* (Dar es Salaam), 12 August 1972, p. 1.

71. Frances R. Hill, "Mobilization and Participation in Tanzania" (Ph.D. dissertation, Harvard University, 1973), p. 279.

72. R. Pole and E. Mollo, "Hombolo Center Is a Step in Ujamaa Development," *East African Standard* (Nairobi), 7 April 1972, p. 8.

73. *Daily News* (Dar es Salaam), 8 September 1972, p. 4.

74. *Ibid.*, 6 October 1972, p. 7.

75. R.H. Rugemarila, "The Economic Impact of Operation Kigoma" (Department of Rural Development, Mzumbe, Morogoro, 1976; mimeo), p. 29.

76. *Daily News* (Dar es Salaam), 2 August 1973, p. 5.

77. Press Release B/5/74, 14 February 1974.

78. *Nchi Yetu*, No. 129, October 1974.

79. Hill, "Mobilization," p. 263.

80. Juma Mwapachu, "Operation Planned Villages in Rural Tanzania: A Revolutionary Strategy for Development," *Mbioni* 7, 11 (1975): 15.

81. "Taarifa ya Ujumbe Uliotumwa Dodoma Kujifunza matatizo na mafanikio ya Operation Dodoma Kwa Manufaa ya Operation Kigoma," 1972; DCO [District Cooperative Office]: Kigoma.

82. "Muhtasari wa Uhamiaji Katika Vijiji vya Maendeleo Mkoa wa Mwanza"; DCO: VVU CD 102/8, Same.

83. Mwapachu, "Operation Planned Villages," p. 16.

84. Michaela von Freyhold, seminar, University of Dar es Salaam, January 1975.

85. "Maelezo juu ya Vijiji vya Ujamaa—Dodoma—(W), 1971/72," mimeo; DCO: D30/3 VVU, Dodoma.

86. Mimeographed letter, 24 March 1971, to Wajumbe wote Kamati ya Maendeleo Mipango Wilaya Kigoma from Mtendaji Mkuu Halmashauri ya Wilaya Kigoma; DCO: DC/81, Kigoma Ujamaa Villages general, Kigoma.

87. See note 82.

88. Simeon Mesaki, "Operation Pwani Kisarawe District—Implementation Problems" (M.A. diss., University of Dar es Salaam, 1976), p. 91.

89. See note 82.

90. See note 81.

91. See note 82.

92. Document dated 17 May 1974; DCO, Iringa.

93. Mesaki, "Operation Pwani," p. 86.

94. Mwapachu, "Operation Planned Villages," p. 16.

95. Document dated 17 May 1974; DCO: D Coop/32, Iringa.

96. See note 82.

97. *Uhuru* (Dar es Salaam), 8 October 1974, p. 6.

98. *Ibid.*, 10 October 1974, p. 6.

99. *Daily News* (Dar es Salaam), 22 August 1972, p. 3.

100. A.K. Maziku, Student report, University of Dar es Salaam, December 1975.

101. *Daily News* (Dar es Salaam), 15 April 1975, p. 4; *Sunday News* (Dar es Salaam), 17 November 1974, p. 7; *Uhuru* (Dar es Salaam), 26 December 1974, p. 6.

102. Instructions to leaders; RCO: Vijiji vya Ujamaa General, RD/KD UvU/G, Kondoa.

103. E.M.E. Mbuta, Student report, University of Dar es Salaam, 1975.

104. "Repoti ya Ziara ya Mwanza Kuona na Kujikunza Shughuli za Uhamiaji Katika Vijiji vya Maendeleo, 24/9/74-3/10/74," mimeo, p. 2; DCO: VVU CD 102/b, Moshi.

105. R.R. Matango, " 'Operation Mara': The Paradox of Democracy," *Maji Maji* 20 (January 1975): 17.

106. *Ibid.*, pp. 18 and 19.

107. Kemal Mustafa, "The Development of Ujamaa in Musoma: A Case Study of Butiama Ujamaa Village" (M.A. diss., University of Dar es Salaam, 1975), p. 204.

108. M.P. Dabana, Student report, University of Dar es Salaam, 1975.

109. A.P.L. Ndabakwaje, Student report, University of Dar es Salaam, 1975.

110. Mbuta, Student report.

111. R.A.B. Byarugaba, Student report, University of Dar es Salaam, 1975.

112. A.K. Maziku, Student report, University of Dar es Salaam, 1975.

113. J. Mkomangu, Student report, University of Dar es Salaam, 1975.

114. Mesaki, "Operation Pwani," pp. 93 and 94.

257

115. Mwapachu, "Operation Planned Villages," p. 21.

116. Mesaki, "Operation Pwani," p. 94.

117. Mwapachu, "Operation Planned Villages," p. 21.

118. Matango, "Operation Mara," p. 19.

119. Mesaki, "Operation Pwani," pp. 102 and 103.

120. Ndabakwaje, Student report.

121. *Ibid.*

122. Mwapachu, "Operation Planned Villages," p. 16.

123. Ndabakwaje, Student report.

124. Mesaki, "Operation Pwani," p. 114.

125. Mbuta, Student report.

126. Mwapachu, "Operation Planned Villages," p. 31.

127. Von Freyhold, seminar, January 1975, pp. 8 and 9.

128. *Ibid.*, p. 9.

129. Raikes, "Ujamaa Vijijini," pp. 19 and 20.

130. See Adhu Awiti, "The Development of Ujamaa Villages and the Peasant Question in Iringa District: A Study Outline" (Economic Research Bureau, Paper 73.4, University of Dar es Salaam, September 1973; mimeo), and Harry Chale, "Emergent Large Farmers and the Problems of Implementation of Ujamaa Vijijini Policy in Usangu (Mbeya District)" (Ph.D. dissertation, University of Dar es Salaam, 1973; mimeo).

131. Hill, "Mobilization," p. 268.

132. Based on movement data from *Daily News* (Dar es Salaam), 17 November 1973, p. 1.

133. Press Release A/949/72, 22 April 1972.

134. Figures for families moved from Rugemarila, "Economic Impact," p. 37.

135. *Ibid.*, pp. 34 and 37.

136. Calculated from data in *Daily News* (Dar es Salaam), 15 April 1975, p. 4.

137. *Ibid.*

138. Calculated from data in *ibid.*, 22 September 1975, p. 3.

139. Calculated from data in *Uhuru* (Dar es Salaam), 3 December 1974, p. 4.

140. Calculated from data in *ibid.*, 20 August 1975, p. 4, and Press Release A/1852/73, 27 July 1973.

141. Mesaki, "Operation Pwani," p. 87.

142. *Ibid.*, p. 98.

143. Mwapachu, "Operation Planned Villages," p. 16.

144. *Daily News* (Dar es Salaam), 2 August 1973, p. 5, and 28 January 1976, p. 5.

145. *Ibid.*, 1 November 1974, p. 4, and *Sunday News* (Dar es Salaam), 15 June 1975, p. 7.

146. *Nchi Yetu* 29 (October 1974).

147. *Daily News* (Dar es Salaam), 15 April 1975, p. 4.

148. *Uhuru* (Dar es Salaam), 26 December 1974, p. 6.

149. Mwapachu, "Operation Planned Villages," pp. 22-28.

150. *Ibid.*, p. 26.

151. Ndabakwaje, Student report.

152. Mkomangu, Student report.

153. From instructions to leaders: DCO: Vijiji vya Ujamaa General, RD/KD/ UvU/G, Kondoa.

154. Raikes, "Ujamaa Vijijini," pp. 9 and 10.

Chapter VI

1. *Nationalist* (Dar es Salaam), 28 October 1971, p. 3.

2. *Daily News* (Dar es Salaam), 24 September 1975.

3. Julius Nyerere, "Socialism and Rural Development," in Nyerere, *Freedom and Socialism* (Dar es Salaam: Oxford University Press, 1968), p. 357.

4. See Samuel S. Mushi, "Modernization by Traditionalization: Ujamaa Principles Revisited," *Taamuli* 1, 2 (March 1971), and Crescent C. Ndunguru, "Ujamaa: A Comparative Study of Perceptions and Orientation in Kilosa and Mpwapwa Districts" (M.A. thesis, University of Dar es Salaam, 1973), p. 312.

5. S.O. Odede, "Some Notes on Tanzanian Rural Development Strategy: A Case of Vijiji vya Ujamaa of Tanga Region," in *Strategies for Improving Rural Welfare*, eds. M.E. Kempe and L.D. Smith (proceedings of workshop at the Institute for Development Studies, University of Nairobi, 31 May-3 June 1971, Occasional Paper No. 4), p. 306.

6. Audun Sandberg, "Socio-Economic Survey of Lower Rufiji Flood Plain Rufiji Delta Agricultural System," BRALUP Research Paper No. 34, p. 50.

7. L.J. Mshana, Regional Planning Officer, Kigoma; personal communication, February 1976.

8. J. Bugengo, "Ujamaa in Mara Region" (paper presented at East African Universities Social Science Conference, 18-20 December 1973), p. 14.

9. Dean McHenry, Jr., "Peasant Participation in Communal Farming: The Tanzanian Experience" (paper presented at the African Studies Association meeting, Boston, 3-6 November 1976), p. 5.

10. *Daily News* (Dar es Salaam), 22 September 1976, p. 4.

11. The statements come from the following villages: Ilambilole, Ipalamwa, Usokami, Kitowo, Udumuka, Kidabaga, Mvumi Makulu, Zashe, Mahembe, Kisada, Kifura, and Wambi, respectively.

12. *Daily News* (Dar es Salaam), 1 September 1975, p. 12.

13. Saidi Mwamwindi v. R. Crim. Sess. 37-Iringa-72, 2/10/72, Tanzania High Court Digest 6, 5 (September-October 1972), p. 259.

14. *Nationalist* (Dar es Salaam), 17 December 1970, p. 4.

15. *Daily News* (Dar es Salaam), 8 February 1972, p. 1.

16. *Ibid.*, 21 October 1975, p. 1.

17. *Ibid.*, 31 December 1975, p. 1.

18. L. Gambi, student report to author, July 1975.

19. *Sunday News* (Dar es Salaam), 22 September 1974, p. 4.

20. *Nationalist* (Dar es Salaam), 19 November 1971, p. 4.

21. Interview with District Agricultural Officer Tuni, Mufindi district, 10 April 1975.

22. *Ujamaa* 16, pp. 3-6.

23. R.H. Rugemarila to all ujamaa village chairmen, Kibondo district, 19 April 1973; DCO: RDD2 Uvs General, Kibondo.

24. Letter to District Ujamaa and Co-operative Officer from District Development Director, Iringa, 8 November 1973; DCO: DCOOP 32 Uvs, Iringa.

25. R.H. Rugemarila to all ujamaa village chairmen, Kibondo district, 19 April 1973; DCO: RDD2 Uvs General, Kibondo.

26. *Standard* (Dar es Salaam), 21 February 1972, p. 1.

27. From Katiba ya Kijiji cha Ujamaa, Seri Chini, 4 January 1974; DCO: VvU CD102/B, Moshi.

28. *African Development*, July 1974, p. T9.

29. *Standard* (Dar es Salaam), 18 October 1968, p. 7.

30. *Daily News* (Dar es Salaam), 24 July 1971, p. 1.

31. *Ibid.*, 21 November 1974, p. 5; *ibid.*; *ibid.*; *Sunday News* (Dar es Salaam), 24 November 1974, p. 1; *Daily News* (Dar es Salaam), 12 February 1975, p. 5; *ibid.*, 1 August 1974, p. 7; *ibid.*, 10 March 1975, p. 1, respectively.

32. From Kikao cha Wanakijiji cha Tarehe, 6 August 1972; DCO: KcU Kimunyu RD 63/1, Same.

33. Francis Fanuel Lyimo, "Problems and Prospects of Ujamaa Development in Moshi District" (M.A. dissertation, University of Dar es Salaam, June 1975), pp. 191-92.

34. Personal communication from J. Sakumba, student at University of Dar es Salaam, July 1975.

35. *Daily News* (Dar es Salaam), 17 July 1972, p. 5.

36. *Ibid.*, 21 July 1976, p. 1.

37. *Ibid.*, 22 July 1976, p. 1.

38. *Ibid.*, 24 September 1975, p. 4.

39. Kiwawa, "Madaraka Vijijini," in Ofisi ya Waziri Mkuu na Makamu wa Pili wa Rais, *Sheria ya Kuandikisha Vijiji na Vijiji vya Ujamaa* (Dodoma: Printpack, 1975), p. 5.

40. Julius Nyerere, "Education for Self-Reliance," in Nyerere, *Freedom and Socialism*, p. 269.

41. Julius Nyerere, "Socialism and Rural Development," in Nyerere, *Freedom and Socialism*, p. 339.

42. For an assessment of the problem in Mwanza Region, see James R. Finucane, *Rural Development and Bureaucracy in Tanzania* (Uppsala: Scandinavian Institute of African Studies, 1974), pp. 63-64.

43. Clyde Ingle, "Compulsion and Rural Development in Tanzania," *Canadian Journal of African Studies* 4, 1 (Winter 1970): 85-86; see also Ingle, *From Village to State in Tanzania* (Ithaca: Cornell University Press, 1972), pp. 101-2. Ingle's analysis is insightful. The leaders he studied were not as low in the hierarchy as those examined in the four-region survey; hence the results are not perfectly comparable.

44. Concerning the situation in Kigoma, see R.H. Rugemarila, "The Economic Impact of Operation Kigoma" (Department of Rural Development, Mzumbe, Morogoro, 1976; mimeo), and C.K. Omari, "Operation Kigoma: Kibondo District, A Preliminary Appraisal" (Rural Development Committee, Report No. 2, University of Dar es Salaam; mimeo).

45. *Daily News* (Dar es Salaam), 23 January 1974, p. 1.

46. Press Release A/207/74, 19 January 1974; *Daily News* (Dar es Salaam), 21 January 1974, p. 3; Press Release A/591/74, 14 February 1974; *Daily News* (Dar es Salaam), 23 June 1972, p. 5.

47. Press Release A/2325/73, 5 September 1973.

48. Press Release A/2931/72, 1 November 1972.

49. Press Release A/3172/73, 29 November 1973.

50. Gerhard Tschannerl, "Rural Water-Supply in Tanzania: Is 'Politics' or 'Technique' in Command?" (Paper No. 52, East African Universities Social Science Conference, 18-20 December 1973), p. 24.

51. *Daily News* (Dar es Salaam), 1 March 1976, p. 1.

52. "Taarifa ya Utekelezaji wa Mipango ya Maendeleo Pamoja na Operation Kigoma," 6 and 7 February 1974 (mimeo), p. 11; DCO: OK/p/111, Op Kig, Kigoma.

53. *Daily News* (Dar es Salaam), 1 March 1976, p. 1.

54. Tanzania, *The Economic Survey and Annual Plan, 1970-71* (Dar es Salaam: Government Printer, 1970), p. 24.

55. By the end of 1977 no villages had yet been registered as ujamaa villages; see *Daily News* (Dar es Salaam), 28 December 1977, p. 1.

56. *Ibid.*, 26 April 1976, p. 1.

57. See G. Hyden, "The Politics of Cooperatives in Tanzania," in *Cooperatives in Tanzania: Problems of Organisation*, ed. G. Hyden (Dar es Salaam:

TPH, 1976), pp. 7-20, and Audun Sandberg, "Socio-Economic Survey of Lower Rufiji Flood Plain Rufiji Delta Agricultural System," BRALUP Research Paper No. 34, p. 50.

58. Cooperative Union of Tanganyika, Ltd., "Shughuli za Vyama vya Ushirika Katika Vijiji vya Ujamaa," n.d., p. 7.

59. Tanzania, *Economic Survey 1970-71.*

60. Letter to District Development Directors from Regional Development Director, Iringa, 12 October 1973; DCO: DCOOP 32, Iringa.

61. *Daily News* (Dar es Salaam), 9 August 1972, p. 1.

62. *Sunday News* (Dar es Salaam), 20 October 1974, p. 1, and *Daily News* (Dar es Salaam), 25 November 1974, p. 5, respectively.

63. *Ibid.,* 10 October 1974, p. 1.

64. *Ibid.,* 16 October 1974, p. 9.

65. *Ibid.,* 12 August 1975, p. 1.

66. Reported in *Uhuru* (Dar es Salaam), 8 March 1976, p. 4.

67. *Daily News* (Dar es Salaam), 12 November 1975, p. 3.

68. *Ibid.,* 17 February 1976, p. 1.

69. *Ibid.,* p. 3.

70. *Ibid.,* 18 February 1976, p. 1.

71. *Ibid.,* 22 March 1976, p. 1.

72. *Ibid.,* 20 February 1976, p. 5.

73. *Ibid.,* 19 February 1976, p. 1.

74. *Ibid.*

75. *Ibid.,* 23 February 1976, p. 1.

76. *Ibid.,* 3 April 1976, p. 5.

77. *Ibid.,* 10 March 1976, p. 4.

78. *Ibid.,* 3 April 1976, p. 4.

79. *Ibid.,* 2 April 1976, p. 5.

80. *Ibid.,* 21 May 1976, p. 3.

81. *Ibid.,* 20 May 1976, p. 1.

82. *Sunday News* (Dar es Salaam), 23 May 1976, p. 6.

83. *Ibid.,* p. 1.

84. *Daily News* (Dar es Salaam), 22 September 1976, p. 4.

85. Joseph Angwazi and Benno Ndulu, "An Evaluation of Ujamaa Villages in the Rufiji Area, 1968-1972" (Paper No. 3, East African Universities Social Science Conference, Dar es Salaam, 18-20 December 1973), p. 17.

86. Report from an international organization which has requested anonymity.

Chapter VII

1. Dispatch in the *Christian Science Monitor*; reprinted in the *San Jose Mercury-News*, 12 January 1975, p. 21.

2. A Copley News Service report in the *San Jose Mercury-News*, 7 March 1975, p. 42.

3. *Washington Post*, 7 February 1977.

4. *Sunday News* (Dar es Salaam), 22 December 1974, p. 6.

5. Julius Nyerere, "The Arusha Declaration: Ten Years After" (Dar es Salaam: Government Printer, 1977), pp. 1, 5, 41, 42, and 43.

6. *Daily News* (Dar es Salaam), 21 September 1977, p. 1. Sokoine had replaced Kawawa as prime minister on 13 February 1977 in a cabinet reshuffle.

7. *Ibid.*, 28 December 1977, p. 1.

8. Issa Shivji, *Class Struggles in Tanzania* (Dar es Salaam: Tanzania Publishing House, 1975), p. 108.

9. A.C. Coulson, "The Evolution of Rural Policies in Tanzania, or Can a Government Bureaucracy Bring about Development?" (Economic Research Bureau, University of Dar es Salaam, 21 January 1975; mimeo).

10. P.L. Raikes, "Ujamaa and Rural Socialism," *Review of African Political Economy* 3 (May-October 1975): 48.

11. Ralph Ibbott, "The Disbanding of the Ruvuma Development Association in Tanzania," November 1969 [mimeo].

12. J. Angwazi and B. Ndulu, "Evaluation of Operation Rufiji, 1968" (Bureau of Resource Assessment and Land Use Planning, University of Dar es Salaam, 1973), p. 18; cited in Shivji, *Class Struggles*, p. 109.

13. J. Rald, "Ujamaa, Problems of Implementation (Experiences from Westlake)" (Bureau of Resource Assessment and Land Use Planning, University College, Dar es Salaam, Research Report No. 10 [May 1970]), p. 33.

14. Lionel Cliffe, "The Policy of Ujamaa Vijijini and the Class Struggle in Tanzania," in *Socialism in Tanzania*, eds. Lionel Cliffe and John Saul, vol. 2 (Nairobi: East African Publishing House, 1973), pp. 208-9.

15. John Nellis, *A Theory of Ideology: The Tanzanian Example* (Nairobi: Oxford University Press, 1972), p. 191.

16. *Daily News* (Dar es Salaam), 15 June 1973, p. 3.

17. Reported by research assistant H.J. Kivina, July 1975.

18. *Daily News* (Dar es Salaam), 23 January 1978, p. 3.

19. Coulson, "Evolution of Rural Policies in Tanzania," p. 109.

20. Jonathan Barker, "The Debate on Rural Socialism in Tanzania" (University of Toronto, February 1977; mimeo), p. 12.

21. Shivji, *Class Struggles*, p. 108.

22. *Ibid.*, p. 122.

23. Cliffe, "Policy of Ujamaa Vijijini," p. 198.

24. Goran Hyden, "Ujamaa, Villagisation and Rural Development in Tanzania," *Overseas Development Institute Review* 1 (1975): 60.

25. Barker, "Debate on Rural Socialism," p. 3.

26. Henry Mapolu, "The Social and Economic Organization of Ujamaa Villages" (University of Dar es Salaam, September 1973; mimeo), p. 110, and Shivji, *Class Struggles*, p. 121.

27. *Ibid.*, p. 118.

28. James MacManus charged in an article entitled "Rising Price of Principles" in the *Guardian*, 14 December 1974, that the World Bank had threatened to withdraw $30 million in aid if Tanzania persisted in the ujamaa village policy and in establishing its new capital in Dodoma. Needless to say, the charge embarrassed World Bank officials and brought emphatic denials. The author has seen no evidence to substantiate the charge.

29. Nyerere, "Arusha Declaration," p. 47.

30. Raikes, "Ujamaa and Rural Socialism," p. 45.

31. See McHenry, "The Ujamaa Village in Tanzania: A Comparison with Chinese, Soviet and Mexican Experiences in Collectivization," *Comparative Studies in Society and History* 18, 3 (July 1976): 347-70.

32. *Daily News* (Dar es Salaam), 26 July 1975, p. 1.

33. Raymond Wilkie, *San Miguel, A Mexican Collective Ejido* (Stanford: Stanford University Press, 1971), p. xi.

34. *Ibid.*, p. 156.

35. *Ibid.*, p. 71.

36. *Ibid.*, p. 157.

INSTITUTE OF INTERNATIONAL STUDIES
UNIVERSITY OF CALIFORNIA, BERKELEY

CARL G. ROSBERG,
Director

Monographs published by the Institute include:

RESEARCH SERIES

*International Integration Series

INSTITUTE OF INTERNATIONAL STUDIES MONOGRAPHS (*continued*)

POLITICS OF MODERNIZATION SERIES

POLICY PAPERS IN INTERNATIONAL AFFAIRS

Address correspondence to:
Institute of International Studies
215 Moses Hall
University of California
Berkeley, California 94720